CROSSING THE DESERT OF DEATH

Through the Fearsome Taklamakan

CHARLES BLACKMORE

With a Foreword by Peter Hopkirk

D1375047

JOHN MURRAY
Albemarle Street, London

© Charles Blackmore 1995

First published in 1995
under the title
The Worst Desert on Earth: Crossing the Taklamakan
by John Murray (Publishers) Ltd,
50 Albemarle Street, London W1X 4BD

Reprinted 1996

Paperback edition 2000

The moral right of the author has been asserted

A catalogue record for this book is available from the British Library

ISBN 0-7195-6020 9

Typeset in 12½ on 14pt Bembo, by Servis Filmsetting Ltd, Manchester
Printed and bound in Great Britain by The Guernsey Press

CROSSING THE DESERT OF DEATH

To the Chinese the fearsome Taklamakan was always the 'desert of death' – 'You go in but you never come out.' Steeped in legend and seemingly uncrossable, this desert is an empty vastness 5,000 feet above sea-level, with treacherous dunes often rising 1,000 feet higher. For centuries the Silk Road, the ancient trade route linking Imperial Rome to China, skirted the edge of the desert to north and south, following the line of the isolated oasis towns along the foothills of the towering Tien Shan and Kun Lun mountain ranges. Even so, many caravans of merchants (with silk, gold and other precious cargoes), soldiers and also pilgrims lost their way between these oases never to be heard of again, often engulfed in the terrifying and all-devouring *karaburam*, or black hurricane.

Charles Blackmore, together with thirty camels and a party of British, Chinese and Uighurs, set out to cross this daunting desert for the first time ever, from end to end, a distance of 780 miles. For sixty days the party, often pushed to the limits of their endurance and out of reach of all help, moved relentlessly forward, overcoming sickness, injury and extremes of temperature in an awesome wasteland that sustains no life or water. Despite the loss of camels and moments of near mutiny among members of the crossing party, they emerged triumphant to take their place in the history of exploration.

This absorbing and at times deeply personal book tells a story of outstanding endurance, of survival against all odds. It also describes the excitement at the discovery of one of the lost cities of the Taklamakan that had lain buried for centuries beneath the desert sand.

Charles Blackmore read archaeology at university before spending fourteen years as an army officer. He now works in a merchant bank. His first book, *In the Footsteps of Lawrence of Arabia*, was published in 1986. He has travelled extensively and has led three significant expeditions. He lives in Hampshire with his wife and three sons.

In memory of my father,
and to my mother who inspires me

Contents

Illustrations		ix
Acknowledgements		xi
Foreword by Peter Hopkirk		xv
Map		xviii
1.	The Lure of the Taklamakan	1
2.	The Planning	15
3.	The Send-off	35
4.	Entering the Desert	53
5.	Dysentery and the Sand Mountains	71
6.	The Silk Road	85
7.	Triumph over Hedin	91
8.	Mazartagh	114
9.	The Chinese Prison Camp	124
10.	All Men Dream	136
11.	The Uyghurs	152
12.	Water Crisis	165
13.	Discovering an Ancient Site	175
14.	The Chinese	185
15.	No More Star-gazing	192
16.	Coping with Suleiman	206
17.	A Costly Error	215

viii   *Contents*

18. Camp of Death   229
19. A Sinister Twist   243
20. A Desert Conquered   256
     Epilogue   261

Appendix: Members of the Joint British-Chinese Taklamakan
         Desert Crossing   267

Illustrations

(between pages 76 and 77)

1. Farewell at Markit as the expedition sets out
2. Crossing the sand mountains to Mazartagh
3. Evening campsite
4. The never-ending ocean of sand
5. Mazartagh
6. Desert rendezvous
7. Nursing the camels
8. East across the desert
9. Water carriers
10. Finding water
11. Vertical sand walls
12. Extra rations
13. After the 'camp of death'
14. The desert conquered

(between pages 172 and 173)

15. The author
16. Rupert Burton
17. Carolyn Ellis
18. Keith Sutter
19. Richard Graham
20. Mark Kitto

21. Guo Jin Wei
22. Lao Zhao
23. The Uyghur camel handlers at Markit
24. Esa Polta
25. Lucien
26. Abdul Rasheed
27. Suleiman
28. Barney White-Spunner
29. Francis Seymour
30. The Silk Road party
31. Kirim
32. Loading the camels
33. The ancient site at Niya
34. The Desert of Death

The author and publishers would like to thank the following for permission to reproduce photographs: Plates 1, 3, 5, 6, 7, 8, 9, 14, 16, 17, 19, 22, 23, 26, 29, 30, 32, 33, Keith Sutter; 2, 4, 11, 18, Carolyn Ellis; 10, 21, 24, 25, 27, 28, 31, 34, Mark Kitto. The remaining photographs were taken by the author.

Acknowledgements

It is obvious but still must be said that only I know the full extent of the teamwork and spirit behind this expedition. It was through the team members, British, Chinese and Uyghur, that my initial dream was fulfilled. This is especially true of Barney White-Spunner, whose handling of logistics and people could not have been more accurate or sensitive.

The best tribute to everyone's courage, tenacity and endurance is that we all survived. My account of the journey in these pages is a personal one. Inevitably I have not recorded each incident as the others would have remembered it; but they were indulgent of shortcomings then and I trust they will continue to be so now.

An undertaking on the scale of the Joint British–Chinese Taklamakan Desert Crossing required extensive support, in cash, kind and advice, from companies, individuals, friends and relatives. I would like to thank everyone who helped us, and only regret that space does not permit me to list them all.

Of the many companies who sponsored us, the generosity of the following in particular should be recorded: Automotive Technik UK (Steyr Pinzgauer); Barings plc; British Airways; BP Exploration Operating Co. Ltd; Cazenove & Co.; Enterprise Oil plc; The Excelsior Hotel (Hong Kong); Hiram Walker Group Ltd.; Hutchinson Whampoa (Hong Kong); ICI Taiwan; International Petroleum Exchange; Laceys Solicitors, Bournemouth; Marine Technology International; Matthew

Gloag; Motorola; Olympus; P & O Containers; Panasonic Business Systems UK; President Enterprise Corporation (Taiwan); Racal Group Services; Saffery Champness Chartered Accountants; Synpac Chemicals Ltd.; United Biscuits (China); Wogen Group Ltd.; Asia Satellite Telecommunications Ltd.; The Rank Foundation; and the YHA. I hope that the publicity from the Taklamakan Crossing justified their support, without which we would never have left these shores.

We were honoured in having HRH The Duke of Edinburgh, KG, KT, as our Patron, and the Rt. Hon. Sir Edward Heath, KG, MBE, MP, as the Expedition Director. Sir Edward helped unlock doors which might otherwise have remained closed and we welcomed his close interest, as an old friend of China, in our endeavour.

I like to think ours was a classic British undertaking; it was a 'first' and we are proud of the achievement. But above all it was a joint venture with the Chinese and I would like to thank the different Chinese authorities for their assistance; not least Mr Tiemur Dawamat as Chairman of the Xinjiang Autonomous Region, and the People's Liberation Army. We could not have undertaken the expedition without their co-operation. Thanks, too, to the remarkable Guo Jin Wei, leader of the Chinese team, and the staff of Xinjiang Nature Travel Service.

One of the expedition's objectives was to raise money for the Leonora Children's Cancer Fund. I wish to thank everyone who contributed to this cause. The accounts are still being finalized but we hope to have raised over £25,000.

We were grateful for the advice and support of the Royal Geographical Society, the Scientific Exploration Society (Colonel John Blashford-Snell, MBE), the British Museum, the British Library, and Oxford University (School of Geography).

A special mention must be made of Bella Birdwood who, with Charlotte Bethell, worked long hours behind the scenes pulling the organization of the expedition together. I would also like to thank Tracy Codrai for typing the original manuscript and the endless redrafts.

I am grateful to John Murray for publishing this book, and

for his infectious enthusiasm which made me dig deeper into my memory to records events, and to Gail Pirkis for her meticulous editing.

Finally, I must thank Tina and my three sons, Oliver, Jack and Toby. For the last three years they have shown remarkable forbearance and understanding in the face of my obsession with the Taklamakan. With this book finished, I am now, at last, back with them.

Charles Blackmore
Hampshire
May 1995

Foreword

When Charles Blackmore told me that he was planning to walk across the Taklamakan Desert from end to end I thought at first that I had misheard him. For no other traveller in history had ever before attempted this awesome feat, and having myself seen its mountainous sand dunes from the air, and studied the accounts of the few travellers who had risked their lives in it, I assumed a horizontal crossing to be impossible.

True, both Sir Aurel Stein and Sven Hedin, explorers from an earlier era, had crossed this vast, egg-shaped ocean of sand, but they had done so vertically, by a considerably shorter and easier route. Both, moreover, had made use of a river which flows half-way into the desert before it vanishes into the sands. Thus the distance they travelled across totally waterless desert was less than a quarter of Charles Blackmore's proposed route, and took them largely between the sand dunes rather than across them.

Stein's and Hedin's other Taklamakan expeditions, while undoubtedly highly dangerous, had involved cutting across corners of the great desert, and operating around its fringes, in their search for archaeological treasures and lost cities. Even so, on Hedin's first such venture – which would form the initial leg of the British expedition's route – he lost two of his men, most of his camels, and very nearly died of thirst himself.

All the same, nothing that Stein or Hedin did can be compared to the two-month-long, 780-mile camel trek across

range upon range of towering sand dunes undertaken by
Blackmore and his intrepid party. By crossing the
Taklamakan from west to east, rather than east to west, they
had, moreover, made their task infinitely more difficult. The
reason for this the reader will discover – as did Blackmore
himself – as the desert crossing nears its end.

Although Major Blackmore, the expedition leader, was an
experienced desert traveller, having ridden in Lawrence's footsteps in *Seven Pillars* country, nothing would have persuaded me
to march with him into this desert (whose name translates as
'Go in and you won't come out'), although he did, jokingly I
hope, invite me to. My own such travels – camel patrols in
Somalia and northern Kenya while serving with the King's
African Rifles – were a picnic by comparison to what
Blackmore was proposing.

Here, perhaps, I should issue a health warning about this
book and its remarkable author. Anyone tempted to follow in
his footsteps should think again. For the dangers and hardships
experienced by Charles and his companions – who included
one extraordinarily intrepid woman – are constantly played
down. To Blackmore, a British Army professional to his very
fingertips, such considerations seemed to be of minor importance once their task had been accomplished. The only thing
that mattered was that he had led his party, which included
Uyghurs and Chinese, from one end of the Desert of Death
to the other, without any casualties. When writing this book
Blackmore, I know, had to be coerced by his editor into
including any moments of danger at all.

Anyone who has read of Stein's or Hedin's ventures into
this nightmarish landscape, or has stood on its fringes and
witnessed a *karaburan* – a 'black hurricane' – turn day into
night within minutes, will know just what an astounding feat
this first lengthwise crossing of the Taklamakan was. It is true
that, unlike Stein and Hedin, the expedition enjoyed the use
of the latest navigational and communications technology to
prevent them from vanishing without trace – like so many
caravans over the centuries – into this frightening void. But
that does not in the least diminish the extraordinary courage

and determination shown by Blackmore and his companions in pulling off a feat that can, arguably, be compared to the first ascent of Everest, or rowing single-handed across the Atlantic.

The options today for the serious explorer, or those seeking to pull off a 'first', have all but run out as the world's great deserts, mountains and oceans are systematically conquered. But if there is a challenge left which has somehow gone unnoticed, then Blackmore, I feel certain, will already be planning to take it on.

Peter Hopkirk

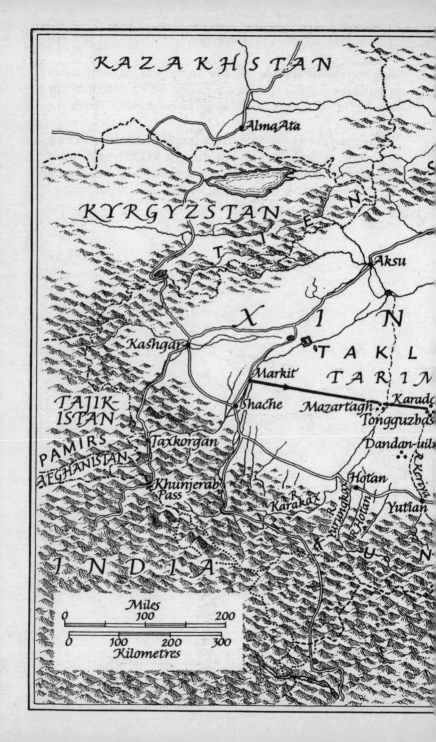

KAZAKHSTAN

Alma Ata

KYRGYZSTAN

T I E N

Aksu

X I N

Kashgar

TAKL

Markit

TARIM

TAJIK-
ISTAN

Shache

Mazartagh

Karadç

Tongguzbas

PAMIRS

Taxkorgan

Dandan-uil

AFGHANISTAN

Hotan

Khunjerab
Pass

R.
Karakax

R. Yunangkax

R. Hotan

R. Kenya

Yutian

I N D I A

K

U

N

Miles
0   100   200

0   100   200   300
Kilometres

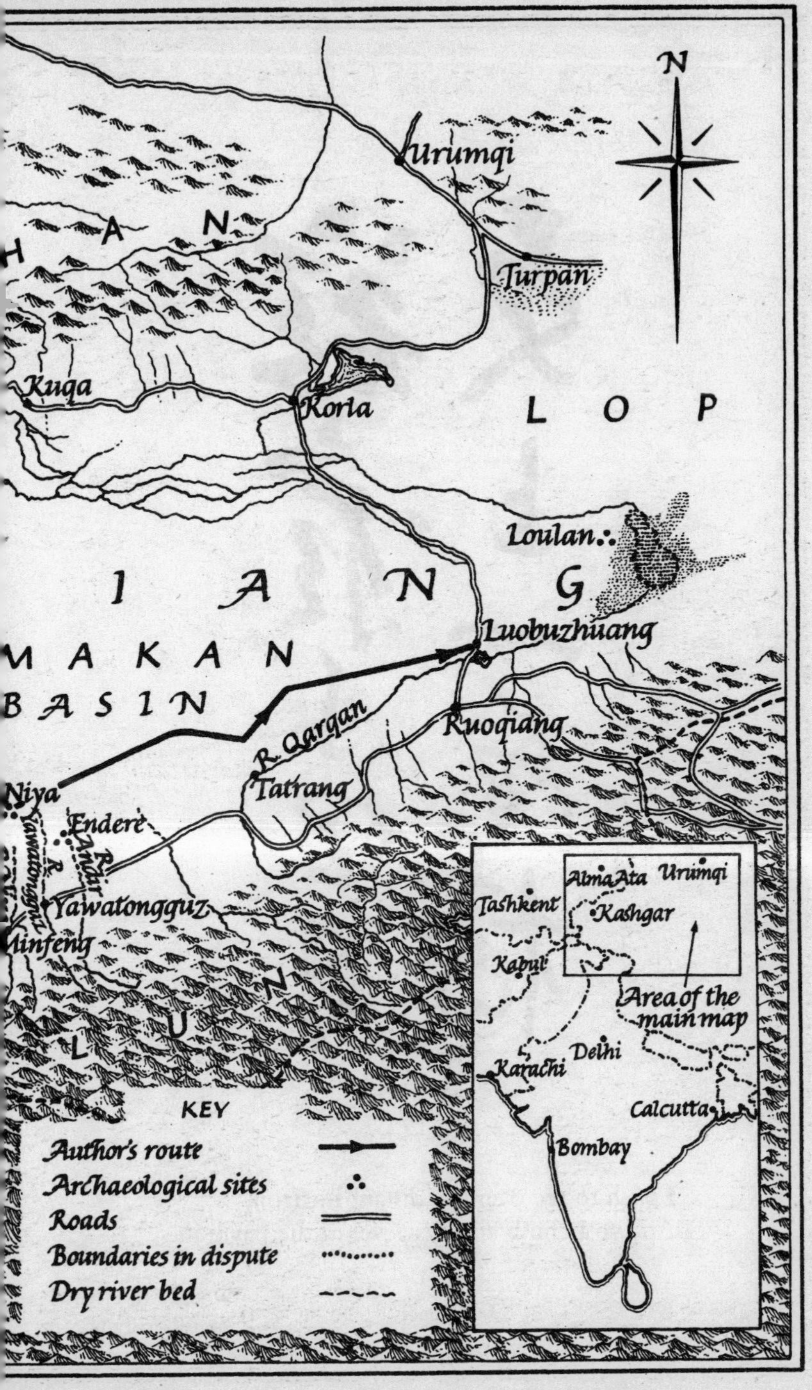
N
Urumqi
Turpan
H A N
Kuqa
Korla
L O P
Loulan
I A N G
Luobuzhuang
M A K A N
B A S I N
R. Qarqan
Ruoqiang
Niya
Tatrang
Endere
R. Andir
R. Yawatongguz
Yawatongguz
Minfeng
N
U
L
KEY
Author's route
Archaeological sites
Roads
Boundaries in dispute
Dry river bed
Alma Ata
Urumqi
Tashkent
Kashgar
Kabul
Area of the main map
Delhi
Karachi
Calcutta
Bombay

欲窮千里目
更上一層樓

I wish to see over the distant horizon,
And so I climb another level of the pavilion.

WANG ZHI HUAN
Tang-dynasty poet
eighth century AD

ONE

The Lure of the Taklamakan

Suleiman knelt in the sand beside the camel. Carefully he sharpened the long, thin blade of the curved dagger that he wore around his waist attached to a length of cord. He did so with the actions of a man familiar with the ritualistic preparation for the killing of an animal. His hawkish, bearded face was more noticeably lined and haggard, for he had been up much of the night nursing the injured camel. It lay impassively on its side, its eyes open but with only the faintest rising of its rib cage indicating that it was still alive. It was the largest of the thirty camels which were carrying our water, grain, foodstuffs and essential equipment for the desert crossing. The night before, the animal had fallen down the steep side of a soft dune and had either dislocated or broken its neck when the saddle became entangled simultaneously around its front hump, legs and neck. We could not be altogether certain about the prognosis, but whatever the nature of the injury, its long neck had rolled uncontrollably from side to side as it struggled to get up again. Despite its desperation it was unable to overcome the weight of its body which anchored it to the ground. As we toiled by torchlight to assist its increasingly confused and feeble efforts, I knew that our attempts were in vain and that the camel would be unable to continue the journey.

My instinct was to put it out of its misery immediately but a consensus among our four camel handlers had been against that. They preferred to wait until dawn in case its condition improved overnight. Undoubtedly they were influenced by Suleiman's belief that the camel would probably die naturally before then. For its nose had already gone cold and that, he told us, was one of the first signs of death. Suleiman had the greatest knowledge of camels after a lifetime breeding and trading them near the southern Silk Road. Although he wasn't our head camel handler, he was the oldest and the most experienced which meant the others naturally looked up to him. Though it was clear to me that they knew I was talking sense, they stuck to their line as if, by collectively avoiding the issue, they would be spared any direct responsibility for ending its life. 'In sha Allah' ('It is the Will of God'), they repeatedly said, as though absolving themselves of all blame. What a desolate and fatalistic phrase that could be.

It was obviously the Will of God, therefore, that the camel actually survived through that long, cold night. The temperature plunged to minus 20° Fahrenheit, for it was then November and the beginning of the Turkestan winter. The animal became ever weaker as it lay helplessly on its side, its massive weight slowly compressing its rib cage and its strength ebbing away with each unsuccessful attempt at rising.

With morning came the moment of reckoning. I did not mind because I knew what was ultimately right. Time was my chief enemy and I could not afford to delay our departure from the campsite by so much as an hour. The desert winter was setting in, our personal physical condition had deteriorated, and our reserves of strength had long ago been burnt off. On top of that, our equipment was in poor shape, having finally succumbed to the sand which penetrated even the most perfectly sealed components and subsequently degraded their performance. More seriously, we had been unable to find water for the camels in the last three days and we could only continue eastwards in the hope of discovering a source before the condition of the other animals deteriorated still further. But I feared the effects of the weather. The cruel north-easterly wind that gusted up to thirty miles per hour, carrying with it its fine sand particles and a chill factor of minus 5° Fahrenheit in the day, had already taken its toll on our depleted reserves. In the circumstances, there was no choice other than to press on through the seemingly never-ending and desolate sand hills at best speed. This meant there was no alternative but to kill the camel if it could not stand up and regain its place in the caravan.

For a brief moment, I had thought of just leaving it behind in the hope that it would somehow recover sufficiently and survive on its own. It was a foolish, naïve thought which ignored the eagerness of the desert to devour the weak and the helpless.

Once the decision had been made it was to Suleiman that the other handlers naturally turned that morning. Only he knew what had to be done and how. I was surprised, however, at the speed with which they distanced themselves from the final act once the preliminary preparations had been completed, melting away as shadowy figures across the cold sand back to their sleeping areas and the remaining couched camels near the main camp.

Alone, Suleiman appeared to notice neither the absence of his fellow handlers nor the imperceptible thin face of dawn which stole over the dunes to the east. Once his knife was sharpened, and in spite of the freezing cold, he removed his thick, quilted black coat and rolled up his sleeves for the gory task ahead. Crossing over to the camel, he first adjusted the constraining rope from the camel's head to its legs and then knelt down hard on the prostrate beast with all his weight upon its neck. The large brown, watery eyes of the camel registered nothing; neither surprise nor pain, nor any apparent sense of its impending fate. The eyes were as empty as the cold young light of day that faintly touched them for the last time. There was no resistance. The fight was through. The executioner, after all, was not a stranger.

I watched with little emotion. I searched within and found nothing but a twinge of guilt that we had no name for the camel which was about to be slaughtered. It was odd, for it had faithfully carried our precious 80-litre tin water containers for the last 700 miles, and without these our chances of survival in one of the world's most awesome wastelands would have been nil. I was not sure whether the camel handlers even had a name, not that it made any difference any more.

With a last gesture of respect, Suleiman leaned reverently forward until his lips were close to the uppermost ear of the camel and prayed aloud. It was an act of utter and touching simplicity. The tears welled in his eyes until the droplets broke and trickled down his sandy cheeks as he prayed, whilst all the time the knife in his right hand gently stroked the thick fur around the camel's throat with sinister intent. Whether he was asking forgiveness for himself in the eyes of Allah, saying a prayer for the camel soon to be dispatched to His safe-keeping, or both, I never discovered. Suleiman faced west in the direction of Mecca and I realized then why so much fuss had been made over the arrangement of the camel's body beforehand; the crude manner in which it was tugged about, rolled over and dragged through the sand by a rope tied to its stiffly outstretched legs had all been in order that its head should also face towards Mecca.

The prayer over, Suleiman sat back on his heels and wiped the tears from his eyes with a scrawny forearm. He sighed deeply, sniffed and adjusted his dirty cloth prayer hat. Then, with a sudden speed that caught me by surprise, my emotions having lingered on the moving act I had just witnessed, he lunged forward and cut savagely in a line just below the animal's chin, expertly seeking to sever the main arteries and windpipe in one. The poor creature half rose in a desperate last bid for survival, bellowing in shock, pain, disbelief and betrayal, and its legs punched the air and the surface of the sand in a panic-stricken search for a footing. I watched, transfixed, as Suleiman was pitched from side to side while he clung with his left arm hooked around the neck of the struggling camel. His right arm became almost a blur as it slashed back and forth with the rhythm of a hand saw as the blade cut through the strong neck muscles. They were locked together in a primitive and frenzied contest until, when the main artery was finally severed, a geyser of blood shot high in the air. The noise from the velocity of its release under pressure reverberated around the foothills of the dunes. The lips of the camel drew back tightly in a last grimace of pain and revealed a skeletal, haunting set of clenched teeth that were the only outward sign of its suffering to affect me.

The gurgling of the hot blood as it poured from the camel's throat became less frequent until there was a final spurt, a gasp and a sigh. It was over. A pool of bright crimson bubbling blood seeped slowly into the sand, and the steam from its heat rose above the dead camel whose last sight on earth had been the vapour from its own lifeblood gently ascending towards an opaque dawn sky.

I turned away with a heavy heart and contemplated the outline of the sand hills to the east. They looked more threatening than ever before: jagged lines of dunes interspersed with soft, dark curves from the shadow cast by their height; dunes thrown into confusion by the elements and the working of some invisible and mighty hand. There was no obvious route through them: ugly and distorted, cruel and forbidding, they appeared to laugh over the death of our camel and deliberately mocked our challenge to become the first people ever to make a complete crossing of the full length of the Taklamakan Desert, one of the largest sandy deserts in the world whose name translates from the local language as 'Go in and you won't come out'.

To explain why I came to be standing in a remote Chinese desert on that fateful morning, a silent and reluctant spectator of the final minutes in the life of one of our best camels, I must go back to a very different scene. The embryo of the idea for the expedition arose from a combination of restlessness and a personal craving for wide open desert spaces planted within me by an odyssey I had undertaken some years before. Then, with three companions and two Bedu tribesmen from the Howeitat tribe of Wadi Rumm in southern Jordan, I had covered more than 700 miles by camel as I retraced Lawrence of Arabia's journeys during the Arab Revolt in the First World War. We spent two months travelling among the nomads across the Jordanian and Arabian deserts. I discovered much about myself and still more about the myth of 'El Aurens' whose exploits with his irregular army of Arabian tribesmen had, by then, been all but eclipsed by the later achievements of the colonial soldier Glubb

Pasha.* For me it had been sharing the lives of our Bedu camel handlers which remained the most enduring memory, a gift unknowingly imparted by them as I relished the abandonment of the uniformity of modern life. I have always treasured that gift. They were nature's gentlemen. I wept openly when the time came to part, leaving behind the companionship of days spent together in the freedom of a vast desert landscape scoured by the wind, its sands scorched by the sun, and of nights under the canopy of stars listening to stories of desert folklore passed down by generations of Howeitat around one camp fire after another.

The renowned explorer Wilfred Thesiger is the only person to have successfully encapsulated everything I felt as a result of that experience. In *Arabian Sands* he wrote: 'No man can live this life and emerge unchanged. He will carry, however faint, the imprint of the desert, the brand which marks the nomad; and he will have the yearning to return, weak or insistent according to his nature. For this cruel land can cast a spell which no temperate clime can match.' A romantic part of me, deliberately or otherwise, used Thesiger's words to convince myself that I would one day return, even if by so doing I vindicated his claim. His words became my excuse and my alibi; through them I found the strength to pursue my ideal, particularly when the pressures of domestic life and work could too easily have persuaded me not to. I was fortunate enough to meet Thesiger once at a friend's house. I told the great man that I thought his description the most beautiful and distinctive paragraph in all his writings, so much so that it stood as his legacy to later generations. I asked whether he could remember writing it or if there had been anything specific which had inspired the poetry of his words, for I felt them to be more profound than any other in *Arabian Sands*. He looked at me through those piercing eyes which have witnessed so much. He could not. And then, as I quoted the passage from memory, he joined in, and smiled knowingly.

---

*Lieutenant-General Sir John Bagot Glubb, KCB, CMG, DSO, OBE, MC, commanded the Arab Legion from 1939 to 1956. When I was seconded briefly to the Jordanian Army in 1980 the soldiers still referred to Glubb as 'the father of our Nation and founder of our Army'.

It was in this frame of mind that I found myself in the summer of 1988 away from active soldiering and attending instead a year-long Army course at the Royal Military College of Science at Shrivenham. To say that I was uninspired by science and technology, and bored by hours of lacklustre lectures and tutorials, would be an understatement. One afternoon, in deliberate search of escape and solace, and playing truant from lectures, I went to the College Library and found myself looking through a copy of *The Times Atlas of the World*.

I flicked through its pages, seeking out any blank spaces on the maps, any outlet for my energy and restlessness. I tried to find a spot in the world, no matter how small, which offered a challenge: somewhere unknown, different, possibly uncharted and sufficiently remote to be hailed as breaking the last frontiers of exploration. To begin with, my attention was not particularly focused upon the deserts of the world, and in my mind I indulged in wandering freely over the brown of the mountains, up and down the blue lines of the rivers, and through the thick, hot and swampy green of the jungles as well as across the clean, open sweep of the deserts. I searched at random for inspiration for a new adventure; something challenging, dangerous and novel, also something which would be impressive in a modern world increasingly shrunken in size by the very accessibility of so many supposedly 'remote' places.

Then I saw it. In the far west of China, nestled between the snow-capped mountain ranges of the Tien Shan to the north, the Pamirs to the west and the Kun Lun to the south, was an egg-shaped blank expanse of yellow that beckoned me from its splendid isolation. Across its width were written the words 'Taklamakan Desert'. To its east, and geographically separated from it, lay the vast Gobi Desert about which I already had some knowledge. This Taklamakan, however, was different. The name alone sounded distinctive. Following an impulse, I referred to the *Encyclopaedia Britannica* and read with growing interest: 'A desert of Central Asia occupying the central part of the Tarim Basin in the Xinjiang Province of China. The desert area extends some 700 miles from east to west and has a maximum width of 350 miles. The desert reaches altitudes of

5,000 feet and windborne sandcover is as much as 1,000 feet thick.'

My interest increased as I read on: a place of extremes of temperature, low precipitation and sparse vegetation, its massive chains of sand dunes rise a thousand feet and no life – human or otherwise – is sustained by its desolate wastes. Its novelty and obscurity lured me further into its hidden secrets. I repeated the name slowly, Tak . . . La . . . Ma . . . Kan, and enjoyed the emphasis. There was something there which was intangible, crude and unrefined. As a desert it was already drawing me in. The basis of a plan unfolded before me, to cross the length of the Taklamakan, a distance of 800 miles, from west to east. I had found, in those few minutes alone, the scent of a challenge which I had sought so impulsively. It was to change the course of my life.

Two thousand years ago, the ancient Han records of China knew the Taklamakan as the Liu Sha, or 'Moving Sands', on account of the movements of its deep dunes that are relentlessly in motion, driven by fierce winds, shaping and forming the soft sand into an impenetrable maze. Modern-day Chinese writers have referred to it more starkly and dramatically as the 'Desert of Death'. There are many legends and dark secrets surrounding 'the worst and most dangerous desert in the world' as the young Swedish explorer, Sven Hedin, described it after his first venture into the Taklamakan in 1895 nearly cost him his life. Two of his four Uyghur camel handlers and seven of his eight camels were less fortunate: they all perished from thirst amongst the unforgiving dunes.

Sven Hedin's experience served to fuel the evil reputation of the desert. For centuries, the ancient trading route, the Silk Road, had skirted the edge of the desert by hugging the line of isolated oases along the foothills of the Tien Shan and Kun Lun mountains. Even so, many caravans of merchants, soldiers and pilgrims lost their way between these oases and wandered off into the desert, never to return.

More often, tragedy befell travellers who were caught out in the open by the dreaded *karaburan*, or black hurricane. Another early European explorer of Central Asia, the German Albert von Le Coq, recorded a story of how an entire caravan of horsemen perished after being hit by the *karaburan* whilst escorting a consignment of silver ingots in 1905: 'The sixty Chinese horsemen galloped into the desert where some of the mummified bodies of men and beasts were found later on, while the others had utterly and entirely disappeared, for the sandstorm likes to bury its victims.' Von Le Coq was to experience the *karaburan* at first hand during one of his journeys:

> Quite suddenly the sky grows dark . . . a moment later the storm bursts with appalling violence upon the caravan. Enormous masses of sand, mixed with pebbles, are forcibly lifed up, whirled round, and dashed down on man and beast; the darkness increases and strange clashing noises mingle with the roar and howl of the storm. The whole happening is like hell let loose . . . Any traveller overwhelmed by such a storm must, in spite of the heat, entirely envelope himself in felts to escape injury from the stones dashing around with such mad force. Men and horses must lie down and endure the rage of the hurricane which often lasts for hours together.

Many of these incidents, terrifying though they were, occurred on the periphery of the desert where the height of the dunes is less formidable than that of those in its interior. Von Le Coq's reference to pebbles and stones suggests an incident that would have taken place on the stony wastelands between the soft dunes and the rocky foothills of the surrounding mountain ranges. It was through that area that the Silk Road threaded its precarious trail from one small settlement to another along the edge of such emptiness. Von Le Coq was still in the desert, as one would define such a barren wilderness, but this was nothing as compared with the vastness of the interior, its soft but towering sand dunes stretching for miles in all directions. That sort of desert existed: that was the true interior where lost travellers could not hope to find a way out. And it was this area which made up the egg-shaped, empty blankness on the map of western China that first caught my attention.

I decided to read up as much as I could about the area, for it had already cast its spell on me. Nearly all the historical references that I found to the Taklamakan came from writers, travellers, explorers and historians who had travelled the desert's fringes. Many of their stories are second-hand, at best. But they are the ones responsible, in part, for creating an aura about the desert. In reality, they knew nothing of what really lay beyond those first or second lines of dunes; nothing about how vast and frightening the interior could be. It was an unmapped and uncharted area because no one had ever been there, an area upon which no human eye had ever settled nor human foot trod. Only a handful of explorers are known to have deliberately entered that forbidding wasteland and attempted to navigate their way through a landscape virtually devoid of any features except the massive belts of sand hills and an occasional dried-up, ancient river bed.

As if black hurricanes and oceans of treacherous sand were not enough, other legends included the Chinese belief that there were demons in the desert who would lure a man to his inevitable death. The great Chinese Buddhist explorer Hsuan-tsang travelled along the southern line of the Taklamakan in the seventh century AD and left this description: 'At times, sad and plaintive notes are heard and piteous cries, so that between the sights and sounds of the desert, men get confused and know not whither they go. Hence there are so many who perish on the journey. But it is all the work of demons and evil spirits.'

Hsuan-tsang recorded another important footnote in the history of the Taklamakan – stories, gleaned from the oasis dwellers along its perimeter, of strange legends about ancient towns that lay buried in its midst. Such stories encouraged local prospectors to risk their lives in order to discover the desert's secrets and the riches of gold and silver which supposedly lay in hoards among the yellow dunes: most never returned.

Such accounts captivated my imagination, and my excitement about the quest grew. I had stumbled upon a secret and the more I discovered, the more I feared that someone would steal my plan and beat me to it. There could be few places left on earth like the Taklamakan with its unconquered sands, its buried cities, and its mystery. In my research I came upon Peter Hopkirk's masterly book, *Foreign Devils on the Silk Road*, which captures all that and more. Knowing Peter had a very detailed knowledge of the region's history and its many travellers and explorers, I tracked him down to his London home.

'You must bear in mind', he told me, 'that the early Taklamakan explorers were looking for the remains of the ancient settlements. None of them planned anything as daring as your venture and I can assure you that a complete crossing of the Taklamakan from end to end has never even been attempted, let alone achieved. If you can pull this off then your crossing will be the first.'

That meeting with Peter, and those that followed, inspired me still further. I drew strength from his support and from the knowledge that I really was on virgin territory. At least temporarily; the discovery of vast reserves of oil beneath the sands of the Taklamakan threaten eventually to open the desert up once and for all. My race soon became a dual one – against others with similar ideas of achieving a 'first', and against the world's major oil companies. The latter's active interest in the possibility of extracting oil from the Tarim Basin, in which the Taklamakan lies, threatens to end the enigma of the desert forever. But it was to take me more than five years to reach the desert's edge. Of that period only the last two years involved really detailed and full-time planning; I had started before then, but the events of Tiananmen Square prevented me from going to China as an Army officer. So I could only wait for the timing to come right. During the intervening period I kept the plan alive in my mind, did a spell on active service overseas with my regiment, and increased the size of my family.

Stories of the 'lost cities of the Taklamakan' first lured such pioneering explorers as Sven Hedin and Sir Aurel Stein to the region. Their names are synonymous with the great era of exploration in Central Asia which became fashionable towards the end of the nineteenth century. At the height of his fame, Sven Hedin was a revered and famous explorer whose painstakingly drawn maps, detailed geographical and archaeological observations, and penetration of that little known area of the world brought him universal acclaim and recognition. In those days, merely reaching the fringes of the Taklamakan was a perilous undertaking; between 1890 and 1899 Hedin made four such journeys that yielded discoveries with enormous archaeological implications. Aurel Stein, a Hungarian by birth who adopted British nationality, did not make his first great expedition across the Karakoram mountains and into the Taklamakan Desert until May 1900 when he was 37. He was accompanied by the redoubtable Ram Singh from the Survey of India who helped him with his mapping. There then began a race between Hedin and Stein and other erstwhile Central Asian scholars, including von Le Coq, to unlock the secrets of the desert's hidden treasures. It was a race which assumed mammoth proportions – there were four German expeditions between 1902 and 1914 alone – and which only ended in the 1930s when the Chinese authorities, frustrated by the success of these international treasure-seeking expeditions and the consequent steady flow of priceless Buddhist antiquities out of China, finally slammed the door on the West.

What Hedin and Stein had discovered were the ancient Buddhist settlements which had prospered from the growing volume of trade along the Silk Road in the early centuries AD. The background of how Buddhism gradually spread into China from India is partially explained by the trade links between East and West along the Silk Route. The gradual spread of Buddhism also brought a new style of art known as Serindian, a term coined by Stein. Along with Buddhism, this Graeco-Buddhist style of Indian art which depicted Buddha in human form for the first time, gradually crept into Chinese Central Asia around the beginning of our era. It slowly permeated eastwards along the Silk Road, resulting in a proliferation of stupas, grottoes and monasteries among the settlements. Not all the sites existed on the edge of the desert. Some were to flourish far within the interior. That they could do so was due to the meltwaters of the Kun Lun mountains to the south which drained northwards under the sands. These formed the

Hotan, Keriya and Endere rivers which penetrated into the desert carrying water to the settlements. In most cases, the rivers were wide and fast-flowing on the desert's edge but became merely a narrow trickle some fifty to eighty miles into the sands. By skilful use of this water through elaborate irrigation systems the people of the oases were able to make themselves agriculturally self-sufficient.

It was during the Tang dynasty (AD 618–907) that the art and civilization of the Silk Road achieved their greatest glory. With the decline in the fortunes of the dynasty there was a commensurate decline in the civilization of the Silk Road leading, ultimately, to the disappearance of the Buddhist art, religious buildings and many settlements. The decline was so complete that entire communities and the once glorious chapter of Buddhist history in Chinese Central Asia disappeared virtually without trace. It was to fall to Hedin and Stein, foremost in the history of nineteenth-century archaeological exploration in Central Asia, to rediscover this lost civilization. The outstanding works of art and manuscripts which they excavated from the sites of Hotan, Niya and Dandan-uilik, to name a few, and brought to the West, now lie virtually forgotten in the dusty recesses of national museums.

There were two main reasons for the reversal of fortunes along the Taklamakan. The first was the gradual drying up of the glacial meltwaters from the Kun Lun which fed these isolated communities. Many of the now well-known ancient settlements in the desert, like Niya, were abandoned towards the end of the third century, although some of the better watered oases survived longer. The second reason was the invasion of the Arabs from the west in the ninth century. The local populations were forcibly converted to Islam, all their priests and monks were put to the sword, and their deserted shrines and temples were gradually buried by the continually shifting dry sands. Finally, in the fifteenth century, the Ming dynasty of China severed the trade routes to the West and shut the door on unwanted foreign influences. The settlements and trading posts around the Taklamakan dwindled and the region became a backwater. Its sand-buried ruins, dating back to the pre-

Islamic era, were to lie undisturbed until the end of the nineteenth century.

Sven Hedin recalled something of the excitement felt on discovering their remains in his first excavations at the site of
Dandan-uilik in January 1896.

> This city, of whose existence no European had hitherto any
> inkling, was one of the most unexpected discoveries that I made
> throughout the whole of my travels in Asia. Who could have
> imagined, that in the interior of the dread Desert of Gobi [it was
> then common to combine the name of the Taklamakan with that
> of the Gobi], and precisely in that part of it which in dreariness
> and desolation exceeds all other deserts on the face of the earth,
> actual cities slumbered under the sand, cities wind-driven for
> thousands of years, the ruined survivors of a once flourishing civil-
> isation? And yet there stood I amid the wreck and devastation of
> an ancient people, within whose dwellings none had ever entered
> save the sandstorm in its maddest days of revelry; there stood I like
> the prince in the enchanted wood, having awakened to new life
> the city which had slumbered for over a thousand years, or at any
> rate rescued the memory of its existence from oblivion.

The more I learned about the reputation of the desert the
more I felt daunted by the prospect of actually tackling it. Why
had no one undertaken a complete crossing before? Surely it
had not lain there for centuries unheeded by explorers of
greater courage and imagination than I? My questions gave rise
to inner doubts that made me realize the near impossibility of
being able to carry it off. But the more my doubts grew the
more compelling the idea became.

The fearsome qualities of the Taklamakan, and the gauntlet
that I was deliberately throwing down in my challenge,
assumed huge proportions in my mind. I felt like those explorers who first pitted themselves against the Empty Quarter in
Arabia. I knew I was no Bertram Thomas, Philby or Thesiger,
but from the scant information I had gleaned the task was not
that different. And the consequences of failure would be the
same.

TWO

The Planning

Such thoughts preoccupied me as I sat on the late-night train from London to Winchester one week before our departure to China in early September 1993. We had just had our final expedition meeting and I found it difficult to grasp that eighteen months of planning had gone by and that we faced the prospect of being in the desert in ten days' time. We were committed. Short of unforeseen complications with Chinese officialdom there could be no turning back and I felt as though I was teetering on the edge of a precipice.

In this mood I took from my briefcase a copy of my Will which needed amending before I left. In the soft light of the summer night sky outside, I asked myself what in the event of my death I should leave Toby, our third son, aged only four months? I wondered if he would ever forgive a father he had never been allowed to know for losing his life in an apparently impossible attempt to conquer the legends of the Taklamakan Desert. And what about Jack, our 4-year-old, or Oliver aged 6 who was just developing into such a caring, confident and interesting boy? I remembered him at the expedition press conference the week before standing beside his mother, when a journalist asked why I was undertaking such a hazardous trip. I gave a suitable but clearly unconvincing response, for Oliver's little voice piped up in the silence which followed.

'But Mummy, I still don't understand why Daddy is going to the desert. Why *is* he?'

My mind raced with the many details of the expedition plan that were still outstanding. Amidst all that, I had barely had time to consider some of the more personal and practical implications of my going. If I lost my life on the crossing, where should I be buried if my body was recovered from the desert and returned to this country? Would it be in the small, tranquil graveyard of Kilmeston, the Hampshire village where we once had a cottage for five years and where all three sons were brought home within days of their birth, or four miles away in the village in the Meon Valley to which we had recently moved? That house overlooked the churchyard and the boys would see my plot from their bedroom windows. Worse still, every time they scampered through the graveyard on their short cut to our neighbour's indoor swimming pool, they would pass the cold headstone representing a final link with their irresponsible father. They would never understand my sacrifice just when their little lives were beginning. That would be the ultimate price of failure. Would it be worth it? I couldn't say – I was too far down the line. The only detailed information I had found in researching conditions inside the Taklamakan came mainly from Sven Hedin's account of his disastrous attempt at crossing just 200 miles from west to east. Our route was nearly 600 miles longer. Although his expedition had taken place almost a hundred years ago the desert would not have changed. Ultimately, I had to accept that our expedition would face the same obstacles. The stark reality of that, now we were so close to leaving, made me even more aware of what I would be putting my family through. I did not want my sons to grow up without me.

My own father had died in a far-off place, the eastern foothills of the Himalayas in Nepal, when I was 19 and my brother Christopher was three years older. He had been serving with the Brigade of Gurkhas at the time of his fatal heart attack at the age of 49. My mother had been living in the farmhouse in Norfolk that they had recently bought and expected to join him in Nepal within the month. It was their first proper home after a lifetime of travelling the world, living in one Army hiring after another. Father had been pleased with the farmhouse and looked forward to settling there when he retired. He never returned to it. The shock of his loss was lessened at first by nature's own protective shield which closed automatically around me; the challenges of my twenties and the need to carve a niche in life also helped. However, I found that I missed him more as the years went by. Then I met Tina and we were married a month before I was posted to Hong Kong where I served with a Gurkha regiment for two years. During our time in the Far East, I took Tina to Nepal and to my father's grave in Dharan. We stood together beside his stained and neglected headstone and I cried; not so much for his loss but more for the time in my life he could no longer share. He would never meet Tina: neither would he see his first grandchild who was born five months later. I felt cheated.

What then, I asked myself as the train bore me homewards that night, would Tina and the boys feel if the desert lived up to its reputation? For the first time I felt scared of the unknown and the ferocious power of the desert which had claimed countless lives over the centuries. Why should I or any member of my team be different? Our plan was untested and relied upon Hedin's and Stein's experiences which, when put together, stacked the odds heavily against us.

There had been a time, right at the beginning, when I had thought of undertaking the journey alone, apart from two or three local people to help with the camels, just as Hedin and Stein themselves had done. Then I realized that I did not have the inner strength and moral courage necessary for such an undertaking, an admission for which the likes of Thesiger would despise me. And so I planned a fully fledged party of four, each member responsible for the primary roles of medic, interpreter, radio operator and navigator, one also doubling as photographer.

I knew, too, that I could not possibly get the whole way across without some assistance in the guise of a support team. Their responsibility would be to ensure that we were resupplied at the two most accessible points of the desert along the line of our traverse. The occasional purist in me felt this was cheating and I dabbled with the idea of going unsupported, a popular phenomenon amongst people trying to prove they can escape from the technological reach of the modern world and somehow return to a bygone age. I abandoned that idea.

My first priority then was to recruit suitable team members with the right skills and, as important, people who would help me get the venture off the ground. The list of requirements was never-ending. I needed the permission of the British and Chinese authorities, detailed information about the Takla-makan (if it even existed) and help from China, the support of the Royal Geographical Society (and other academic bodies) if I was going to carry out any useful scientific and geographical projects, and nearly £400,000 in cash and kind to cover the financing of the project and the necessary equipment. The development of a structured and credible plan, before I could approach companies for sponsorship, was in itself a major undertaking.

Barney White-Spunner, a serving officer in the Blues and Royals, was the first to become properly involved. We had completed officer training at Sandhurst and Staff College together but had seen little of each other thereafter until we ended up in the Ministry of Defence. One morning, eighteen months before the crossing took place, he came into my office on his way to a briefing elsewhere in the building.

'That's not Army work you're doing there, Blackmore!' he teased in a high-pitched voice, followed by his characteristic chuckle as he leant over my desk.

'No, for a change it's not. I'm planning an expedition.'

'Where are you off to this time?'

'China, to try and walk across a desert that no one has ever crossed before.'

'What's the name of this desert?'

'The Taklamakan.'

'Never heard of it. Are you going on your own?'

'No, there will be eight of us including camel handlers and about thirty camels carrying the rations and equipment.'

'Are the camels Bactrian or dromedary?'

'Bactrian, two-humped jobs, but on the Silk Road 200 miles to our south I'll have a vehicle party which will try to enter the desert at intervals and resupply us.' I showed him a map of the region.

'Who have you got coming so far?'

'No one at the moment, this is just the initial planning stage to get clearance from the Foreign Office and from the Chinese authorities.'

'I wouldn't mind leading your back-up team. This part of the world fascinates me and I've always wanted to travel the Silk Road.'

From that moment Barney's commitment was total, and it is unlikely that we would have got through the early, chaotic days and their endless difficulties without his logical, clear-headed approach, and his extensive network of contacts. In Barney I found the best qualities of a deputy leader. I confided in him, and whenever problems arose he always had a remedy to hand and a way of reassuring me in his calm and unabashed manner.

He was keen to find a role in the support party for his life-long friend, Lord Francis Seymour, who at 36 was a year older than both of us. A month after my first conversation with Barney I met this unlikely looking explorer in a Chelsea wine bar. I could not immediately think how I could use him. The first thing I noticed was his threadbare tweed coat worn over his suit and, when he later gave me a lift home, it did not sur-prise me that there was a coat-hanger where the aerial should have been on his car. Next was his habit of tilting his head slightly to the right as he studied me intently from beneath two large, bushy eyebrows. What struck me afterwards was the practical and determined mind which lay behind his delightful, relaxed and somewhat dishevelled exterior and which sought to escape the confines of a financial job in the City. I soon discovered that Francis had no side to him and personified modesty, and the full measure of his commitment to the project became apparent when we met early the next morning in the foyer of the Royal Horse Guards Hotel in Whitehall, the first of many interviews I held there. Francis, having declined a coffee, sat silently reading my expedition file for fifteen minutes until he fully understood the plan. He believed it was achievable. He then asked some pertinent questions before dashing off to work, leaving me with no more idea of whether he was keen, or how I could use him, than I had had the night before. In the end he drove one of the support team vehicles and acted as Barney's deputy, primarily responsible for equipment and communications.

Later that summer I met Carolyn Ellis after a talk in London by Ranulph Fiennes on his latest book, *Atlantis in the Sands*. Attractive, adventurous and exuding confidence, Carolyn had an infectious laugh and a simple, uncomplicated attitude to life. She had recently left the Army after ten years as an officer in the Queen Alexandra's Royal Army Nursing Corps, which included service in the Gulf War. I had been looking for someone with medical experience and Carolyn was eager to come along. Virtually up until the day we departed I had reservations about having a woman in the crossing party; not that I doubted her physical stamina or her ability as the expedition medic, but I was cautious lest a romance should cause the teamwork to break down.

My wife had her own doubts, too, fuelled by a postcard she found from Carolyn that I'd left on the table. It read, 'Dearest Charles, I couldn't sleep last night for excitement thinking about the desert and the expedition – let alone our dashing blond leader! Thanks for supper. Lots of love, Carolyn.' Tina was pregnant at the time and, if I've learnt nothing else during my marriage, it is that women become extremely vulnerable and quite unpredictable at such times. Unfortunately, I had not explained my marital status to Carolyn beforehand.

'What's this? What's this?' Tina demanded with an indignant look, adding, with utter finality, 'You're certainly not taking *her* to the desert.'

I adopted the tactic of saying it was harmless and unintentional and then dropped the subject, but carried on with my plan regardless. Thus many things happened unbeknownst to Tina, yet it was the only way of protecting her from sleepless nights as I slogged through the problems of putting together 'this absurd schoolboy adventure that will surely kill you', as she sometimes called it.

Next to join was Keith Sutter. Tall and quietly spoken with an engaging smile, Keith was a handsome 25-year-old Californian photographer who happened to be in London receiving an award for mountain photography when we met in November 1992. There was something about him that prompted me to consider him as our official photographer. I can remember his reaction; a blend of enthusiasm tempered by native shyness and respectful politeness towards someone he perceived as an archetypal English eccentric.

The continual problem we faced in planning everything was that Barney, Francis and myself were in full-time and demanding jobs. Furthermore, except at the very end when Enterprise Oil came to our rescue, there wasn't an expedition office, a telephone, a filing system, secretarial backup or any focus for raising the funds, obtaining the equipment and co-ordinating the detailed preparations. There was only us at our normal place of work, or in our free time at home. Snatching phone calls, sending faxes and typing our own letters to potential sponsors all had to be fitted into everyday work and domestic needs.

Just when it seemed as though things were about to fall apart, we found a saviour in Bella Birdwood. She told me outright that she would be useless at raising money but that she would help with letters and the general organization. In time she came to do much more. To our sponsors and the close relatives of the crossing party, Bella became the official mouthpiece for the expedition and kept them informed with regular and amusing bulletins during some difficult times. Later, with Charlotte Bethell, who took the pressure off Bella on those occasions when she thought she was about to lose her job, her husband, all her teeth and even her hair from sheer worry, the two of them formed the expedition rear link and organized everything from press conferences and freighting out equipment for the support team to gifts for the Chinese and fund-raising. Additionally, Charlotte ran the expedition accounts. They asked nothing for the hours of work they put in and the expedition would have been near impossible without their unselfish and unstinting support.

Throughout the winter months of 1992 and early 1993, Barney, Bella, Francis and myself were the core who planned the expedition which now had a start date of September 1993. We met once a fortnight after work in each other's London homes to co-ordinate an increasingly heavy workload. There were many evenings when Barney's and Francis's wives, Moo and Paddy, patiently produced a meal, watched it disappear under a bombardment of expedition conversation and then saw us retire to another room, having neglected the clearing up. We would then continue to plan until we were red-eyed with fatigue and finally would disperse in the early hours with long lists of things to do before the next meeting. There was never enough time. The whole task seemed so overwhelmingly large that I left on many of those nights with the feeling that I was swimming against a current which was too strong. Because there was so little time for preparation I grew increasingly concerned that my research into the desert and its conditions was woefully inadequate. I knew I should have been planning things in the utmost detail, because our very lives depended on that, but it was all I could do to keep up the pressure of targeting sponsorship. Letter after letter came back with the same words, 'Unfortunately we are unable to support you on this occasion. We would, however, like to wish you luck with such an epic and enterprising feat.'

My confidence took knock after knock with the stream of rejections. I envied the apparent ease with which the likes of Stein found favour with Lord Curzon, the Viceroy of India, and the British Museum who advanced him generous grants of money; similarly, Hedin had had the backing of the King of Sweden and financing from the Royal Court. Theirs was a golden age of exploration when national interests were at the fore.

All the sceptics said it couldn't be done. They were gloomy days. Furthermore, a Civil Service branch of the Ministry of Defence was being particularly unhelpful in handling the clearance for an expedition that involved military personnel. I was told the Chinese would not agree to the proposal. In the 'very unlikely' event that they said yes, 'there is no doubt that such a high profile trek by British military personnel would be used for maximum propaganda purposes'. They questioned whether the British Army would gain anything meaningful from this expedition and concluded, 'Major Blackmore should put his considerable energies into developing alternative proposals. To sum up, the answer is no.' This narrow-minded and entrenched view coincided with a time when I was already questioning my own future in the Army. In fact, the question was more one of whether the Army offered any future after the savage and swingeing Treasury cuts which only caused more overstretch and fewer opportunities. I began to look at myself out of the context of the Army and realized that, in many respects, I had probably had my best and most active days of soldiering.

The personal pressure on me mounted. The plan for the Taklamakan was so fraught with unknowns that no two pieces of the jigsaw fitted together. I feared the consequences of failure – not physically in the desert itself but in failing to bring the disparate components of the expedition together in sufficient time for it to have even a chance of succeeding. Failure in that context would be attributable to my poor handling of the planning phase because I had spread myself too thinly. After months of agonizing I eventually decided to resign my commission after fourteen years in the Army and to look at second-career opportunities. I had no idea what I wanted to do. As if that was not enough, Tina gave birth to our third son two months before we moved house. In short, we had both thrown all the cards into the air and waited to see which way up they landed. The final burden was the news I received concerning my mother: she had breast cancer which was well advanced. I knew that in going to China for four months I risked never seeing her again.

In the midst of these fundamental changes to everything I had known, and the stress and uncertainties they created, I clung to the belief that I could launch an expedition across the other side of the world and achieve something hitherto believed impossible. I fought a continual battle within myself against self-doubt and on many occasions contemplated giving up despite the overwhelming challenge and lure of the desert. There were other moments of deep satisfaction, the tentative feeling that the hard work might be worthwhile after all when some strands of the plan started to come together. From the outset I had intended that there should be more to the expedition than walking across the desert. I reasoned that if I was to risk my life in such an enterprise then someone should, at the very least, benefit from that. With this in mind, one of the objectives of the crossing was to raise funds for a charity for every mile that we collectively walked. After some deliberation I chose the Leonora Children's Cancer Fund. In order to capitalize on the expedition's unique opportunity to contribute towards scientific research, we secured the backing of Oxford University for a project aimed at studying the movement of the desert's sand by taking measurements and samples across the length of our traverse. Finally, the British Museum and the British Library engaged us to survey and record some of the known ancient sites that we wanted to reach on the crossing, and others nearer the Silk Road which the support team hoped to investigate. These projects, and other minor ones which followed, including looking for evidence of meteorites and any trace of Prejevalsky's wild horse (last seen on the fringes a hundred years ago), afforded us the support of the Royal Geographical Society and the patronage of HRH The Duke of Edinburgh. With such a framework in place the targeting of commercial sponsorship became easier.

In June 1993, three months before the planned crossing, I flew to China for a preliminary reconnaissance to make contact with the Chinese on the spot, for without their support the crossing could not happen. I took Mark Kitto with me as my interpreter. It was a calculated risk since both of us were still serving officers and neither had secured the prerequisite military clearance for such a visit to a Communist country. But, above all else, I had to get there and translate some of the rhetoric into reality.

I had recruited Mark, then a Captain serving in the Welsh Guards in Northern Ireland, for his fluent Mandarin which he had studied at the School of Oriental and African Studies in London. Mark was tall, with a quiff of blond hair, and he had an air of mischievousness and boyish charm. He was 26 years old. I liked him immediately because he had similar mannerisms to James Bowden who had accompanied me on two previous expeditions.

In Beijing the pair of us transferred to a tired-looking Russian aircraft hired by the Chinese from Kazakhstan Airways. With the uncertain combination of a Chinese pilot at the controls and a Russian cabin crew, we flew at less than 15,000 feet across the length of China to Urumqi, the capital of Xinjiang Province, where I had been put in touch with the required authorities and the People's Liberation Army whose co-operation (including providing permits and access along the Silk Road for our support party) was essential to the plan. Apparently, the aircraft would not fly higher or the wings would threaten to detach themselves from the mainframe. My excitement mounted as every hour brought me closer to the land of the Taklamakan for the first time. Our Chinese hosts took full advantage of our disorientation and jet lag on arrival by promptly taking us to a huge banquet, liberally washed down with countless toasts of *bai jiu*, the inflammable white rice spirit, before finally showing us to our hotel beds in the early hours. Talks, they said, would start at seven o'clock the next morning (eleven at night our time: we groaned). For three days we were cooped up in a hotel room, smoking foul-smelling Chinese cigarettes, drinking plain hot water or weak tea without milk, locked in negotiations with the Xinjiang authorities. Outside we could see the workers of a factory attending roll-calls and centralized exercise routines in a courtyard in front of the Red Flag. Urumqi was drab and depressing, its Communist architecture uninspiring, soldiers in green uniforms, peaked caps and red stars much in evidence everywhere, dilapidated Kamaz trucks trundling along the streets, horns blaring, and cyclists weaving their way in and out of the traffic to the shrill ringing of bells. A haze of pollution hung

over the city. We were given neither the time nor the opportunity to go anywhere near the desert.

The man at the centre of our talks was Guo Jin Wei, a senior
official in the state-owned Xinjiang travel company, who
would accompany us on the crossing and provided the link
with the People's Liberation Army. More than anyone he
became the man in China who believed in our quest and
ensured that hitherto suspicious officials were brought on side.
For a year Guo Jin Wei had been in touch with me by fax and
telephone. I had met him once before when he came to
London on a business trip, his first ever outside China, having
been put in touch with him on the recommendation of a friend
who had previously travelled in Xinjiang with Guo's company.
Then I had arranged to meet him at a hotel near the Ministry
of Defence. After half an hour he had still not arrived. Just as I
was getting ready to leave, a colleague of mine brought in the
resourceful, chubby and smiling Mr Guo. It transpired that he
had talked his way unescorted into the Ministry of Defence,
had taken the lift to the fourth floor and had found my office.
It made a minor mockery of the civil servants who obstructed
the granting of clearance for our expedition on the grounds of
security. Together Guo and I had worked out the practical
aspects of the crossing, particularly how and where our back-
up team could meet up with us, and now I needed to agree a
final price for my host 'sponsors' as well as the detailed plan.

The route I had chosen for the crossing was from Markit on
the western fringes of the Taklamakan to a first resupply point
at Mazartagh, an ancient site on the dried-up bed of the Hotan
River. That leg comprised 210 miles of high sand dunes. From
Mazartagh it was a further 90 miles to Tongguzbasti. There the
back-up team could meet us, for Tongguzbasti was a settlement
(in fact the only one) of goat herdsmen in the desert that could
be reached from the southern Silk Road. After that it became
more difficult. There were two ancient river beds in the eastern
half of the desert which offered possible access for vehicles
entering from the south, but neither extended into the desert
more than 60 miles. The route from Tongguzbasti to the end
point at Luobuzhuang was over 400 miles long and we would

need at least one interim resupply point. The need for these resupply points presented a problem: there were no records to fall back on and the Chinese themselves were imprecise about the topography and feasibility of the resupply plan. Without resupply at various points along my traverse the chances of success were remote. The paucity of data about the Taklamakan was frustrating. Ours was a unique venture without precedent. The west-to-east crossing had never before been contemplated. The Chinese had only ever heard about the activities of Stein and Hedin but none of them had studied their accounts, nor could they provide any local knowledge about the desert's environment. Inevitably much of our plan was guesswork helped, in part, by my previous experience with camels in the Middle East. That experience, however, could only be viewed as a stroll in the park compared with the highly risky enterprise of tackling the Desert of Death. The Chinese viewed our ambitions with a degree of puzzlement. They could not come to grips with the prospect of an undertaking fraught with so much danger and so little apparent chance of success. To them there was no earthly reason to risk lives in crossing a seemingly uncrossable and uncharted desert simply because it existed; but the pride I took in my daring gave me confidence, at least externally. In that regard the British have the advantage of history as a race renowned for tackling some of the world's greatest challenges of exploration.

On that first morning Guo presented us with the Chinese version of the plan and his attitude was very much that if we agreed to it then our remaining time in Urumqi could be devoted to sightseeing. We quickly realized that the hidden agenda for the Chinese centred around how much profit they would make. No surprises there. Fortunately I had already calculated that the success of our venture depended on their co-operation, for there had been many examples of international expeditions coming to grief at the hands of Chinese bureaucracy in the past. Therefore, when the negotiations became tense and when they refused to reduce the colossal sum that they demanded in US dollars, I played my trump card. It was a letter from Sir Edward Heath, in his capacity as our expedition

director, inviting the Governor of the Province, Tiemur
Dawamat, to become the Chinese Director of a retitled Joint
British–Chinese Taklamakan Desert Crossing Expedition. For
Mark and myself it became a battle of attrition. The Chinese
were cunning negotiators and kept us at it all day. They would
then allow a five-minute break at the end before taking us off
to another banquet for even more officials (everyone in China
is an official of something, or so it seemed) where we were
always the target of never-ending toasts in *bai jiu*, enthusiasti-
cally given as though we would never be seen alive again.

But we stood our ground and eventually left China after four
days well satisfied. The costs had been considerably reduced
and we had reached agreement on the plan as well as on two
points which became critical to our ultimate success. One was
that I would provide the radio equipment, both within the
crossing team and from the crossing team to the support team.
The second was that the British would produce their own integral vehicle support. Neither was an easy task with only three
months left before departure but it did reduce the bill for
Chinese assistance and, more importantly, it meant we retained
a degree of independence from the anticipated bureaucratic
meddling of the Chinese authorities. The necessary compromise for their co-operation was that at least two Chinese would
accompany the crossing (in fact they later raised the number to
four when we reached China in September), and that at least
four Chinese would travel with Barney's team on the Silk
Road.

On our last afternoon in Urumqi we attended a well-orches-
trated banquet and press conference with the Governor in the
People's Hall. Standing beneath large red banners proclaiming
the glorious joint undertaking of the British and the Chinese
to conquer the 'Desert of Death', I attempted a diplomatic and
rousing speech which Mark translated. I repeated a Chinese
proverb: one chopstick on its own is easily broken but a bunch
of chopsticks together are not so easily broken.

'We, on this great and daring expedition, will go through the
desert like a bunch of chopsticks,' I said, holding up my
clenched hands to the audience of bemused Chinese journal-

ists and Party officials. Mark looked at me and raised an eyebrow as though to say, are you sure you really want me to translate all that rubbish? I did. It was greeted by toothy grins and polite clapping which made me stand even taller on my soap box and passionately end with the boast: 'The name Taklamakan means you go in and do not come out. We, the British and Chinese, will go in and we *will* come out. No more will it be called the Desert of Death.'

This was followed by a crescendo of cheering and clapping. If there had been martial music playing as our aircraft flew over the snow-capped Celestial Mountains near Urumqi on our way to Beijing then the film set would have been complete.

Now confident of Chinese co-operation and support, we reached Hong Kong for the second part of our trip aimed at raising funds. Our contact was Richard Graham, an ex-diplomat and Old Etonian, who was small in stature but exuded great charisma, presence and wit. There did not seem to be anything Richard could not do; he had the ability to make you feel like the only person in the world. How unfair that someone could be so clever yet utterly charming and humorous with it. A year younger than I, Richard was about to begin work in Shanghai and wanted to join the crossing party in return for raising funds in the Far East. After two busy days, each with twelve meetings magnificently stage-managed by Richard, he had more than earned his place and we left with over £60,000 pledged by Hong Kong companies and individuals.

Many people involved with expeditions will often say that the planning phase is far more stressful and difficult than the conduct of the actual trip. Without pre-judging the crossing I certainly began to feel that. In order to begin our traverse in late September we would have to ship our support vehicles from England by early August at the latest. That left just six weeks to find and equip the vehicles and obtain the appropriate permission for their use in China. I could not afford to delay the expedition as everything hinged upon the time of year. By

choosing September we would face the end of the summer in
the desert and the transition to its early winter weather: any
earlier and we risked being fried alive by temperatures that can
average 120° Fahrenheit in the interior; any later and the penetrating cold of the Turkestan winter with its bitter winds would
leave us cruelly exposed. We had to get out of the desert by
mid-December: surviving longer than two and a half months
on the crossing after constant exposure to such extremes of
temperature would have serious consequences.

Resolving the problem of the vehicles was where Francis
came into his own. Within two weeks he had made contact
with a 55-year-old Welshman called John Thomas who had
apparently driven across much of the Sahara by vehicle. More
importantly, he owned a six-wheel-drive Pinzgauer made by
the Austrian manufacturers Steyr-Daimler-Puch. John came to
one of our meetings in Francis's house. I liked his frank, matter-
of-fact approach but I detected in him the traits of a self-made
man and individualist who might one day run counter to the
grain of the expedition. He was a shrewd man who thrived on
detail, and I felt uncomfortable because my big-picture planning lacked that. With his neatly swept-back grey hair, John
Thomas (later to be known as 'Little Willie') would sit in our
later meetings saying little, allowing the conversation to flow
along until it reached the point he had selected for his ambush.
Despite my initial doubts about John, he was clearly a resourceful man with vast experience of both vehicles and deserts who
wanted an adventure at an age when most people had hung up
their spurs. His condition for joining the expedition, however,
was that his delightful wife, Anne, should come along as well
since they had done all their other trips together. I wasn't overly
keen on a husband-and-wife relationship in the support team
but it was either that or no vehicle, no John and none of his
expertise.

With John and Francis working flat out to find another
vehicle we had a stroke of luck. The UK representative of the
Austrian manufacturer gave our plan his enthusiastic support
and arranged a meeting with Steyr's European Sales Manager
at Gatwick Airport whilst he was in transit to another country.

That crucial twenty-minute meeting in the departure lounge secured the second vehicle on loan from the manufacturers. All our energies then focused on finding the funds, equipping the vehicles, and preparing them for shipment from Southampton to Karachi. Three weeks remained before the P&O container ship sailed.

In a remote barn on the edge of the Black Mountains in Wales, John and his son Kevin laboured night and day to convert the manufacturer's vehicle for its role. It started as a basic flat-bed with only a cab and chassis; it ended up like an armoured vehicle with a secure storage area on the back accessible only by an ingenious hatch and, under the flooring, a sealed compartment fitted as a safe box inside the reserve fuel and water tanks. Unladen the vehicle weighed 3 tons.

A training weekend was organized at the Thomas's home in late July. The vehicle was nearly finished apart from a respray and it was encouraging to see the tangible beginnings of a desert expedition to China taking shape in such unlikely surroundings. It was not a convincing weekend. Had any of our sponsors and families then seen the disorganized state of our preparations I think they would have put our survival chances at zero. Between them, Barney and Francis were incapable of erecting a tent. The rest of us, helpless with laughter, stood and watched an orange blob on four feet working its way around the garden. Mark Kitto, in the meantime, tried demonstrating the high-frequency (HF) radio link between the crossing and support parties but couldn't even raise Portishead Maritime Radio Service near Bristol. Aside from these minor practical problems, there were many planning difficulties and unknowns which kept cropping up. Could the vehicles reach us in the desert? How much water would we need to carry on the camels between resupply points? Would the HF radio link in fact work from the middle of the desert to Barney's team 150 miles to the south? The more we talked it through, the more questions were raised and the more doubts I had about the likelihood of success. That was the challenge. After all, no one had done this before so the information did not exist: even the map had large areas on it which were ominously marked 'uncharted'. We had drawn, where possible, on Hedin's and Stein's accounts but their goals had been different: they never set out to traverse the entire desert. We were the guinea-pigs. The surety of this, intensified by the many unknowns, bonded us together over that weekend and made us want to taste the true spirit of adventure that only ever touches a handful of people in life.

In an ideal world I would have had several training weekends and also a week away. I was worried in the main about our personal physical preparation and the welding of individuals into a team under testing conditions. There was no time. We had a tiny window of opportunity and, having got thus far, we had to go for it.

Ten days after that weekend, we mustered the team with the heavily laden vehicles for a Press photo call in the Close outside Salisbury Cathedral. Everything had been such a hurry that we were still sticking on sponsors' logos when Sir Edward Heath arrived. It poured with rain. Afterwards, we repacked the equipment before driving the vehicles to Southampton Docks. There John and Kevin were in their element. They had prepared vehicles for expeditions many times before and I was impressed by their efficiency and knowledge of Customs & Excise. I felt a thrill of anticipation as I watched Bella and Thomas (our nicknames for the vehicles, Bella aptly named after Bella Birdwood in tribute) loaded into a P&O container and securely lashed down inside. The container was then placed on to a flat-bed for the SS *Rotterdam*'s passage to Karachi.

Although it was a relief to see the back of the vehicles and the bulk of the equipment, a further £70,000 in funding was still needed as well as the necessary clearances to drive in China and use radio and satellite communications equipment there. I had not waited for these and only hoped things would come together before the ship reached Pakistan, working on the premise that unless decisions were made in the absence of many of the answers the venture would never get off the starting blocks. It was whilst wrestling with the final details of the plan in the last three weeks that I had a setback which nearly ended all involvement for me when I twisted my right knee running through a woodland in the valley behind my house. It had been a glorious run and I had felt magnificent until then. The knee had been operated on twice before and the ruined ligaments replaced by carbon-fibre ones, but the weakness had always been there. Within hours I was on the 'phone to Doctor Andrew Cobb, the orthopaedic surgeon who had carried out the last operation, asking in a mild panic if he could do anything for me. He operated the following day, and on coming out of the anaesthetic I was not reassured to see his serious expression and hear his grim verdict.

'Charles, you cannot go to the desert. Your knee is one of the worst that I've ever seen. If you go ahead with this scheme then I can only say that you will need an entire plastic knee replacement on your return.'

As I had lain unconscious Andrew had tried getting Tina to talk me out of the expedition.

'You should know him by now, Andrew,' she replied, 'he has set his heart on it and nothing you or I can say will change that.'

She was right, up to a point, but I hardly felt like a daring desert explorer when she wheeled me out of the hospital and into the car, my leg thickly bandaged and immobilized from the heel to the hip.

The build-up of the last fortnight became unbearable. Half the team were by now in Pakistan, yet major queries over the plan and the funding lay unresolved. I limped, bad-temperedly, around my upstairs office at home where, at the desk in front of maps and photographs, I could occasionally escape and indulge my fantasy. On other days I was in London in office space lent by Enterprise Oil, where Rupert Burton took on much of the work. He had joined at the last moment to fill the slot of radio operator and check navigator in the crossing party. Rupert was a bachelor, aged 31, and an ex-Parachute Regiment non-commissioned officer who had recently spent eight months in the Pyrenees as a mountain ski guide. He was tall and strong with an easy, confident manner, and I felt more comfortable knowing that his stamina and humour would be a major contribution to our teamwork. A final member of the team was Paul Treasure who filled a role which had not been planned until Tina saw Paul's portfolio of artwork. It was she who suggested he came to China as our official expedition artist and that was what happened, all within three weeks, leaving behind his wife Janie with their two-month-old daughter.

We were all leaving someone behind, whether parents or wives with children, and the responsibility of that weighed heavily; each of us, in our own way, gave it much thought as we measured the risks we were taking. As the only married person in the crossing party I probably attached more significance to my survival than the others may have done; but that was very much a personal feeling since, as befitted the spirit of our undertaking, we never discussed the true consequences of failure.

THREE

The Send-off

A bustle of bureaucratic activity by Pakistani officials in Karachi started off Thursday, 9 September, but it finally ended in an agonizing delay for the advance party of Francis, John, Anne and Mark who had arrived the day before to get the vehicles out of customs for the drive to China. There were problems over the vehicle carnets and the shipping documents. Faxes winged back and forth to the Automobile Association in Basingstoke and to my expedition office at home in Hampshire. A solution was found late in the afternoon but it was too late. The customs office had shut. The following day, Friday, was a religious holiday in Pakistan. Nothing could be done until the Monday. The team sweated and kicked their heels in the Embassy Hotel in Karachi and fumed over the lost days. The crossing party was due to fly into Kashgar on 20 September and the vehicles had to be there then. Timings were tight. Francis, nominally in charge of the advance party, delighted Mark by refusing to get up on that Friday morning because there was nothing to do. Sadly he was right. There was nothing to do in Karachi on a Friday, except pray.

The following Monday was a trial of British diplomacy and patience but, by the evening, the vehicles were finally in the hands of the advance party and heading north with a police escort because of recent civil unrest. After 100 miles disaster struck. John's engine seized up. The vehicle could go no further. Using the MTD 6,000 satellite link fitted in the Bella vehicle, Mark sent a fax which arrived at my home. It read simply, 'JT vehicle engine gone. Request organize for complete new engine to be sent to Islamabad', and finished with an outline plan for recovery and the news that Mark and Francis intended continuing alone to the Chinese border.

The only thing which impressed me back in England as I read the words coming off the fax machine was Mark's brevity. The UK representatives of Steyr, Kevin, Bella and myself spent the next four days, up until the hour I left for Heathrow Airport, arranging for a new engine to come by road to England from the factory in Austria and thence by British Airways to Karachi. It was a slick and expensive operation but within five days John had his replacement. It had not been a good start and I was already questioning the decision to take my own vehicles. Mark and Francis had transferred vital stores and had pushed on to Islamabad to collect Barney who had in the meantime arrived there. For the 800-mile route north through Pakistan, over the Khunjerab Pass, across the Chinese border and into Xinjiang Province, they took it in turns to sit either on the roof or astride the engine cowling in a small cab designed for two. A member of Guo Jin Wei's organization, Xinjiang Nature Travel Service, met them at the border on 17 September; the customs post officials waved them through with barely a glance. The next day they reached Kashgar* and parked triumphantly outside the former Russian Legation where both Hedin and Stein had stayed before and after their Taklamakan forays, although Stein usually stayed at the British Consulate.

On the day the overland party reached Kashgar, Richard Graham met Keith, Rupert, Carolyn and myself in Hong Kong. We drove from the airport to Barney's sister and brother-in-law's colonial house on the Peak where a small reception was held for the Press and our Hong Kong sponsors. The follow-

---

*Officially known by the Chinese as Kashi.

ing morning at four o'clock we sat jet-lagged and bleary-eyed in the Cobbolds' kitchen waiting for a fleet of taxis to take us back to the airport and the flight to Beijing.

'Where's the dog?' asked Rupert, picking up the discarded collar lying on the kitchen windowsill.

'Dead,' replied Rolly Cobbold with a dead-pan face.

The ensuing laughter, shared by Rolly, buoyed us up for the journey ahead. Later, as the taxi drove through the empty streets of Hong Kong, familiar and friendly to me for I had lived there for three years, I realized that control of the expedition was soon to slip from my hands. In China it would be the Chinese and their system which would ultimately hold the key, no matter how good my plan or how determined my leadership.

A banquet was organized at the old Beijing Hotel next to Tiananmen Square for our one evening in Beijing. Huge banners proclaimed the glorious adventure and, judging by the number of First Day stamp covers we signed that had been specially printed, we were already heroes in China though we'd not yet set foot in the desert. Having listened to the translation of lengthy speeches of self-congratulation, shaken hands with half a dozen generals who were veterans of Mao's Long March, and drunk numerous toasts of *bai jiu*, we left the banquet in an almost imperial, conquering mood, determined to do battle with the legend of the 'Desert of Death'. Sorting out details at the British Embassy the following morning for the repatriation of any dead bodies was a more sobering experience.

The entire expedition, less John and Anne who were still fixing their vehicle in Pakistan, finally came together at Kashgar, a colourful, shambolic town combining modern Chinese architecture with ancient mud-walled houses and picturesque bazaars, the meeting-point of the northern and southern arms of the Silk Road. There we took the opportunity of visiting Chini-bagh (or Chinese Garden), the residence of the former British Consul-General in Kashgar. Chini-bagh's heyday was in the late 1800s and early 1900s when George Macartney, a half-Chinese Englishman, lived there

with his young Scottish wife. Macartney served for twenty-
eight years as Britain's representative in that remote, far-flung
corner of the world protecting Britain's interests and acting as
a listening post for Russian and Chinese regional ambitions.
Stein regularly stayed with the Macartneys on his expeditions
to and from the Taklamakan and soon struck up a close friendship with them. When we got to the building we noticed it
was well maintained and decorated but exuded the air of a
crumbling edifice from a bygone era. The immediate surroundings had been ruined by a tarmac drive and a lorry
drivers' hostel which loomed over Chini-bagh, having been
built right up against its walls. No longer was there the 'poplar
lined avenue, and the light of a lantern that showed me the
outer gate . . . as I descended from the spacious courtyard to
the terraced garden I found myself welcomed in the heartiest
fashion by Mr and Mrs Macartney.' Thus did Stein describe his
first visit there in July 1900 after two months travelling over
the mountains from the Indian plains. 'Comfortable quarters
adjoining the garden were awaiting me, and when after a
needful change I joined my hosts in their dining room there
was every little luxury to favour the illusion that I was in an
English home far away from the Heart of Asia.'

There were still beds of old English roses, thickly covered
with Kashgar dust, which stood out like silent sentinels in a
once proud, carefully nurtured garden. We liked to think that
they were planted by one of the wives of the British Consuls-
General, maybe even by Lady Macartney, in which case did
Stein sniff the fragrance of their blooms on one of his visits?
We ventured on to the terrace: there in the spring of 1934,
Mrs Thomson-Glover, wife of the then Consul-General,
had been shot through the shoulder, and a doctor attached
to the Consulate had been killed during the troubles in the
province. We climbed on to the flat roof and held the Union
Jack high with an air of defiance, probably the first time it
had flown there since the Communist revolution in 1949.
The significance of the moment was all the more poignant
because the flag was the one that had been draped over my
father's coffin in Nepal. On the same flat roof Stein enjoyed

perhaps the pleasantest hours . . . after dinner we would sit in the mild evening air . . . from there we would watch the frequent picnic parties of Kashgar families which had gone out early in the day to feast on the profusion of fruit in the orchards owned by almost all respectable citizens in the environs, and who were now gaily returning in long cavalcades of men, women, and children. Their songs sounded to me very melodious, often strangely reminding me of airs I had heard long ago on road and river in Hungary.

Satisfied by our humble pilgrimage, we joined the line of donkeys and camels drawing carts along the poplar-lined road south from Kashgar. The sun and the dust simultaneously rose on another day in Chinese Turkestan. Barney and I drove in the Pinzgauer and we felt tremendous pride as the vehicle, its signboards boldly proclaiming our undertaking, motored towards our ultimate destination of Markit. There lay the true beginning of the adventure.

'Well, Barnstable, if only those damned civil servants in the Ministry could see us now,' I laughed.

'I know. Have you seen my rather smart Chinese driving licence?' He chuckled with glee. Securing those licences for Barney, Francis and John had been a major Chinese concession to the expedition. It was unheard of for foreigners to drive their own vehicles and to do so without a Chinese escort.

'But,' he continued, 'what tickles me is that here we are, two officers with "Top Secret" security vetting, leading a convoy of vehicles through one of the most sensitive and remote military provinces in China. Bloody marvellous.'

We drove past lines of simple mud-walled and wooden buildings. Outside, racks of maize dried in the sun and children in colourful clothing played in the dust and grime with home-made toys amidst black pigs and scrawny chickens. We flashed past their simple lives, technologically advanced travellers infused with the comfort of another age, fleetingly aware of the culture gap and the timelessness of their existence. Local people seated on their donkey carts looked at us with astonishment. They could seldom have seen anything like it. Once, when we halted for a break, Barney called out the traditional Islamic greeting, '*As salaam alaycum*', to two men cycling past on the same bicycle. They promptly fell off in amazement, got up, dusted themselves down and stood staring at us both in silence before continuing their journey.

Our eyes gazed at the southern Silk Road, with its line of oasis towns set amidst barren surrounds, seeing the same scenes that Hedin and Stein had witnessed almost a hundred years before. Little had changed, except for one obvious thing: large blue trucks called 'liberation lorries' headed towards us at reckless speeds, their drivers taking up the road's width before blocking out the view for some minutes afterwards with thick clouds of dust. Modern perils for modern travellers.

We reached Markit wearing our layers of dust like battle honours as we filed through the greeting line of local girls in traditional costume outside our accommodation. We were tired and thirsty after the hot day's journey from Kashgar, the last three hours of which had been along sand tracks. The building was adjacent to the main street and within a small compound. Inside, the rooms had bare walls and concrete floors and were equipped with iron bedsteads and naked light bulbs. Each had a hole in the ground – the toilet. Next to it stood a rusty barrel of water – our washing facilities. And in my room two large frogs hopped around on the floor.

It was no surprise that local hospitality was primed and ready. It included the usual banquet with familiar speeches and by then still more familiar *bai jiu*. Nevertheless, it was the first real opportunity for me to meet the other Chinese members of both teams apart from Guo Jin Wei, the Chinese team's leader.

Ranked next to him was the impressive frame and cheery smile of Zhang Bohua, more usually referred to as Big Zhang. His qualifications for being in the crossing party were his apparent fluency in Uyghur and his prowess as a climber of supposedly immense fortitude and endurance. He certainly looked the part initially, but unfortunately that impression did not match his later performance. Then there was a 56-year-old government scientist called Lao Zhao who apparently had experience of research in the desert. I had observed him since we first met at Urumqi airport and had decided that he was probably tough, resourceful and self-contained, despite the fact that he looked like a schoolmaster taking his students for a Sunday morning nature stroll. Within a few days of the crossing Richard had nicknamed him 'Calculus' after one of the characters in Tintin. It was an apt title for someone who was to wander across the Taklamakan in a bright orange kagool, occasionally and inadvertently blowing up himself and others on the temperamental petrol stove that we used for cooking.

Finally, there was Qiu Lei, a thin and pale, spotty-faced individual in his late twenties who was the official Chinese photographer, or so we were told. With his buck teeth, long hair and unathletic build, I immediately looked upon Qiu Lei as a liability and knew I wouldn't get on with him. I protested strongly against his participation the following day but the Chinese line was uncompromising to the point of confirming that he was actually a representative of the Central Government; in effect, the man sent from Beijing to keep an eye on us. Keith quickly verified that Qiu Lei had little idea about photography and the sham of his cover story aggravated me still further, especially as I had only planned on taking two Chinese in the crossing party, but he and the government scientist had been forced on us as a *fait accompli* at the last moment.

The arrival of thirty handsome-looking male Bactrian camels and their six Uyghur handlers accompanied by their families caused a great stir in our compound the next morning. The courtyard was soon thick with camel droppings and the air filled with the pungent smell of the animals and the sounds of their bellowing. They were fat and well rested after a month's grazing nearby. The Chinese had organized their purchase with the local people from the area south of the Taklamakan, between the oasis towns of Hotan and Yutian, and then they had been herded 300 miles along the Silk Road to Markit. The appearance of the camels, and the condition of their flesh, looked splendid enough but we had no way of knowing if they were accustomed to moving over sand and enduring heat and other privations. Ranged along the wall beside our vehicles and other equipment they looked incongruous and archaic, as though belonging to another era of travel history. It was not easy for anyone without camel experience to appreciate the full extent to which our survival in the dunes depended upon them.

'Well, General,' remarked Richard, 'I reckon you now own more camels than anyone else in Central Asia.'

'What are we going to call them?' asked Carolyn. 'We must give them names. Sven Hedin did.'

In fact Hedin's preparations for his 1895 expedition were never far from my mind. He too chose to make the crossing from Markit to Mazartagh, a disastrous attempt from which only he, two Uyghurs and one camel survived by heading north out of the dunes and leaving the other two Uyghurs and seven camels behind in their sandy graves. At Markit he had assembled the provisions for the journey, including 'four iron water tanks and six goatskins to carry the water . . . and sesame oil to nourish the camels in the desert'. His camels were also males and all but one were Bactrian: 'We named them, in Jaggatai Turki, the language of the country, as follows: "The White", "Boghra" (the stallion), "One-Hump", "Old Man", "The Big Black", "Little Blackie", "Big Fawnie" and "Little Fawnie".' He was not to know that only Chong-kara (The Big Black) was to survive his brave attempt. Until our arrival no one had ever repeated it and, except for advanced technological communications, little or nothing had changed in all those years.

There was a great deal of sorting and preparation to be done on 22 September. We were due to establish a base camp on the edge of the dunes six miles east of Markit after the festivities of the following day and then begin the crossing on the 24th. Leaving the others in the compound to arrange the stores, Rupert, Mark and myself took the Bella vehicle to the edge of the dunes and tested our radio, navigation, and satellite equipment. We were stunned by the ferocity of the heat, and having walked only half a mile in the sand I returned to the vehicle sweating profusely and with a badly aching knee. It dented my confidence slightly but I dared not dwell upon the reality of actually having to walk in that inferno, each day taking us further away from the support team. Worse still, Rupert could not get the satellite data link working and he discovered a large crack in the casing. Without it we were down to the portable Ultralite voice-link that was powered by a petrol generator as our only emergency means of communicating with the UK and the Embassy in Beijing. That didn't work either. On top of everything, Mark was unable to get through to Francis who was in Markit manning the second high-frequency radio. The only things which functioned were the Motorola handheld radios with a range of about two to three miles for use between the front and rear of the camel caravan. Even Rupert's and my Global Positioning Satellite (GPS) navigation aids gave different readings when we came to check our exact location on the ground.

I returned to the compound in a sour and deflated mood and inspected the crossing party's personal and team equipment. This led to my first clash with the Chinese. When I got to Qiu Lei's equipment Guo insisted it was against Chinese custom for me to look inside his bags. I reasoned with him that any of them could check my team to satisfy themselves that only essential equipment was being taken into the desert.

'But, Charles, I have to say that this really is not our way,' insisted Guo as he stood between Qiu Lei and myself. I curbed my temper as Qiu Lei looked at me with his usual weasel-like, self-satisfied expression.

'It must be a joint effort,' I countered. 'No one will carry on the camels more than is necessary or we will all suffer. There must be a bare minimum. It may not be your way but I'm leading the expedition and I must be sure everything is correct.'

Richard sensed we were heading for a confrontation and knew I was in no mood for diplomacy after my earlier abortive communications reconnaissance.

'As a matter of interest, Charles, will you let Guo check your bags?' he asked, seeking a different tack against Chinese intransigence.

'Of course,' I replied.

'In which case, Mr Guo, would you mind then if Charles looks in your personal bags?'

'No, that is all right.'

'Then why can he not look in Mr Qiu's?'

'Because that is not the Chinese way,' replied Guo.

The charade was acted out several times and in the end I gave up. I knew that even if I did strip their kit down to nothing most of the items would creep back before we actually entered the desert. Therefore I decided to tackle the issue again once we were on our own as a crossing party, when common sense might prevail among the Chinese. The incident confirmed what we had suspected all along: Qiu Lei was a government agent and we had been deliberately obstructed from seeing the equipment in his heavy bags. They weighed twice as much as everyone else's, even those of Keith who was the professional photographer.

The entire situation began to frustrate me because the Chinese were transfixed by publicity and ceremonial stage management for our send-off. They could not grasp the need for diligent preparations and approached everything like a group of package tourists off on a happy hiking holiday in the sand in the delusion that someone else would take care of the arrangements. I doubted if any of them really knew what lay ahead. There again, neither did the rest of us: and I was to wrestle with that fear on and off for the entire duration of the journey.

I looked at the crossing party standing around in the courtyard. They were hot and restless. Piled nearby were our provisions, including the tin water tanks, sacks of food and camel saddles. There was no semblance of order and, in the midst of it all, locals in Lenin-style cloth caps milled about nosing into everything, the Chinese television crew got in the way, and hordes of Party officials clutching Taklamakan Crossing First Day covers pestered us for signatures. One support vehicle was still somewhere south of Islamabad and the communications equipment was not yet working properly. It was hardly surprising that I felt control of the expedition was slipping out of my grasp.

Richard laconically summed things up in his diary entry for the day:

After lunch there were rows over baggage, an inspection and the Chinese crossing party membership. It boiled down to this. We (the foreigners) basically saw the expedition as British-planned. The Chinese saw it differently – a joint venture in which the Chinese predominated, with a little technology for international flavour (and tourism promotion). In micro, there is a journalist who doesn't write, who doesn't take photographs and yet who seems imposed on us by Beijing. All rather rum. Will he come? I suppose so, but it will lead to friction. Meanwhile there was a fair amount of being marched up and down the hill by the Duke of York, or kit going in and out of rooms, vehicles and storage places.

By the early evening we had achieved some semblance of order. More importantly, Rupert had finally got through on the vehicle link to our satellite communications sponsor, Marine Technology International (MTI) at Chessington in southern England, and they sent back instructions for rectifying the Ultralite's problems. It felt good to be in touch with the outside world again and we were able to send a detailed update for Bella Birdwood to pass on to our sponsors and families. Mark and Francis, in the meantime, had also done wonders with the HF radio link which was now up and running.

The Mayor of Markit had decreed the following day a local holiday to honour our departure into the desert. Our farewell march through the streets was preceded by a deafening cannonade of firecrackers at the gates to our compound which caused panic among the camels. They had just eaten their fill of good hay, a luxury they enjoyed for the last time.

'Blar! Blar! Blar! (pause) Blar! Blar! Blar! (pause) De da da! De da da! Blar! Blar! Blar!' Bands of schoolchildren blowing battered, tarnished horns and banging their ancient drums marched ahead of us as we filed behind the British and Chinese flags, respectively carried by Captain Ho of the People's Liberation Army and Barney White-Spunner, conceivably the only British Army officer to lead a parade in China carrying their national flag. Behind the flags walked the members of the crossing party, then an entourage of senior Chinese Army officers in uniform, county and local officials splendid in their Sunday best, the support vehicles led by Bella, and finally the laden camels flanked by their dignified Uyghur handlers.

The crowds lining the hot and dusty streets were four deep by the time we had covered the short distance to the compound of the People's Hall, above which hung a vast red banner with white letters proclaiming, 'The send-off ceremony of the China Britons on the United exploration passing through Taklamakan Desert'. Everything had a dream-like quality to it. I had not been prepared for the scale of the occasion and I relished a temporary escapism that let me forget the awesome nature of the desert and the dangers that lay ahead.

Long tables decked with cloth bunting and Chinese ornamental lanterns overhead had been arranged on a platform at the front of the hall. From there we looked down on the colourful pageantry of hundreds of people packed into a compound decorated with flags and banners of all descriptions. There were parades of schoolchildren in bright turquoise, crimson, yellow and green uniforms; floats representing boats crossing the sea of sand; and lines of Uyghur dancers in their more traditional black and white costumes. Seated in honour among the senior Chinese officials we watched the bewildering clashes of noise and colour dominated by the strains of martial music from the brass bands. 'Blar! Blar! Blar! (pause) Blar! Blar! Blar! (pause) De da da ! De da da! Blar! Blar! Blar!' The phrase was repeated over and over again until our ears screamed in protest.

'If this is the send-off,' I shouted above the din to Richard beside me, 'what on earth will happen if we actually come out the other end?'

'Heroes of China, old boy,' he replied with a smile.

After rousing speeches in Chinese, Uyghur and English, the Mayor of Markit led the crossing party to the base of the dais where Uyghur women stood shyly with traditional costumes in their outstretched arms. We lined up facing them. They came forward demurely but solemnly and dressed each of us in turn in the traditional dark blue Uyghur robe with its wide red velvet sash around our waists and then the men completed the ceremony by placing a black and white Muslim prayer hat on each of our heads. They bowed before withdrawing and we smiled self-consciously, feeling for all the world as though we were lambs ready for the slaughter. Next came people carrying brown leather cases which were individually opened in front of me. They contained four locally made wooden musical instruments of the finest quality, presented as gifts to the British from the people of Markit. I was impressed by their attention to detail, for on the side of each instrument were delicately inlaid the words 'Royal Geographical Society'; underneath was our expedition logo of the Union Jack with a camel in the centre and the letters CCCC, one under each of the camel's hooves, which stood for Camel Crossing for Children's Cancer. I felt a warm surge of personal triumph. My mind flashed back to the moment when I had designed that logo whilst seated on an aeroplane *en route* to Germany on a visit to an Army establishment. In those hectic days of planning everything had had to be jammed in. The result of it all was now transformed into reality: for there we stood, resplendent in our Uyghur robes, being presented with local gifts in front of all those people and amidst the pomp and ceremony of local custom and taste, as though we were Victorian explorers and ambassadors from the Great White Queen across the sea. I had never dreamt that our departure for the desert would be marked by such an occasion and the gesture was deeply touching. My one regret was that no one in England would ever see it, let alone believe that scenes more reminiscent of a hundred years ago could still be acted out in a remote area of China.

The conclusion of the ceremony was a blessing by four solemn imams who entrusted Allah to guide us through the wastelands of death and take us into His keeping. Then, with the bands leading, we began the final procession along the street heading east. It was lined on both sides with schoolchildren in bright uniforms holding bouquets of paper flowers. Behind them stood yet more people. White doves were released in our path and clouds of confetti were scattered over us. The scale of the send-off was humbling and overwhelming: the blaring of bands, firecrackers bursting among us, a myriad of Han Chinese and Mongolian faces wearing expressions ranging from rejoicing to blank incomprehension, curiosity and sadness, all of these flashed past us as we marched along amid a kaleidoscope of colour, noise and emotions.

'*Hosh! Hosh!*' – 'Goodbye! Goodbye!' we called as we waved to the enthusiastic crowds who were now ten deep in places. Many people were crying and some of the women reached out to Carolyn with tears running down their cheeks and begged her not to journey into the Desert of Death. I saw the fear on their simple, uncomprehending faces and for the first time it occurred to me that they truly knew something we didn't. The emotional bewilderment of the attention we received brought home to me just how potentially fatal the local people thought our boasted exploit was. This was our funeral march. As I walked through lines of outstretched hands, the blur of impassioned faces and the noise of the cheering, I found myself swallowing hard to suppress an overwhelming desire to cry. Suddenly I feared never returning and I did not want these strangers to be the last ones to see me off: I wanted my own people there, the ones I loved, to witness the powerful spectacle and give me a final hug. I caught glimpses of Rupert, Keith, Carolyn and Richard absorbed in the clamouring attention and the frenzy of excitement. Their bearing, their pride and their very vulnerability to the ravages of the challenge before us made me seriously doubt whether we could pull it off without loss of life. Would we all be there at the end? I asked myself. If not, the blame would be mine. Mine alone.

Once again the legend of Sven Hedin's own journey was never far away. He too had experienced a similar send-off from Markit ninety-eight years previously.

> On the morning of April 10, our eight stately camels and their leaders marched out of Markit. The camels were heavily laden and the bronze bells tolled solemnly, as if for a funeral. The villagers had assembled on the roofs and in the street. They all looked grave. 'They will never come back – never,' we heard them cry one to another. 'The camels are too heavily laden; they will never get through the deep sand.'

The sound of the bands, the singing and cheering finally faded away as we reached a small bridge where the town proper and its solitary tarmac road both died. This was the signal for the procession to end. I felt exhausted by it all and the sweat poured off me. Then, as Richard recalled in his diary:

> There was a sort of separation of goats from sheep: only families of the Uyghurs (fairly extensive, still wailing), officials, vehicles, camels and us remained in the brief, blissful shade of a white poplar avenue. We were all hoarse from shouting and I couldn't imagine walking all day in this heat. The 'medium cheeses' hastened back via Kashgar to Urumqi, doubtless to their own great relief, and I can imagine the stories they swapped on the back of how awful these dusty Uyghur outposts were. The smaller, 'local cheeses' also looked relieved. In clapped-out PLA jeeps, aircon and windows having long ago ceased to work, we bumped and choked our way down sandy lanes, stopping from time to time to ensure the clouds of dust enveloped us all. A taste of a sandstorm? Perhaps the Lawrence of Arabia/Yasser Arafat scarves would have a role after all. Then I remembered mine was in a warehouse in Markit. Ah. We stopped in dunes, reeds and a terrifying silence. It was like the beginning of a war. Everyone was there to witness something heroic: only the enemy hadn't been identified. We foreigners strode around purposefully with binoculars, maps, briefing notes, check lists and communications equipment.

After the excitement and colour of the send-off from Markit, and the emotional build-up over the last few months, it was frightening to be poised on the edge of the infamous desert. Until then it had been a plan, which we had marketed successfully. In the process I had even convinced myself that it would be possible, providing fate was not against us. I looked back at the patches of green scrubland, the lines of poplar trees in the distance, and the cultivated fields around Markit to the west. In the opposite direction, to the east, in a haze of shimmering heat, was nothing; only a vast and unknown ocean of sand, its waves the gentle but sometimes jagged dunes that became entwined and interlocked as though forming a barrier to anyone who dared attempt a passage. The reflected glare off the sand was too bright for the naked eye and the heat was drier and heavier than I'd ever experienced before. The task which lay ahead was daunting.

An antiquated water-carrier had reached our base camp at the desert's edge and we filled the 80-litre tin water containers. There were twenty in total. I was more annoyed with myself than at any other time when I found that six leaked badly. It was entirely my fault for not having checked them back at the compound but the whole fiasco of the Chinese obsession with publicity for our departure had thwarted my preparation attempts. The only thing I could do was send them back to Markit with Zhang Bohua in the hope that a local welder could repair them before we started the crossing the following day.

That evening, as the desert thankfully cooled, our camel handlers invited us for a final feast. The British teams, the Chinese teams, the local officials who had stayed to witness our send-off, and the camel handlers with their families, all sat together around the edge of a blue tarpaulin sheet in the middle of which were plates of melon, the legs and the heads of sheep, local bread and rice. I studied the faces of the camel handlers: this was their moment and it was done with such touching simplicity and gentleness as to capture a different significance than the jamboree of Markit.

Our six handlers were all from the same village, the Seven Stars Commune, on the outskirts of Markit. It was only later in the journey that we were to understand fully the relationship between them, their complex personalities and something of their backgrounds. But at that moment, the last evening on the desert's fringes before we entered its uncharted depths, they merely represented yet another ethnic culture that the British had to get to know as members of an overall team dependent on each other for success.

Nearest in age to Esa Polta, the head camel handler and clearly the respected elder without such temporary status, was Emir, who looked like a gentle herdsman suddenly brought into the limelight of the 1990s. Then there was Abdul Rasheed, a tiny fellow with an impish smile and drooping eyes just like Dopey in *Snow White and the Seven Dwarfs*. I glanced around at the others. Kirim Yunus had a young and intelligent face matched by an athletic physique. Something about his bearing and manner suggested that he was more than just a simple Uyghur camel handler. Beside him was Rosa, Esa Polta's nephew, who led every conversation with the sharp humour and confidence of a London Cockney. He said he was 31 and had two daughters.

'I have three sons,' I replied.

'Excellent, excellent. Very strong!' was his enthusiastic reply.

Finally, seated beside Esa Polta, was Lucien, whose face reminded me of a young Nepalese tribesman with its tightly drawn Mongolian features and strong jawline. He was the youngest but nevertheless claimed to have four children and was Esa Polta's son-in-law. He had a quick smile and animated speech.

By the morning Zhang Bohua had still not returned. When he did finally arrive at ten o'clock he looked as though he had had a bad night on the town. More importantly he had failed to get the water containers repaired and instead offered thirty flimsy plastic 20-litre containers. I was furious. We filled them anyway, only to discover that the seals on the tops were no good and water sloshed out with the slightest movement. We improvised by cutting strips of cloth which marginally improved the fit of the seals. The next complication was that only two plastic containers would go into one camel sack which caused a loading problem when distributing the weight.

I had calculated on carrying 1,800 litres of water for the three-and-a-half-week crossing to Mazartagh, providing just under 5 litres a day for each person's needs – 2 litres of drinking water, 1 litre spare in our backpacks, and 2 litres for communal cooking and sweet tea. That was without wastage and left a fine margin for safety with temperatures rising into the hundreds. My prime concern, however, was the camels. Their chances of being watered were very much in the lap of the gods. There was no information on whether water could be dug for in the desert except some scant references in the accounts of Stein and Hedin. The local people said it was possible to find water on their hunting forays into the interior but they were not specific as to whether that would be the case all the way to Mazartagh. My satellite charts and maps were not an aid in this regard.

Since each camel would need up to 40 litres every three days there was no possibility of it being carried. My entire plan, therefore, rested upon a huge gamble: that we would be fortunate enough to find places where we could dig for sub-surface water in the desert itself. This was its best-kept secret and it would be a hit-and-miss affair. Would we find it? Hedin had dug successful wells deep in the sand at certain points where the ground signs were favourable but it could never be guaranteed.

Slowly and gradually the sand grew moister. It was evident there was water. When we got down about 6 feet, the sand was so moist that we could squeeze it into balls . . . The camels, waiting patiently, stretched their long necks over the sides of the well and sniffed at the cool wet sand. We were all standing in a ring around the gaping hole watching Kasim when all at once he stopped, letting the spade drop out of his hands. Then, with a half smothered groan, he fell to the ground. 'What is the matter? What has happened?' we asked. 'The sand is dry!' came a voice as if from the grave. We literally collapsed, conscious of our weariness, and realised how much of our precious strength we had wasted during the three hours we had toiled in vain. For three days the camels had not tasted a drop . . . we sought rest, leaving the patient, docile camels standing in a circle around the mocking well, waiting in vain for what they could not get.

Our lives were to depend on finding water for the camels hidden beneath the sands.

FOUR

Entering the Desert

My decision to strike out into the desert at midday on 24
September was not taken lightly for I was aware that it was
the hottest time of the day and that we had been in China
less than five days and were not acclimatized. Also, the altitude
of the desert at 5,000 feet above sea level would affect our
metabolisms.

Our preparations up to that point had admittedly been inadequate. Some would have argued that it was irresponsible to
lead men and beasts into such a formidable desert without
being fully prepared. There was no time to familiarize ourselves
with the camels and the loading and unloading techniques, the
water containers were far too vulnerable, and the rations and
equipment had not been comprehensively checked and tested.
To any onlooker it would have appeared that we had simply
thrown together thirty camels, three different ethnic cultures,
some containers of water, sacks of camel fodder and other
sundry items, topped off with the odd piece of sophisticated
technical equipment, and called it an expedition. Should anything go wrong, I would justifiably be accused of incompe-
tence and poor leadership.

On the other hand, I knew from experience how important
it was to get started and how things would then fall into place.
There were bound to be many testing incidents which we
couldn't hope to replicate in training. I remained confident
that by taking the first few days slowly and getting the routine

established things would work out. The only doubt remaining
was that of water for the camels and this lay in the hands of fate.

Already there were more echoes of Hedin's 1895 disaster. A
camel broke loose just before we left and tossed its two containers to the ground. One landed upside down, crushing its top.
We rushed over to restrain the other camels who were unsettled by the clamour, only to see the last of the water disappear
into the surface of the hot sand. The second container fared less
badly and we decanted the remaining water into three plastic
jerrycans.

'At this rate, Charles, everything is going according to schedule for a repeat Hedin performance,' Carolyn joked. She gave
no hint of fear that this might be an omen of disaster. 'First the
wailing women in the streets of Markit and then the accident
with the water containers. What next?'

'I don't mind skipping the next bit, including how he drank
camel urine and blood to stay alive,' added Richard.

With the truant camel placated and the loads readjusted we
struck out into the desert. Newly shaven, blessed, and in new
dotus, or Muslim prayer caps, our Uyghur camel handlers
looked splendidly proud.

'You would think they were ready for a *jihad*,' commented
Richard. 'By comparison, we look like a ragged line of beaters
about to walk up partridges in Spain!'

I was burning to set off. Hastily scribbled last-minute letters
were handed over to the support team, and the inadequacy of
my clumsy mixed-up thoughts to Tina filled me with guilt. I
checked the map for the third time that morning and confirmed with Rupert a compass bearing of 84° magnetic.
Shouldering his backpack, he set off into the distance as lead
scout, checking our direction line in the absence of landmarks
among the contours of the dunes. The heavily laden camels
stretched in a line behind us with the handlers at the head of
each train. It was a wonderful and exciting sight. The slow,
ungainly but graceful motion of the camels set the tone and
speed of our departure. It was camel miles per hour from now
on, and the weakest one dictated the daily progress of the entire
caravan.

I had mixed feelings as we entered the desert. On the one hand, there was the thrill of achievement. The germ of an idea, sown that morning in the library at Shrivenham, was now flourishing. On the other hand, I fully appreciated my personal responsibility for the outcome of the crossing, however far we got, and the lives of the team members, be they British, Chinese or Uyghur.

Barney, Francis and Mark accompanied us for a short distance. Barney walked beside me and joked, 'Now, Blackmore, make sure you come back alive as I don't want to be the one who breaks the news to Tina!'

'Well, as godfather to Toby you'll have to look after his future and pay his education,' I replied. 'So it is in your interests that I come out the other end!'

Barney chuckled but said nothing. He became more serious and I wondered what he was thinking. We had discussed my chances of success before. I recalled a number of occasions, back in England when we were alone, when Barney had looked at me and asked in that soft and confidential tone of voice, 'Do you really think you'll make it?' My reply had always been positive. 'I wonder,' he'd then say. 'I'm not actually convinced you will.'

It had never done my self-confidence much good hearing the inner doubts of a man I had grown very close to as a friend, a respected adviser and leader of the team responsible for trying to extricate us in an emergency. However, I never believed that Barney thought we would all die or mysteriously disappear and reinforce the desert's name and legend; instead I interpreted it to mean that we would not complete the crossing on account of the hardships and apparent physical impossibility of such a feat. In any case, he never elaborated and I never asked.

I was already sweating. We had covered less than half a mile up and down small undulating dunes. The sand was soft and my knee was painful in spite of the pills Carolyn had given me to ease the discomfort. The injury was constantly on my mind, making me mistrust my suitability for the crossing, never mind my leading it. I suppressed such fears and misgivings, concentrating instead on savouring the historic moment of the expedition's beginning.

I remembered Tina's brave words just before we said our goodbyes, only eight days earlier at Heathrow Airport, about ensuring I relaxed and enjoyed the experience. 'It is a bold and exciting adventure,' she had said, 'the like of which you will never repeat again.' I could still hear her soothing my pent-up anxieties. 'Remember, darling, you have put this whole thing together from scratch. Even to get to the edge of the desert will be an achievement. So go out there and do your best, it will be a unique feat, and don't worry about the boys and me, we're fine, we'll cope.'

Barney stopped and said that he would see us off from there. We shook hands and he wished me luck. 'See you at Mazartagh,' he shouted as I walked away from him at the head of the first train of camels. Then I was alone with my task in hand. Barney had his own worries and responsibilities: he had to get John's vehicle back in the expedition, move east along the Silk Road whilst maintaining communications with us in the desert's interior, contrive a rescue bid if the situation arose (although how he was going to do that we never decided: certainly the topography prevented access to us by vehicle), and try to get into the desert as far as Mazartagh for the first resupply. Between the two of us lay two or three months of testing leadership on which ultimately rested the fate of the expedition.

I noticed the silence of the desert for the first time – a desolate emptiness broken only by the trudge of my feet in the sand and the low resonant toll of the cylindrical bell around the neck of the lead camel. I checked Rupert's bearing again. He cut an impressive figure of strength and fitness as he probed ahead among the sand dunes. There was something indefinably reliable about him which I sensed would be needed in the future. I limped to ease the pressure on my knee which became particularly bad when climbing the dunes. How long would it hold out? I looked back. Mark and Barney's distant figures resembled a last contact with the outside world, watching as we entered the fearful void knowing nothing of what lay ahead except sand, and more of the same. After half an hour they had disappeared and we were on our own; thirty camels and fifteen people with sufficient water and rations for twenty-five days to Mazartagh. We continued for two hours. Richard chatted with everyone down the line of the caravan like a contented Jack Russell on a country walk. In between he would either sit upon the crest of a dune or stand and sketch a scene, pen-top in mouth, Barings baseball hat on head, a small and wiry figure in knee-length shorts and a dark blue shirt.

The atmosphere among the team relaxed as we wound our way slowly through low dunes forty to sixty feet high. There was a feeling of relief that we had finally got under away and that the serious business of crossing the desert could now begin. But it was hot, a blinding, searing heat of such ferocity that we did well to walk a few miles. Nearly another 800 to go suddenly seemed an eternity. Lao Zhao pointedly disagreed about the route and compass bearing which temporarily unsettled me at a time when I was feeling vulnerable over the responsibility of the massive undertaking we had embarked upon. Some would have suggested that ours was a death wish.

Within an hour the caravan had spread out over such a distance that it seemed unlikely it would ever come together again. I climbed to the top of a dune in the hope of finding a vantage point to survey the scene but I was disappointed: even thirty camels each some ten feet high were no match for the interlocking and overlapping maze of dunes which dwarfed them. Where the dunes were small and flat the caravan had gone straight over but where the slopes became steeper the handlers led them along a meandering path around the base and out of my sight.

In the mid-afternoon, another water camel went on the rampage, breaking free from its companions before the handlers could intervene, ploughing alone down the soft side of a dune in a cloud of sand and dust. Reaching the bottom it half rolled before Rosa and Lucien caught up. Too late. One of the 20-litre containers was crushed and its contents lost.

'At this rate there won't be a container left in three weeks'
time,' muttered Keith, shaking his head.

'Putting things into perspective,' Richard said, coming over
to me, 'Sven Hedin's departure was rash, his handlers were
dubious, his water preparations inadequate and his navigation
worse. I know it isn't the same, but the problems haven't
changed much.'

'Very encouraging, Richard, thank you.'

'Pleasure, old boy. Just thought I'd let you know. Maybe our
technology will make things better?'

'Hardly. The fact that we can talk to our support team or
people back in the UK doesn't mean we will get across the
desert.'

'True,' added Carolyn, who'd come across to where the
camel's baggage was being reloaded. 'If we are to come out alive
it will be because the people and the camels worked and the
water lasted.'

'I wouldn't want to hear a bookie's odds on that,' laughed
Richard.

I thought briefly of turning back to the support team for
more containers and spending a day longer training the camels
and ourselves in the routine of the crossing. It was an instinc-
tive reaction, based on a human tendency to gravitate to what
is familiar and secure rather than face the unknown and indefinable. I cursed myself for not having taken more care over the
preparation of the water containers. In most respects I had
drawn literally on the lessons of Hedin's experiences but this
aspect I had inadvertently overlooked. I had considered it at
length during the planning phase in England. Then, with so
much to do in such a brief space of time in China, I had allowed
it to slip my mind. Hedin had written that his tanks 'were surrounded by a wooden grating to protect the thin iron plates
against damage from knocks. Grass and reeds were packed in
between the tank and the grating, to prevent the sun's rays from
beating directly upon the iron.' Not that the padding lasted
long: within the week his handlers were forced to feed their
starving camels on it.

We continued the march and, after a while, the silence was

punctured by the sound of singing. It was one of the camel handlers. I remarked to Richard that things could not be too bad if they had something to sing about. It was a slow and haunting song which we were to hear nearly every day on the crossing.

By six o'clock we had covered six miles in five and a half hours. It was good progress by desert standards after a late and inauspicious start. I halted the leading camels in a flat area between a belt of dunes ranged on either side and waited for the rest to catch up. It was half an hour before the last camel reached us and we commenced unloading them or, rather, observed the Uyghurs so that we could do it the next time. The morale of the party soared when the stop was ordered and there was confident chatter now that the first tentative steps into the legendary desert had been safely completed. It had not been as bad as expected. The camels roamed from the camp after they had been unloaded, leaving the stores in untidy lines with baggage, camel sacks and sleeping bags spread like the possessians of a guerrilla army over the jagged valley.

As the sun settled behind the dunes, the colour of the sand turned grey and the shadows of evening stretched themselves slowly and luxuriously across the ground. We welcomed them. It was a pleasure to walk about bare-footed and savour the sand's cool and gentle softness between one's toes. The Uyghurs were busy digging an exploratory water hole and, after a while, there was a shout and they beckoned us over. The hole was only six foot deep and its sides were surprisingly firm but there, at the bottom, was a small pool of water gradually seeping through the dark, moist sand.

'*Su! Su!*' pointed Esa Polta, who was directing the efforts of his handlers. Rosa, in the bottom of the hole, scooped some into his hands. He sipped and then spat it out. '*Ella yukshe*', he said with a broad grin. I took that to mean it was good. Tonight, at least, the camels would drink; what would happen tomorrow we didn't know, but it was encouraging to find water and see that the water-hole technique worked. Everyone relaxed as the slow routine of evening camp naturally evolved. Lao Zhao sat beside the petrol cooker and stirred a large frying pan filled with sizzling meat. Rupert tried reaching the support team on the radio but failed. Richard was on top of a gently sloping dune forty foot high overlooking the camp with a sketch pad on his lap. Off to one side, Carolyn inspected the split nostril of a camel, caused by its wooden nose peg being ripped out by the leading rein. These pegs were thrust through the cartilage of the animal's nose to take the rope fastened from it to the tail of the camel in front. In such a way the camels were tied together in strings of four to six each. The knot was supposed to be sufficiently loose that, if the next camel fell, the knot would come undone of itself. Clearly, in this case, it hadn't.

Keith took photographs and I busied myself with the navigation for tomorrow's route. Richard came down from his dune.

'General,' he announced, 'I think it would be hygienic to have a proper toilet.'

'Good idea, Richard,' I replied, 'why don't you take a shovel, go downwind a few hundred yards around that dune and dig one?'

He set off with a shovel over his shoulder and, on his return, briefed us at length on the toilet routine and how it was the job of the last person to fill in the hole, even though we could never be sure who the last person would be. On account of Richard's enthusiasm for the chore I made him responsible for camp sanitation and water monitor in charge of checking and measuring our daily supply.

After the evening meal I got everyone together to discuss each individual's role and how we would operate as a team. The night air was warm and still, and a three-quarter moon cast shadows over the faces and figures of our group as we huddled together like the plotters of some great conspiracy. After all, we were: we planned to rob the desert of its mystery and legendary name once and for all.

'This campsite would have been a sensuous place,' reflected Richard later, as we lay in our sleeping bags, 'enlivened by dancing girls, Muslim rugs, flagons of chilled wine, roasted goat on a spit, and musicians echoing the controlled drama of the sunset. But with stew and rice, the prayers of the Uyghurs and the belching of the camels, it is still glorious.'

I gazed at the canopy of brilliant stars which seemed as vast and countless as the many dunes of the desert. The unknown open spaces which sandwiched our little caravan made us afraid and ashamed to flaunt our smallness in their presence. Other than the occasional cough of a camel in the distance or the clang of a bell as the animals moved about, the entirety of the silence brought with it my first feeling of inner peace and contentment for many months. I had truly arrived. The melancholy desert night wrapped itself around me and I did not wish to be anywhere else in the world.

'How are your feet?' I eventually asked Richard.

'They'll hurt like hell tomorrow. And your knee?'

'The same.'

The sun's sharp and intense heat early the following morning quickly removed the comfort and security of our night's camp. It hit us with all the ferocity of a hammer striking an anvil. Keith woke everyone before tackling the precarious task of getting the petrol cooker working without setting fire to himself. It was some time before the Chinese stirred and this made me cross; they had agreed to organize breakfast but they were incapable of waking up unless one of us stood over them shouting '*Niahow! Niahow!*' ('Hello! Hello!'). As the expedition went on they increasingly loathed this abrupt end to their slumber, but never once did they have the discipline to get up without it, let alone be the first up. That was another chore which fell to us.

As the camp stirred to life I watched the Uyghurs take themselves off to a fold between the dunes to find some privacy for their morning prayers. They stood shoulder to shoulder and faced Mecca as they chanted in unison. After a few minutes they knelt reverently and leaned forward until their foreheads touched the sand. Finally, they rose again, dusted themselves down and went to round up the camels that had strayed from our valley during the night. I had been surprised that the handlers had not hobbled the front legs of the camels with rope after dark to prevent them wandering. In the Middle East it had been a standard routine for my Bedu since a camel can roam many miles away from camp and, on one occasion, it took us a whole day to find them. There again, there wasn't much incentive to go walk-about in the Taklamakan, not even for a camel.

The camels were couched by the lines of stores to repeated shouts of '*Jugga! Jugga!*', the command used for getting them to kneel down. A sharp whack with a camel stick on the knee joints encouraged the less willing ones. One camel turned, drew back its lips and spat a large gob of regurgitated food straight at Emir. It hit him square on the back. He took up his stick in a rage and beat the poor beast on the head — it responded with screams of indignation. The initial loading of the baggage on the camels was an important task. It could not be rushed otherwise the imbalance of equipment and poorly secured loads would cause frequent delays during the day's march. We watched the skilful handlers that morning and learned from them the subtle art of load distribution and of tying the camel bags, water containers and grain sacks. The majority of the camels were co-operative and placid in spite of being tugged about and having heavy weights dumped on them; others were less docile. A camel branded with the figure 8 on its hind leg was the worst: it spat and bellowed, kicked out, and shot to its feet at the slightest touch of any downweight, creating such a fuss that he became impossible to load at times.

The loading operation required the help of everyone, but even with us all working flat out it still took nearly two hours each morning throughout the expedition. Thirty camels to manage are a lot. Someone had to round them up as they frequently strayed far during the night. They had to be marshalled in an area near the stores and selected for the right load, whether it was water, grain or baggage. Then they had to be brought forward, couched, placated and loaded before being taken to one side and joined to an appropriate train with five others. Good teamwork was vital and I was unimpressed to see Qiu Lei that morning seated off to one side, apparently busy with his camera equipment. He looked ridiculous in his white cotton one-piece zip-up jacket with trousers. Instinctively, I knew we were in for a show-down. As far as I was concerned, this was my expedition and I had handpicked the team. I had not asked to be lumbered with a political agent posing as a photographer who had probably never spent a night under the stars before. I had marked his card 'passenger' right from the moment I set eyes on him that night in Markit. Richard spotted the cause of my distraction and promptly strode across to Qiu Lei with a barrage of Chinese words that provoked a sharp, loud and heated argument. Richard turned away in barely concealed disgust and we knew the matter could not rest there. Qiu Lei needed careful handling and it was important not to alienate him at the outset. Somehow I had to find the key with which to unlock him, thereby bringing him into the team rather than allowing him to work in isolation.

By 10.30 a.m., after two hours of loading, we were ready to continue the crossing. The thermometer registered 90° Fahrenheit. There was no wind. The sensation of thirst was very strong and I longed to drink from one of the two water bottles we each carried.

The morning's march was frustrating because of the slow pace of the camels and the many deviations around the increasingly wide sand dunes. Too frequently the inadequate rope between the camels would break and there were regular halts to bring them together again. We had yet to learn which camel was best suited to which load, and by midday there had been three accidents after the animals had run amok and dumped their baggage. Fortunately, there were no water containers among them but two of the grain sacks were split open and had to be painstakingly stitched up again. The third time we sat down apathetically and rested. The heat was intense and I felt utterly drained. Then Rosa dug into a camel sack and, with a triumphant smile, unexpectedly produced a large watermelon for us. We gazed longingly as he expertly cut it into slices, our eyes watching each drop of juice as it teasingly fell to the ground and instantly disappeared. Casually, feigning indifference despite the scorching sun and burning hot sand, we took the fruit and savoured each bite of the red flesh, spat out the pips and gnawed its freshness right down to the thick green skin. Every mouthful was bliss and I held the moisture for as long as possible before reluctantly swallowing.

By this time Rupert and Keith, who had been ahead, had disappeared from sight. I took two slices and followed in their tracks. My knee hurt and my head throbbed from the heat, which was made worse by its reflection off the sand. I felt lethargic and faint. Could we survive for 780 miles across the entire desert like this? My thoughts were sober as I plodded ever onwards across the shimmering line of white dunes which stretched endlessly ahead to the horizon, dotted with the occasional tamarisk shrub. It was only the second day and my respect for the immense power of the desert had grown by the minute. I looked at the two slices of watermelon in my hand and longed to devour their dripping juice. It was a hard test. Would Keith and Rupert ever know? After all, I could claim that I had dropped them in the sand. The very devil tempted me but my integrity held out. Just. I found Keith after ten minutes. He too was suffering from the heat but he was cheerful. 'Rupert's further up ahead,' he said. We exchanged few words, each of us unwilling to expend any energy in unnecessary talk. I walked on. The temperature was stifling as the sun blazed down from a clear sky. Ten minutes later I came across Rupert, half lying under a tiny area of shade provided by a convenient lone tamarisk shrub. With the sun nearly overhead there was little shadow. He thanked me and took the melon. I did not tell him how difficult it had been not to eat it myself during those last twenty minutes. We sat together in companionable silence and waited for the head of the caravan to emerge from the jigsaw of dunes.

All that day we headed on the bearing and my strength began to fade. I knew that I was dehydrated but we were all in the same situation, although none of us dared show it. I unscrewed the top of my aluminium Army water bottle and looked miserably at the tiny amount of warm water left in the bottom. I calculated that there were three mouthfuls left. Not enough for three more hours walking. We had to cover twelve miles that day and I was determined to achieve that.

Rupert seemed unaffected and strode out far ahead of the caravan on a perfect bearing. Behind him we led the camels a meandering route by choosing the less difficult ground. Where

Rupert went straight over a dune, keeping to his direction line, we went around the sides. He was a walking powerhouse and I admired his strength. My diary for the remainder of 25 September read:

Esa Polta asked me to stop at about 5.30 p.m. He said that from here (Desert Camp 2, 38° 51.30′N and 78°06.08′E) there would be no water for the camels for two days. We had done only 8.2 miles since Desert Camp 1. I was actually quite ready to stop, being close to dehydration. I had no energy for anything. I collapsed under the shade of a tamarisk shrub and cooled off. Dreadful feeling. My worst fear is whether I personally can pull this off. Rupert and Carolyn are fine. Richard was tired and Keith was flat out. The Chinese fared no better. It was an effort unloading the camels. We let them wander free while taking it in turns to dig a water hole. The others may have been different, if not they equipped themselves well, but it took all my self-discipline and the last of my energy to handle a shovel with visible manliness. At the start the sand effortlessly swam back to reclaim the temporary indentation left by my shovel and it seemed improbable we'd ever clear it fast enough to dig the well. The only clue to it being a suitable spot had been the imperceptible thin white crust on the surface in the leeward and windward hollow between some dunes. The signs were not commonplace and we had marched all day before finding any. It appeared the moisture from the depths below the sand had been sucked by a capillary action to the surface and there evaporated over a long period of time to form the salt crust. We worked in shifts of two digging and two resting. Stripped to our waists and wet with perspiration we toiled under the late afternoon sun with a unity of purpose. Once the softer sand had been excavated from the sides of the square it became possible to take the hole deeper. That night we were fortunate and the sand became moist at a depth of three feet. At five feet I took a handful of wonderfully cold sand and squeezed it hard until tiny bubbles of water appeared. Then at seven feet the brackish water seeped into the hole and stayed there. That was but half of the backbreaking chore. The next part was to prevent avalanches of sand pouring into the well whilst buckets were laboriously filled and passed up to waiting hands who carried them to the thirsty camels. Thirty animals are a lot to water and the shift went on until the early hours of the morning.

Richard wasn't interested in digging a latrine tonight! As I write this now, in my sleeping bag by moonlight, he is to my right, Rupert is on my left (attending to his blisters by sewing cotton thread through the bubble – a Parachute Regiment trick, he said) and Keith is fast asleep. Carolyn patched up my blisters. Felt much better after some food. Carolyn and I have just heard voices singing in the desert miles away. Perhaps, as the legend goes, these are the desert demons calling us. We could not reach the support team on the radio.

For the next six days we traversed sand mountains up to 1,000 feet high in places. Lao Zhao said there would be seven of them but we eventually crossed twenty-four. Ahead the landscape was the same: two-mile-wide valleys of dunes up to 200 feet high which we fought our way across until the beginning of the ascent of another massive 1,000-foot sand mountain that lay across our route. We gave up counting them. We had no information from our maps* or from the Uyghurs about where we might possibly find water for the camels so there was no alternative but to continue pressing eastwards in the hope of finding somewhere to dig.

The British members of the team surpassed themselves. They were always right at the front, leading the camels or coaxing them up sheer dunes, struggling to help them through the soft sand and never relaxing for a moment. I observed them with pride. By contrast, the Chinese appeared almost to give up, as though the sand mountains and the heat were too much for them. With the exception of Lao Zhao, they walked at the rear of the caravan, favouring the narrow footpath of compressed sand formed by the passage of one hundred and twenty camel feet in a line. It was easier at the rear. Rupert coined a saying: 'He who walks at the rear has camel shit on his boots.' It was true. At the front the sand was soft and virgin; each person strained their leg muscles and expended precious energy forging a route through or break-ing off to help a camel train ascend a high dune. The sand

---

*Tactical pilotage charts with a scale of 1:500,000, prepared by the American Defense Mapping Aerospace Center. The maps showed no relief data and the squares of longitude and latitude were simply shaded yellow. In places were the less reassuring words, 'uncharted' or 'topography unknown'.

mountains stretched to the horizon and beyond. There was no way out.

On 26 September, only our third day in the desert, Rupert, Richard and I were afflicted by attacks of acute diarrhoea. The initial scene was amusing: Richard bolted over the crest of a dune whilst Rupert and I made a dash for another spot. We were half-way through loading the camels that morning.

Rupert and I smiled across at each other, squatting in the sand, as a symphony of loud farts accompanied by simultaneous releases of hot, gravy-thin fluid cascaded from within. The smell was revolting.

'Better out than in,' quipped Rupert.

'This could be the beginning of a real test,' I replied. It was. Our condition deteriorated slowly over the following six days until each of us was experiencing bowel movements every hour. The illness became very debilitating and dehydrated us even more. There were some mornings when we barely had the strength to lift the heavy loads on to the backs of the camels. The cleft between my buttocks became painful as sand mixed with moisture rubbed as I walked until the skin became raw and then cracked and bled.

Eventually, the experience was more a humiliation than a joke. Rupert, still out at the front blazing the trail, would disappear from sight for some time and I knew he was quietly suffering. He never complained. I became concerned that he was pushing himself too hard in those early days. He refused to drink any more than two water bottles a day, even though we each carried a third as a reserve in our day sacks. His stubbornness and refusal to admit or show any signs of physical weakness annoyed me. I did not want him suddenly to go down on us. Carolyn always said that the way to cope with sickness or sunstroke was prevention rather than cure, yet Rupert insisted upon tackling his problems alone and would not let any of us assist. Richard's strength was the first to go. Regardless of his condition, he displayed tremendous stamina and courage, and maintained his wonderful sense of humour throughout. Yet, by the fifth day, he was clearly very ill and Carolyn diagnosed a case of amoebic dysentery.

His eventual decline came quickly. We had been leading the caravan on a difficult passage through a maze of small sand dunes so soft, and with such sharp ridges, that it had taken two scouts up front to select the best route for the camels. Richard had taken turns with Rupert and me, dashing left and right, up and down the dunes, calling out directions and simultaneously keeping ahead of the front camel train to avoid any hold-ups. In temperatures reaching 110° Fahrenheit, and on a meagre diet and self-imposed water rationing, the task proved a formidable one.

On that day we collapsed for a rest, our energy and enthusiasm quite spent. There was no protection from the sun which beat down remorselessly and dried out our skin. We were covered in fine sand – it was in our hair, all over our bodies, in our ears, eyes and mouths. Always there was the continual crunch of grit between our teeth. We lived in it. It was a natural extension of our existence. Rupert and I then took the lead. There were times that afternoon when I could willingly have caved in. I could not believe that we would survive such punishing conditions. But we kept on, trudging eastwards, knowing that each step brought us nearer to our goal. After an hour only half the camels were in sight. We halted. One of the camels carrying two water containers backed into another and a container was punctured. Water gushed from the hole. We watched, reacted slowly and, with visible lethargy, struggled to our feet and attempted to repair the damage. Everything was a tremendous effort. No one wanted to give up their last ounce of energy in case they went over the top. It was almost tempting to lie there in the hot sand and pretend it had not happened: to have done so, shedding all responsibility, would have been wonderful. With Keith's help I eventually plugged the hole with strips of cloth wrapped around a piece of wood from a camel stick. It was rudimentary but it worked. We lay there afterwards, too exhausted to contemplate the remaining hours left before the happy release of the cool of evening. But while daylight remained we had to continue. The pace had to be ruthlessly maintained if we were not to be beaten by the sand mountains. It would have been easy to have halted early or taken longer breaks, but that would not get us out of our desert prison any quicker: ours was a race against the rapidly diminishing supply of clean drinking water that we carried. Once that was gone we would survive for no more than three days in that punishing temperature. Travelling at night was one way of reducing the risk but I had discounted it after careful thought. Keeping thirty camels and fifteen people together in the darkness would be very difficult: the risk of someone becoming disorientated and separated was too high. Besides, navigating through the dunes by day was hard enough – by night it would be even more awkward, and slower. At least marching by day our bodies created a slight cooling breeze which was preferable to lying at rest under a pitiless sun that would sap our energy and dehydrate our bodies.

The remaining camels with the Chinese had caught up but Carolyn and Richard were missing. I had not noticed their absence before. It was unusual for them not to be near the front. The Chinese sat together despondently around the last camel train. They said nothing. The weariness of the situation was overwhelming and no one was in the mood for chat. Our isolation and vulnerability amid the colossal landscape were depressing. I was cross that the Chinese had not helped lead the camels over the dunes that day – it had been all they could do to keep up. That fact particularly grated as I watched the valiant efforts of my team as they struggled to set the pace and direction through the dunes, three out of five of us fighting off repeated attacks of dysentery. We had not told the Chinese. There was no point; they did not have the teamwork or even the strength to help us, let alone understand our intense physical suffering and degradation. On the other hand, I pitied them because they had not volunteered to risk their lives for the vanity of achievement; they had been ordered to accompany us and I often felt the sadness in their eyes and wondered what they were thinking. Two races could not have been less alike – the bravado and devil-may-care insouciance of the largely irrepressible British spirit and the suspicious, distrustful and almost childlike insecurity of the Chinese. Their strengths were different, but then so were their background and history.

After forty-five minutes Carolyn and Richard appeared, small figures dwarfed by the dunes, the shape of their bodies distorted by the waves of rising ground heat. At first it looked as though they were strolling along having a good talk, oblivious to us waiting. Not until they came closer and Richard nearly collapsed as he sat down did I sense that something was wrong.

'Charles,' Carolyn called, 'you'd better come here'. With an effort I got up and walked over to them. Richard's bearded face was lined and haggard.

'Sorry,' he said, 'didn't mean to hold you up but I went all funny and our marvellous Doc here came back to rescue me.' Carolyn then told me how she had realized that Richard had dropped far behind the trail and had gone back to look for him. She found him lying in a depression between two dunes talking to himself. Richard described the scene less dramatically later with his characteristic humour, relating how he'd had an appalling attack of diarrhoea, the bloody discharge from which left him so weak that he had been unable to move.

In that state he began thinking back to the time when he was lying on a beach in Mombasa on his honeymoon, looking across the blue sea to the Portuguese fort on the peninsula and watching his wife, Anthea, walking across the sand towards him. He spoke to her. That was when Carolyn reached him. Richard made light of his condition and refused to ride a camel. Carrying his brown moccasin shoes in one hand and a water bottle in the other, he presented a comical caricature of an explorer walking barefoot through the sand with short, uncertain steps. After ten minutes I saw him half stumble and half run as he sought the cover of the nearest dune where he could relieve himself with some dignity. He was clearly suffering badly and the conditions we faced were not likely to improve his state. This was just the beginning.

FIVE

Dysentery and the Sand Mountains

The sand mountains were our greatest test on that first leg to Mazartagh. We prided ourselves on each day's progress, knowing that the same obstacles had defeated Sven Hedin and killed off virtually his entire caravan. Aurel Stein had even turned back after reaching the first of the high dunes, believing them to be totally impassable. Yet the desert had its own magic quality. Occasionally a rare cool wind blew seductively over the top of the highest dunes and dried our sweaty shirts. The great craters of unruffled sand beckoned us, and the play of light and shadow beguiled us. Ahead lay row upon row of further peaks and higher mountains which were separated by brief valleys. Alas, they ran north to south and not west to east – beautiful but frightening.

Under such strained circumstances there were inevitable clashes, most of them between myself and the Chinese. None were serious and all helped finally to consolidate my position as leader. The first occurred towards the end of a day when, due to the extremely difficult terrain, we had gone only seven miles. Everyone was very tired. Esa Polta looked around solemnly and said something to Big Zhang (who spoke questionable Uyghur).

Big Zhang (in Chinese to Richard): 'He says there is no water here. Tomorrow and for three days after in these hills there will also be no water. On the third day the camels will start to die. And on the fourth day they will die.'

Richard to myself (in English): As above plus, 'Sounds promising, doesn't it?'

Myself to Richard (aside): 'It would have been useful to have known this before, really. But there's no point in standing around. We'll keep going.'

Myself to Richard (loudly in English): 'Thank him for his comment. It's hard to be sure of anything out here because no one has been here that we know of. This is not a good place to camp. We have another hour of light left. Let's go on and get lower into the valley. Besides, there might be water there.'

Richard to Big Zhang (in Chinese): As above.

Big Zhang to Richard (in Chinese): 'This is not good.'

Big Zhang then translates to Esa Polta in Uyghur, and at length.

Esa Polta grunts.

Guo Jin Wei (in English and Chinese): 'What's happening?'

Big Zhang (in Chinese): 'He (Charles) wants to go on. He (Esa Polta) says there is no water.'

Guo Jin Wei (in Chinese): 'So?'

Big Zhang (shrugs): 'Crazy.'

Myself (in English): 'Let's go on, Guo, while there's still light.'

And on we went. With that, Richard took up the rein of the lead camel and, despite his frail condition, set off at a spanking pace towards the next line of high dunes. The Chinese fell in behind and muttered among themselves. Rosa and Kirim, however, came up to me as we ascended the dune and told me with huge smiles on their faces how strong the British were, clapping my back and thighs with exclamations of '*Chambar! Chambar!*' which means 'The strong one'.

'*Yukshe dos* (good friend)!' they exclaimed, again patting me on the back. '*Ella yukshe* (very good).' The gesture was flattering but I wasn't sure their enthusiasm wasn't misplaced.

Another situation was potentially more awkward. We had selected a campsite one evening at a spot likely to be good for digging a water hole. Inevitably, at the day's end, the chore of digging was an onerous one which nobody enjoyed nor had the energy for. The camels had been unloaded, Lao Zhao and

Guo were preparing the evening meal, and Rupert was attempting to get through on the radio. Taking the lead I picked up two long-handled shovels and headed towards an undulating patch between the leeward and windward sides of some dunes where a tell-tale white crust of solidified sand salt suggested there could be water if we dug deep enough.

'Digging?' inquired Qiu Lei as I passed him.

'Yes, here you are,' I replied, handing him one of the shovels. He looked at me blankly but I ignored him and carried on to the spot and started digging. I was alone at first until Carolyn, Keith and Emir joined me. I noticed after a while that Emir had the same shovel that I had given to Qiu Lei. I looked back towards the camp, set up on a low flat dune. Qiu Lei was seated by the cooking area smoking a cigarette and talking to the others. Our eyes met briefly. I gave him my best thousand-metre penetrating stare, as I'd describe it, intending to convey exactly what I felt. He turned away without a flicker of recognition or, what was worse, any sign of guilt. I carried on digging in the hope that my example would eventually be followed. It was not.

Then, unable to control my rising anger any longer, I slammed down the shovel, swore loudly and strode back towards the camp, covering the distance in long purposeful strides. I ascended the side of the dune and shouted to Qiu Lei, 'I asked you to help dig a hole. Now get down there and start digging.'

'I'm sick,' he said pathetically, his face a picture of contrived abject misery. 'My leg hurts . . .', he continued, until I cut him off.

'Your leg hurts! Both my bleeding legs hurt and I have a bad stomach,' I interjected sharply. 'Now get down there and dig!'

'You cannot order me,' said Qiu Lei, choosing a different tack.

'I can order you. I am the expedition leader, now dig!' I yelled back, seized by an intense desire to knock his block off.

'You say please,' he replied in a half defensive tone.

'Please!' I shouted at the top of my voice, and then grabbed his arm and frogmarched him to the water hole.

To his credit, he dug for an hour and subsequently always made a semblance of effort. But I knew it could have been a close-run thing; my authority had been on the line and I wasn't sure what I would have done had he continually refused.

There were also light-hearted moments. One in particular happened after Richard lost his temper with Rupert and myself while we were acting as lead scouts. Rupert had gone to the left of a vast dune, looking for the line of least resistance, and I had carried on straight ahead. To our right the dunes continued almost vertically to a false summit with a plateau that tapered off to the south. To everyone but Richard it was obviously the hardest route.

'What's the point of having scouts if they don't get ahead and find the best way?' he asked, annoyed at us for being indecisive over the trail. 'Now where has Rupert gone? He's always buggering off on his own and no one can follow his tracks.'

Before I could reply he turned his six camels sharply towards a deep depression and descended into it. Reappearing on the far side, he headed towards the sheer dune walls of the least impassable route. Carolyn went with him, more concerned for his deteriorating health than out of any faith in his choice of route, and encouraged the camel train with volumes of Devonian expletives.

'Gooan there! Gerrup the dune! Ha! Ha!' and she waved her large Australian bush hat.

To my profound relief, the remaining camel trains led by the Uyghurs did follow my tracks. I watched Richard's small figure at the front, determinedly pulling on the taut tope as he hauled the reluctant camels further up the slope.

'Richard,' I shouted across the dunes, 'don't be an ass, this is the best route, come back this way.'

He ignored me, screaming 'Cha! Cha!' at the camels whilst Carolyn used her long stick to urge them on. Up and up he went with his six camels, higher and higher until he was eventually quite a distance away. It was a magnificent display of grit and determination. He seemed literally to pull those camels up the steep leeward side of the dune.

From where I stood, a few hundred yards ahead, I could see

a sharp ridge around a moon-shaped depression that was clearly a dead-end even to Richard and his fine troop of obedient camels. The first camel attempted it and fell floundering in the sand, bellowing in its effort to stand up as the others drew back and their legs sank to above their knee joints. I looked on anxiously and half expected to see the camels, complete with baggage, roll down the slope. Everything hung in the balance until the ropes snapped between the middle pair. Then total chaos reigned. Richard went back down the line, struggling to keep his own footing on the edge of the high dune, and tried to sort them out with Carolyn's help. It was a tough job for only the two of them.

'Richard!' I shouted at the top of my voice. 'Stop being a f——g idiot and come this way. You really can't get through there.'

He said something that I didn't catch, which was probably just as well. He then threw his camel stick into the sand in a fit of exasperation, took off his hat and sat down. Carolyn went up to him, put her arms around his neck and gave him a kiss. I was half tempted to go to their aid but decided that Richard had to sort out his own predicament. Finally they both managed with great skill to get the camels together again, turn them around and head back down towards the direction line that I had taken earlier.

That night we laughed a great deal about the incident. Rupert teased Richard, saying that at one point he was convinced he saw the camels putting on their oxygen masks as they followed Richard out of curiosity towards the highest summit of the Taklamakan Desert. Richard was suitably apologetic about being so obstinate, and I still have this memory of 'Bright Little Bean' (as the Chinese nicknamed him) with his admirable following of camels marching resolutely ever onwards and upwards. 'Anyway,' Richard said in conclusion, 'it was worth it after all; at least I got a kiss from the Doc!'

That was Richard's last great effort. The following day he succumbed to his amoebic dysentery, the physical strain of his earlier efforts having taken their toll.

A partial explanation for three of us contracting dysentery so early in the expedition lay in the daily cycle of the frying pan. This huge, flat-bottomed pan with its long wooden handle was used for cooking our breakfast and evening meal. During the day the pan was kept in a camel sack where dust and sand stuck to any remaining food deposits. In the evening, once it had been used for cooking, it then mysteriously migrated towards the Uyghur camp near the camels. There, unbeknownst to us, it served not only as a water trough for thirsty camels but also as a bowl for their meal of corn. When everyone had gone to sleep it lay discarded in the open, either in the bottom of the water hole if one had been dug, or by the circle of couched camels. In the morning, since the British were always up before the Chinese, a search would be mounted for the missing frying pan. After a couple of days it became routine to retrieve it from the Uyghurs. The pan was then roughly cleaned with sand before being used for breakfast. Finally, it was returned to the hot confines of a dirty camel sack until the evening, when the cycle began again.

I watched this happen, as we all did, for the first week without even registering its significance. The pan's nightly disappearance still remained unaccounted for and I thought nothing of finding it with the Uyghurs in the morning. Then the penny dropped. One morning I saw the pan being used after breakfast to water and feed the camels again, and the full import of what had been happening finally struck me. I said nothing until that evening, once the stores had been unloaded, when I assembled the crossing party for a simple demonstration.

'This is a bucket – it is for watering and feeding camels,' I said, holding up an aluminium pail.

'This, however, is a frying pan which is for humans to eat from. Bucket – camels; frying pan – humans.'

Of course it was too late by then, but the essential lesson of hygiene and cleanliness was not lost upon us for the rest of the crossing. I did not place sole blame for our condition on the germs from the pan; by any standards our bodies had received a rude shock and the metabolisms of Richard, Rupert and myself had not coped with the stark contrast to their normal

The author says farewell to the crowds in Markit as the expedition leaves for the desert on 23 September. Many people were crying and some of the women reached out to Carolyn with tears running down their cheeks and begged her not to journey to the 'desert of death'

The caravan of thirty camels ascends a 1,000-foot-high sand mountain. Lao Zhao said there would be seven such mountain ranges across our route from Markit to Mazartagh – we eventually crossed twenty-four, each nearly a mile wide with two-mile-wide valleys in between where the dunes were 200–400 feet high

3. The camels are unloaded at an evening campsite in the sand mountains. The next day's route was straight over the top

Crossing the never-ending ocean of sand in temperatures of 100°F. Three of us
struggled with dysentery, and thoughts of Sven Hedin's ill-fated 1895 expedition
were never far away

5. Rupert Burton (*centre*) demonstrates the high-frequency radio link fo contacting the Silk Road party to Carolyn and the author. The Mazartagh mountain line looms behin the only rock formation in the entire desert

6. Rendezvous in the desert one day's march west of Mazartagh. The haze marks the beginning of a sandstorm

'. *En route* to the ancient site of Niya, Carolyn treats the wounds of the camels caused
by the wooden baggage frames rubbing against their bodies as they became thinner.
The suppurating sores were riddled with maggots

. The caravan slowly works its way east across the desert. The silence was complete
except for the tolling of camel bells. 'No man can live this life and emerge unchanged.
He will carry, however faint, the imprint of the desert, the brand which marks the
nomad; and he will have a yearning to return, weak or insistent, according to his
nature. For this cruel land can cast a spell which no temperate clime can match.'
(Wilfred Thesiger, *Arabian Sands)*

9. Emir leads camels each carrying two 80-litre tin containers of precious water. Nearly 160 litres were lost in the first few days because of camels breaking loose and rolling down the dunes in their panic

10. Finding water for the camels was a continual gamble. Once we went for seven days without finding a suitable place to dig a well. This site was on the route from Tatrang to Luobuzhuan, when the temperature averaged minus 5°F in the daytime. The camel handlers are Kirim, Emir (*seated*) and Suleiman (*in the well*). The water was too brackish and saline for human consumption

1. Vertical sand walls blocked our route in many places during the last 165 miles to Luobuzhuang. There was no choice but to make lengthy and slow detours. Already tired and sick, we felt dwarfed by the immensity of the seemingly impenetrable sand dunes

2. Mark (*left*) watches Suleiman cutting meat from the camel we had killed on the morning of 10 November. We would be needing the extra rations later. The temperature was minus 10°F

13. The afternoon after leaving the 'camp of death' where the camel had been killed. The size and shapes of the dunes were more awesome than the sand mountains *en rou* to Mazartagh and now our reserves of energy were totally spent and the camels were exhausted, often collapsing in the soft sand, unable to rise. We had not found water fo four days. That night we camped at the top of the sand mountain in the centre of the picture and ate the meat of the dead camel. That night, too, the Chinese nearly mutin

14. The desert had been conquered. The author and the Chinese team leader, Guo Jin Wei, celebrate at Luobuzhuang after a 780-mile crossing that took 59 days

routines. Walking for eight to ten hours a day in temperatures of around 100° Fahrenheit through soft sand at an altitude of 5,000 feet above sea level is enough for most people. Add the fact that three litres of drinking water a day are hopelessly inadequate, top it off with a stark and changed diet, and the sum effect of the equation on an unacclimatized body is plain for all to see.

By the end of the first week in the desert we had covered nearly seventy miles. It was a time of growing together and learning each other's strengths and weaknesses. A strong affinity developed naturally between the British and the Uyghur camel handlers. By contrast, we noticed that the Chinese regarded them as almost inferior, an inbred attitude stemming from centuries of Han domination of the minority peoples of Xinjiang.

Esa Polta once told us why he came on the expedition. During the planning stage, a year earlier, Guo Jin Wei had been advised by the Chinese Communist Mayor of Markit that Esa Polta was one of the few men who knew the desert and had experience of camels. Guo went to Esa's simple dwelling on the outskirts of Markit and explained the nature of the journey. Esa listened attentively but said nothing until the end.

'You will all die,' he finally commented in the matter-of-fact and unemotional tone of someone whose seventy-six years had seen hard times and suffering. 'The journey you propose is quite impossible. It has never been done before.' He went on to recount the legends of the desert and the stories he had heard from his father of the generations of men who had never returned from hunting forays into the interior. By way of verification he concluded with the account of Hedin's ill-fated journey. That expedition had departed from his birthplace only twenty-two years before he was born. Perhaps his parents had lined the streets of Markit and said farewell to Hedin's camels and handlers as they filed past on that last occasion.

Thinking that he had to look elsewhere, Guo was surprised when Esa concluded by saying quietly, 'But I will come with you, despite my years, for I wish to see once again the land I hunted over in my youth and the far-off Mazartagh mountain range. I want to see the land of my forefathers before I die. Then I shall rest in peace. *Al hamdulillah.*'

When the story was translated to us around the camp fire one evening, I did not know whether to draw confidence from the fact that Esa was with us or not. Richard firmly believed that Esa had decided to lay his weary bones to rest in the desert. That fatalistic interpretation certainly left us with nagging doubts as to the prospects for our own survival.

The feeling was reinforced towards the end of a long and tiring day shortly afterwards, when we had nearly crossed the last of the great sand mountain ranges. The Uyghurs were becoming excited at the thought of seeing the fabled Mazartagh mountain line before long. At every halt they crowded around my map and demanded to know where we were. Next they asked me to point out landmarks which the map did not show – Loestagh, Hamitagh, Gutentagh and Mazartagh. Each of them jabbed a finger at the brown contour lines of the mountain feature which stood out in stark contrast to the otherwise blank relief of yellow sand dunes on the map. I realized then that these were names which had been passed down through generations. They had never seen them before but they knew that they wanted to see them. Their eyes lit up and they sat back on their heels in the sand as they repeated the names over and over again, the words rolling off their tongues with child-like pleasure.

That evening, we pitched camp and unloaded the camels as usual. Everyone was quiet with fatigue. It had been a punishing day and those of us with bad stomachs were weakened by the physical effort.

'Wow! Great picture. Just look at this, guys,' I suddenly heard Keith say. We followed his gaze and there we saw a tiny figure seated on top of the highest dune to the north. It was Esa Polta. He had detached himself from the caravan before it halted, climbed several dunes, and worked his way along a ridge to the summit. The pyramid dunes were breathtakingly beautiful, their edges sharp, their shadows creeping away from the setting sun amidst the gentle brown hue of the sand. Esa sat there sideways on to us and gazed far to the east. His body formed the perfect, sharp outline of a silhouette. Richard was too weak to take much notice but he summed up the scene in a glance.

'The old boy is making his peace with Allah,' he said. 'He's fulfilled his dream of looking for the last time over the land of his ancestors. Now he will be happy if he pops his clogs. God bless the King of Mongolia!'

Without the luxury of water for washing and shaving we soon looked thoroughly unkempt. Our hair was thickly matted and the sand was so fine that it clung to our bodies like an extra layer of skin. Sand filled every orifice and penetrated the outer cladding of the most tightly sealed equipment, seizing up our cameras and the sound-recording equipment that we had been given by BBC Radio. But daily we grew in confidence as we came through another ordeal and learned how to cope with the desert.

'You know, old Lao Zhao is an interesting chap,' Richard said to me one day as we fell into conversation while walking along. 'He keeps saying that he still wonders why the water stopped coming from the Kun Lun mountains down into the Taklamakan and the Tarim Basin. His theory is that the mountains moved and the water gushed the other way thereafter, into the Indian subcontinent, flooding Bangladesh.'

'The joy of that theory, Richard,' I replied, 'is that it will be hard to disprove. And it's simple enough for non-scientists like me to understand.' He laughed.

'Did I ever tell you of Lao Zhao's find?'

'No.'

'With a proud grin he showed me a little dead animal which he held by the tail. He had found it in the sand. I thought he had dinner in mind and was about to decline politely. "This", he said, "is a rare animal last seen in the Taklamakan by a Russian explorer seventy years ago." It looked like a long-eared mouse, or a gerbil. But, in fact, he said it was a five-toed rat!'

'Amazing.'

The days soon fell into a familiar routine as we mastered the intricacies of camel handling. The animals earned our respect in spite of frequently dumping their heavy loads. The wilder camels were loaded with more durable stores like tents, personal clothing bags and the large cooker. The more placid and trustworthy animals carried the water containers. For extra safety we separated the water camels to prevent a train of six of them stampeding all at once and thereby threatening the survival of twelve containers. It had happened at the beginning but we quickly learned from our mistakes.

The art of loading in the mornings was time-consuming and labour-intensive. We worked in teams of four to one camel. The animals were brought over in ones and twos from where they had been eating their daily corn ration. Abdul Rasheed, the smallest of the handlers, normally had that task. The camels were identified by their size and temperament as either carriers of *cornuk* (grain), *su* (water), or *ubrech* (baggage). The smaller and weaker ones were put into the last category. The methodology seemed straightforward until one of us would enquire of a handler, '*Ubrech?*' and point to a camel. '*Cornuk, cornuk,*' he might reply before moving off to help elsewhere. Sacks of grain would then be positioned ready for loading before another handler came over, waving his hands and saying '*Su, su*'. Much confused, the team normally opted for a different, more readily identifiable camel and left the other for the Uyghurs.

The camel frames on to which the baggage was loaded were simple affairs. Two poles, roughly three inches in diameter, were tied at the top of the saddle and ran parallel to each other on either side of and just below the line of the humps. Suspended from the poles were pads of reeds compacted inside cloth sacking in a crescent shape. These covered the animal's ribs. The whole thing was secured by a rudimentary girth and rope twining around the notches of both poles at each end and under the camel's belly. The twining could then be adjusted to make the frame fit more tightly or more loosely around the humps, depending on the type of load.

The twining would cut savagely into a hump when the frame slid too far forwards or backwards. This was a problem later in the crossing when the camels were thin and the saddles became too big for them, causing some appalling pressure wounds that went septic and filled with maggots.

The first step in loading was to check that the saddle frame fitted correctly and that the girth was tight. Next, a length of rope was doubled and placed over the frame between the humps with the loop on one side below the pole, the two ends hanging down to the ground on the opposite side.

It took two people to lift the grain sacks. To a count of '*ee, er, san*' (one, two, three in Chinese), the sack was lifted to chest height and rested on the camel's side against the two ends of rope. These were then brought from under the sack, stretched tightly over the top, passed to the other side and dropped over the other grain sack. The last stage was to feed the two ends through the loop and hitch it up as high as possible, finally tying off the taut rope between the camel's humps. The sacks were then adjusted for height, the trick being to ensure their correct centre of gravity for the comfort of the camel. If they weren't centred, as frequently happened, the uneven motion of the walking camel soon unbalanced the load. The result was an awkward camel, kicking and spitting whilst trying to shed its burden. That normally caused a simultaneous reaction along the line of camels tethered together from front to rear, until there was chaos, confusion and scattered equipment everywhere.

During the days when we had dysentery the job was very tiring. Richard was excused loading during his illness and would busy himself instead, when he wasn't squatting in wretched misery, by finding the ropes for the trains or clearing up the litter and burying it.

Litter left by the Chinese and Uyghurs became our bugbear. No matter how many times we picked it up, dug a hole and disposed of it, they seemed oblivious to the importance of such basic drills. We never understood how they could wish to litter such beautiful virgin sand. It was a point of pride and principle that every camp site and lunch stop was left clean. They never improved. Right to the end of the expedition the British team would go around picking up the rubbish from under the very feet of those who had dropped it. To begin with it irritated us to the point of distraction; but, as with all such expeditions when people of mixed races and backgrounds learn to live together, we mellowed in our attitude and accepted it as one of the chores that befell us. There was little point in getting worked up about such small things with the more pressing demands of survival constantly hanging over us like the sword of Damocles.

I made a daily discipline of keeping a diary. This, surprisingly, was more difficult than it sounds. There were many occasions when the mere thought of picking up the book and writing an entry seemed too much of an effort. An appalling lethargy would often set in; all one wanted to do was sit and stare at the surroundings. In such moods I never ceased to be impressed by Keith's continual activity with his camera, always looking for the perfect angle and the ultimate picture. Sometimes I was able to keep quite a detailed and varied account, as with this entry for 29 September:

2300 hrs. Desert Camp 6. 38° 54.44′N; 78° 40.93′E
For the first time today I wondered whether this desert would ever end. Ridiculous thought with over 600 miles to go; but I do feel tired of walking over sand!

We have pulled and coaxed camels and struggled over sand dune mountains all day, some of which are 800 to 1,000 feet high. It is like going over virgin snow in Alpine passes. The team worked well and we made up some time after lunch, finally camping at the 9-mile mark. Good going under such difficult conditions.

No wind today. It was 95° Fahrenheit and like a furnace. Richard with v. bad stomach. Rupert likewise plus a poor leg. He perked up this evening so all is OK. Temperatures at night average 20° to 30° Fahrenheit, a blessed relief from the daytime.

Had a long chat on the radio with Barney and compiled a dispatch for *The Times* in London. Another camel had all its nostril ripped out by the rope being pulled. The Uyghurs were indifferent to its pain, and blood spurted everywhere.

Saw a butterfly! What on earth was it doing in this godforsaken place? Rather a charming and colourful sight against the backdrop of emptiness.

Abdul Rasheed appears to have recovered from his sunstroke. I gave him a BP baseball hat from our sponsors to keep the sun off his shaved head. Now we call him BP.

At one point today the caravan divided, with the Chinese team and half the camels heading off in another direction. Richard and I soon checked this and were quite firm about the dangers of such behaviour. Their excuse was that we were not going in a straight line!

My knee hurt but generally it has held out well and the muscles are strengthening. Of more concern are the huge blisters on my feet.

The Chinese worked better today and actually got involved with helping the camels over the difficult dunes.

Had a camel stampede going down a steep dune into a massive depression and one of the tin containers split along its seam. Keith quickly upended it and attempted to save the water. Transferred its remaining contents into two empty plastic containers. We can't afford to lose any more tanks. Water is a serious worry.

I had a session with my team and told them that we must integrate more fully with the Chinese, avoid two camps, not walk all day as a British team etc. I explained that otherwise it would become like a festering sore which would be difficult to cut out.

I'm lying under a canopy of bright stars writing this entry. Lots of thoughts of Tina and the boys. I think of them daily as I walk. How I miss the faces of the little ones. I want to spend so much time with them when I get back. I regret all this lost time but hope they will be proud of what their father has done one day.

I tucked my diary away, turned on my back and gazed at the radiance of the night sky, savouring the immensity of its vastness and relishing the calm after the trials of the day. People have always said that the night skies in Arabia are beautiful to behold and I too have shared them, but in Western China they were no less impressive. Perhaps it had something to do with being in the desert. Here our spirits were free to soar and we had time to appreciate our surroundings. There was an indefinable romance about our adventure, lying in the desert at night surrounded by one's companions and the camels. It was timeless. Then, as I felt the cool night air make the skin on my sunburnt face tighten, I recalled the terrible harshness of the heat, the burning sand and the blinding light, the breath-lessness and weakness of my frail body as it struggled up and down the dunes, and the constant craving for water. Not for the first time I asked myself whether we would ever get out alive.

SIX

The Silk Road

Mark Kitto had stood for some time on the desert's edge at Markit watching with conflicting emotions as our caravan wound its way into the unknown. The achievement of that moment held a special poignancy for him, he told me later. As he gazed out over the sea of sand into which thirty camels and fifteen people had just disappeared he experienced an over-whelming elation that the expedition was actually happening, and also a sudden surge of panic: would they make it? At the same time, bitterly disappointed that he was not with the cross-ing party, he felt left out and isolated, knowing in his heart that his real place was not with the support team, where Barney and Francis were clearly happy with their roles. Mark was to have been in the crossing party but, two weeks before leaving England, I had replaced him with Rupert Burton. My reason-ing was that Mark's linguistic skills would be of far more use to Barney in handling petty Chinese officialdom in the bazaars of the Silk Road than they would in the desert where two of the Chinese team spoke plausible English.

He turned back to his vehicle. The camel tracks on the crests of the dunes had already been obliterated by the wind which had picked up since mid-morning. He had only walked a mile into the desert to see off the camel party, yet just that small dis-tance seemed to have taken him into the heart of the wilder-ness. Mark wondered how the members of the crossing team were feeling as their tracks quickly vanished behind them.

He arrived back at camp to see the Chinese support team slinging the last of their bags on to the vehicles. The Chinese assumed that the British would be joining them at the guest-house in Markit to savour its dubious luxuries after a night in the open. They could not understand the British desire to spend a peaceful night under the stars in the desert. The Chinese need for creature comforts as opposed to the British enthusiasm for the outdoor life was to become a major source of conflict within the support team in the months ahead.

The following morning, to the relief of the Chinese, they returned to Markit and found the half-ruined building that served as a post office. There the old woman behind the counter disappeared to the market, returning with cloth hand-kerchiefs and cotton in which she wrapped and then sewed up the video tapes and camera films for mailing to Bella and the UK Press. The parcel took six weeks to arrive, by which time the contents were no longer newsworthy.

The support team's daily routine revolved around hearing news from the camel party, its most important focus the evening radio schedule. This became Mark's sole reason for existence, it being a point of pride that he would get through. The first time he set up the radio's dipole and sloping wire configuration for skywave was outside a PLA barracks in Yecheng, one day's drive south of Markit. After sifting through the interference of the Pakistani border posts with Kashmir, he was elated to hear Rupert's voice booming through from over a hundred miles to the north. Later, back in the dismal hostel in Yecheng where the Chinese had insisted upon staying for two days, he was visited and questioned at great length by anxious senior military officials in search of a spy. So the next time he needed to communicate he had to drive for miles out of town to a quiet spot where he would not arouse too much suspicion.

The Chinese always insisted on talking to their team in the desert after the British had said their bit. Mark contrasted the tenor of these conversations with those of his compatriots. A common topic was the heat and the conditions.

Mark to Rupert, 'What's the temperature like out there?'

Rupert, 'Not too bad, about 100° Fahrenheit.'

Mark, 'Oh! So it's hot.'

Later, the leader of the Chinese contingent of the support team would ask his counterpart, Guo Jin Wei, a similar question. The reply crackled through the vehicle loudspeaker, 'It's terrible, really, really terrible. We are all dying of thirst.'

Barney's chief concern centred around the arrival of John and Anne Thomas. Without the second vehicle it would be unsafe for him to enter stretches of the desert. The Russian Kamaz truck, hired by us from the PLA, and the other Nissan jeeps of the Chinese support team could not cope with anything like the terrain that Barney's Pinzgauer could tackle. The safety as well as the success of the expedition depended upon the two Pinzgauers working together, carrying the vital resupplies far into the desert along the ancient river lines.

Still without news from John and Anne, on 27 September Barney took the support team further east along the Silk Road to the Duwa valley fifty miles west of Hotan, in the foothills of the Kun Lun. There he was in a good position to monitor the progress of the crossing party which he plotted on a large map after each successful radio contact. On the other end of a radio, listening to increasingly dramatic accounts of the crossing of the sand mountains, the outbreak of dysentery and the search for water, he felt rather as a soldier might in headquarters, monitoring progress on the battlefront. Each piece of information was analysed by the support team and the question asked, what are its implications for us? Barney could only sit helplessly and pray that everything would work out: he knew there was little he could do if something went seriously wrong. At the same time, using the satellite link, he had constantly to reassure the home team in England despite his own frequent misgivings to the contrary.

Nothing seemed too much for Barney. At times he resembled Badger in *Wind in the Willows*, steadfast and sure; at others, he became a furiously busy Mr Toad, bustling about with ideas pouring forth, talking excitedly about this and that, and humming to himself when he was either distracted or under pressure. In the latter respect he and Toad differed: Toad never hummed. During the planning phase I would arrive at Barney's London house after work in the evening and he would greet me at the door dressed in Turkish pyjamas with crimson leather slippers on his feet.

'You made it then?' (pause for a long hum) 'Come in.' (pause for another hum) 'Now what can I get you?' (hum) 'Whisky?' (his favourite drink).

He would then lead the way into the kitchen where his wife Moo would be preparing a meal, probably having been warned of my arrival only minutes before. (I once asked Barney her real name but he couldn't remember.) Being with Barney was always interesting and very refreshing: little bothered him although there were moments on the Silk Road when he felt the exactitudes of a modern expedition to be at odds with his surroundings. In dealing with the local people one could never be sure whether they were adhering to Beijing time (standard throughout China for the running of the country), Kashgar time (two hours behind), or Uyghur time (four hours behind). Usually it was a combination of all three, resulting in misunderstandings and long periods of waiting around for things to happen.

The evocative name of the Silk Road is somewhat misleading. Starting in Chang'an (present-day Xi'an), it evolved as an overland trade route across China and Central Asia to the Middle East, and consisted of a network of caravan trails that eventually linked East and West. It carried much more than silk: the caravans were laden with tea, precious metals and a host of other rare commodities for which there was a lucrative market at either end of the route. Not all goods travelled the entire length of the Silk Road; many were bartered and sold in the oasis towns which were dotted at intervals along its length and provided safe havens for the caravan men who spent their whole lives on the road. Their talk would mainly consist of questions and answers, all of which related to 'The Road'. 'Is the road open?' they asked. 'Is the road peaceful?' 'Are there brigands on the road?' If the caravan man was Chinese his farewell would characteristically be 'A peaceful road to you,' and if he was a Turki his parting benediction would be '*Yol bolsun*'

(May there be a road). This overland trade found one of its best markets in Rome, for as the Romans became increasingly affluent, they developed a corresponding fondness for the products of distant places, and especially for silk.

From Xi'an in the province of Shaanxi, the Silk Road crossed the Gobi Desert to Dunhuang. There, one route struck north-west to pass along the lush oases of the Taklamakan's northern rim which included the cities of Turpan, Kuqa, Aksu and, finally, Kashgar. The southern route turned south-west to skirt the northern foothills of the Kun Lun mountains, and then wound along the southern rim of the Taklamakan with its string of oases – Miran, Ruoqiang (Qarkilik), Endere, Hotan (Khotan) and Shache (Yarkand). At Kashgar the two routes met, then plunged westwards over the Pamirs, on through Iran and Iraq to the Mediterranean, with its sea lanes to Rome.

The support team's campsite in the Kun Lun was idyllic – a fertile valley with lush poplar trees, clear water fresh from the glaciers in the mountains and a few local people to add colour and interest to the scene. Unfortunately the magnificent Kun Lun were obscured by a haze of dust the entire time, a common phenomenon in those parts attributed to the sands of the Taklamakan.

John and Anne arrived there on the third day, 30 September, fully one week after the crossing began, after many adventures and a good deal of luck. They had experienced difficulty getting over the border at Taxkorgan and had spent two days in Kashgar where customs officials impounded their vehicle. Picking up messages left by Barney *en route*, they used their common sense and headed towards Hotan. At the mouth of the Duwa valley they found a final message on a pile of stones. They were then in range to communicate with the vehicle Motorola sets and drove triumphantly into camp for a tumultuous reunion. At last the expedition was complete.

From Duwa the support team continued into Hotan itself, a charming and unspoilt old town with a fascinating bazaar and a great centre of carpet-making, a rare spot in the world that has not yet been touched by mass tourism. Hotan is built around the oasis created by two rivers, the Yurungkax (the

White Jade River) and the Karakax (the Black Jade River), where they flow down from the Kun Lun and spill out on to the plain. The two rivers join fifty miles north of the oasis and form the Hotan river which bisects the desert. Hotan is a big oasis, about fifteen square miles in area, and settlements continue along both arms of the river into the desert where the yellow dunes gradually converge until only a thin line remains. Mazartagh, the first resupply point, lies along that line nearly 120 miles further into the interior. At that time of year the river was bone-dry; as a spate river it is filled only in the spring when the snows melt in the Kun Lun.

Barney's one mission of pleasure in Hotan, to the amusement of everyone, was arranging for the delivery of cases of Famous Grouse whisky, generously donated by Matthew Gloag. The consignment had reached Beijing, and Barney spent hours organizing its eventual delivery to the airstrip at Hotan. Mark recorded in his diary that Barney finally stopped shaking once the precious cargo was safely locked in the back of the Bella vehicle.

In the bazaars of Hotan the support party bought grain for the camels and the foodstuffs necessary for the impending resupply at Mazartagh. That done they could only wait and monitor on the map the progress of the camel party as it battled eastwards, realizing that if any disaster struck at this point there was little that they could do. The crossing party was like a submarine stranded on the sea bed, within radio contact with the surface but out of reach of help.

SEVEN

Triumph over Hedin

The Russian explorer Prejevalsky, accompanied by two English-men, Carey and Dalgleish, were the first Europeans ever to see the mountains of Mazartagh on the left bank of the Hotan river. That was in 1885, ten years before Sven Hedin set off on his attempt to cross the uncharted desert from Markit to Mazartagh. The rationale for Hedin's plan came from Prejevalsky's description of a chain of mountains that apparently stretched from Mazartagh at an oblique angle westwards across the desert: 'we lost sight of the mountains which became blended with the sandy desert. But they bent round towards the north-west, and, increasing in height in the middle, stretched, the natives told me, as far as the fortified post of Maral-bashi on the river of Kashgar. Of vegetation there was not a trace. The slopes of the mountains were buried in drift-sand, half-way up from the fort.'

From such accounts Hedin reasoned, naturally enough, that

> if from Merket [Markit] we steered our course eastwards, or rather towards the east-north-east, we were bound, sooner or later, to come in contact with the Mazartagh; and, like the natives, I was convinced, that we should find a lee side to the range, where the drift sand would not be blown together, but we should be able to make long, easy day's marches on firm ground, and possibly might even discover springs and vegetation, and perhaps light upon traces of an ancient civilisation.

From the maps available at the time Hedin measured the distance as 200 miles 'through the desert as the crow flies; and if we did only twelve miles a day, the entire journey ought not to take us more than sixteen days'. In fact, it took Hedin twenty-six days to escape the desert's clutches; he staggered out of it to the north, barely alive, having failed to cross the sand mountains or link up with the Mazartagh mountain line. Behind him, in the wilderness, he left Mohammed Shah and Kasim Akhun to their painful deaths from thirst and exhaustion along with seven out of the original eight camels who likewise succumbed to the desert. Neither did Hedin's dog, Yolldash, survive.

Driven nearly insane by thirst, the expedition resorted to desperate measures, as Hedin wrote afterwards.

> Islam and the other men gathered a saucepanful of the camel's urine. They poured it into an iron cup, and added vinegar and sugar; then, holding their noses, swallowed the abominable concoction. They offered the cup to me; but the mere smell nauseated me. All the others drank it except Kasim. And he was wise to abstain; for after a while the other three men were seized with violent and painful vomiting, which completely prostrated them.

On another occasion Hedin drank the fuel from their Chinese primus stove, and the last of the sheep they had taken as their mobile larder was slaughtered for its blood.

> At length Islam, with an aching heart, led the poor creature a little to one side, turned its head towards Mecca, and, whilst Kasim tied a rope round its legs, drew his knife, and with one sweeping cut severed the arteries of the neck. The blood poured out in a thick reddish-brown stream, and was caught in a pail, where it almost immediately coagulated. It was still warm when we fell upon it greedily with spoons and knife-blades.

Later, 'gaunt and wild-eyed, with the stamp of insanity upon him, Yollchi sat beside the tent, gnawing at the dripping sheep's lungs. His hands were bloody; his face was bloody; he was a horrible sight to look upon.'*

---

*Hedin's tent was that of an Indian Army officer, given to him at Chini-bagh by Macartney. Within it the young Lieutenant Davidson had died during his journey across the Pamirs to Kashgar in 1892. 'But it had been well disinfected, and I was not superstitious.' Hedin's last sight of the tent at the 'Camp of Death' was of his two dying camel handlers lying inside it as he made his desperate attempt to break out of the desert, leaving them behind to their fate.

Since then there had been no further attempts to repeat Hedin's route; the uncharted desert, with its graveyard of Hedin's dog, his handlers and his camels, lay shrouded in mystery and steeped in legend. Hedin's account of his planning and subsequent experiences were all there for me to draw on, yet it was to be the very paucity of that information and the sheer challenge of succeeding where Hedin had failed that gave me the tenacity and willpower to overcome the desert.

My own camel handler, Esa Polta, claimed at the outset to have travelled some of the route to the north of the Mazartagh mountains as a boy accompanying his father on a hunting trip. Apparently oryx were then plentiful along the desert's fringes. For the first few days of the crossing the knowledge of Esa's experience gave me some grounds for confidence. One evening, however, it transpired from a conversation around the camp that Esa had never in fact been over our route before.

Three days earlier he had emphatically announced that our present position was the last place in which water could be found for the following four days. Fortunately he had been wrong. We found water for the camels at modest depths of six feet for two of those days. I realized then that there was no sub-stance to Esa's recollections. In short, we were travelling blind, not knowing what lay ahead, and this imbued in us a tremen-dous pioneering spirit. We were going somewhere and seeing things that no man had seen before.

I could only plot the fix from the hand-held Global Positioning Satellite (GPS) navigation aid on the featureless map as a means of checking our position amid the vast expanse of dunes that stretched on every side to the horizon. This remarkable equipment worked by picking up the position of satellites, normally a minimum of three for triangulation, and fixing a ground position accurate to 100 metres in longitude and latitude. It was battery operated and its sensor converted the information into a reading in less than three minutes. But on the scale of my map, which was simply coloured yellow, delineating sand, and criss-crossed with lines of longitude and latitude, it told me nothing more than that our progress was steadily eastwards and we had not veered too far north or south.

Hitting the extreme eastern end of the Mazartagh mountain line was the only way in which I would eventually confirm that we really were on course. It was, therefore, a moment of tremendous excitement when at mid-morning on 1 October, seven days after setting out from Markit, we reached the crest of the highest point and saw, right across a plain of small dunes, the Hamitagh, Loestagh, Gutentagh and Mazartagh mountain line. The feature was only just discernible amid the heat haze on the skyline and it would take another day to reach the flatter ground that Sven Hedin had been aiming for but had never reached.

As the camels descended the steep slopes of soft sand, I became somewhat wistful over leaving the sand mountains. We had been amongst them for five days. Their shapes had been stunning and we had grown used to living within their forbidding presence. In many respects we had relished the challenges of each day; seeking routes around the deep sand depressions and along the ridges ever upwards for nearly an hour until the highest point was reached; resting in a flattish area wide enough for thirty couched camels; living day by day in the fine sand, constantly exposed to the ferocious sun which seemed more scorching because of the altitude; pushing, encouraging and hitting the camels in each train as they were urged on through deep sand, up and down extreme angles which, under normal circumstances, would have been avoided. Dust, sweat, heat, strained leg muscles, blistered feet, weakness and light-headedness, dehydration, the glare off the sand, hot air in the lungs, cracked lips and gushing, unreliable bowels which allowed one little dignity – all these were features of our struggle. With justifiable pride in our achievement, we emerged from the sand hills.

Richard quoted the Chinese saying, 'Time makes a hero', to me one day. With the Mazartagh line at last in sight, I couldn't help feeling that there was a touch of destiny in the headway we were making. We had carved a route through the seemingly impassable sand mountains whose sheer size and barrenness were so awesome to any but the most determined, or insane. It had, for us, been a singularly British achievement. We had set the pace and length of each day. We had found the best route through the dunes and had navigated safely. We were always either at the front or going back down the long line of camels, encouraging the Uyghurs, checking the loads and ensuring that the camels kept together and did not shy at the obstacles ahead. It had been exhausting work, and Rupert, Richard and I had done it whilst our precious reserves of energy and fluid were drained by dysentery. We gave of ourselves to those sand mountains. By contrast, the Chinese were notable only for their reluctance to get up in the morning and tackle the day's business, and the way in which they would always walk together at the back of the caravan. Richard soon coined a phrase for this: 'clip boarding', he called it, and his name for the Chinese was the 'irregulars'.

'I see the irregulars are clipboarding at the rear again,' he would say in his marvellously spirited and humorous voice. Lao Zhao was the exception and we developed a growing friendship with him as well as respect for his desert knowledge. He was always the first member of the Chinese team to get up in the morning and he happily undertook the cooking of breakfast and dinner. Guo Jin Wei wanted to become more involved but his lack of fitness and weight problem hampered him.

Early on, I had been aware of the importance of avoiding two camps and constantly reminded my own team of the fact. Richard was superb in continually patching up Anglo-Chinese misunderstandings or intercepting them before they grew. He worked endlessly and tirelessly, his enormous understanding of people's characters ensuring that the two teams bonded together. His sensitivity worked within our team as well. He became my gentle adviser and prompter. In return he acted in a subtle way as the mouthpiece for Rupert, Keith and Carolyn who did not always view situations in a wider context. I already knew that I would miss Richard when he left at Mazartagh. From the outset his work with a merchant bank had only permitted him a month on the expedition after which he was off to set up a new business office in Shanghai. The combination of my military style of leadership, which, in the circumstances, was exactly what was required, and

Richard's delicate blend of diplomacy, intellect and cunning made us a good team and a formidable force for the less worldly Chinese. The situation was ideal because it allowed the British the uninterrupted and unchallenged job of leading the expedition with the Chinese assisting and following in our steps. We did not seek to change it.

We found no water for the camels on the day that the Mazartagh mountain line was sighted. We checked our own supply and discovered that only 900 litres remained. We were but half-way to our first resupply point, still 100 miles further east. Despite this, the morale of the Chinese and Uyghurs in particular was higher than ever before now that there was a feature to head for which they had heard about.

Under a magnificent full moon, the light of which gave the dunes an almost surreal quality, Guo Jin Wei and I sat together and discussed our progress and the conduct of the crossing. He suggested that I refrain from barking at the Chinese and Uyghurs in the mornings, a trait I had developed while trying to instil some order and urgency into the long, drawn-out procedure of packing up the camp and loading the camels. It increasingly frustrated the British element that we seldom got going until ten or ten thirty even though we had roused everyone four hours beforehand.

I was developing an affinity with Guo. As his fitness and confidence slowly improved I saw more qualities in him as the leader of the Chinese. He was different from the others in that he understood our Western mentality, and I realized what a powerful ally he would be. He went on to tell me that he was in fact half Korean and had been brought up in Manchuria before his parents were sent to Xinjiang during the Cultural Revolution. His father had been a soldier in the Chinese infantry and had fought in the Korean War. My father had also been an infantryman in that war and I joked to Guo that perhaps our fathers had shot at each other near the banks of the River Imjin. If they had, they would never have believed that forty years later their sons would live together for three months surrounded by desert wastes and dependent upon each other for their survival. After the war his father remained in North Korea and married a farmer's daughter before returning to Manchuria. The whole family was deported to Urumqi when Guo was 7 because his father was a fluent Japanese speaker and was thus considered a destabilizing influence. The father was then sent to an open prison somewhere in the remote outback of Xinjiang and Guo did not see or hear from him for ten years. Indeed the family did not even know whether he was alive. During the Cultural Revolution, Guo worked on a farm and learned to drive a tractor when he should have been studying at school. He told me how much he resented having his education taken away from him.

At this point our conversation was unfortunately interrupted by an urgent call of nature and I sped barefoot across the cool sand to the privacy of a nearby dune. Barely having time to lower my green shorts I squatted in relief as yet another hot liquid discharge formed a pool between my legs. My stomach ached and turned over in waves: nothing relieved that feeling and I was always left spent and exhausted afterwards. The dysentery was in its sixth day and I could feel my whole body weakening in its grip. Then I heard the noise of further liquid farting nearby and I made out Richard squatting in similar misery. 'One day we'll look back on this and smile,' he said, 'and we'll remember sharing the beauty of a desert night together under the radiant moon in positions of total humility!' We both laughed. Afterwards we lay side by side on our backs looking up at the canopy of bright stars, sprinkling the fine sand through our fingers and talking of home and the future. The deep silence of the desert was broken only by the occasional sound of a camel bell as the animals wandered in search of small tamarisk scrub. It was a shared moment.

The next day brought us close to the westernmost rocky crags of Hamitagh. There the going was flatter and the dunes easier to circumvent. I set a bearing of 110° magnetic which would take us east north-east towards Mazartagh. The outcrops of rock were striking, their red, pink and brown colours contrasting with the yellow sand dunes. Here and there fault lines of clear white, dazzling crystal rock protruded above the sand and ran through the exposed surface until they disappeared again. We broke chunks off and stored them in our pockets until we were as heavily laden as diamond hunters. Thinking that we were running parallel to the south side of Hamitagh, we ascended vast dunes of fine red, yellow and white sand and looked south over the flatter land with fresh eyes. We were entranced by the lure of the hills. In this enchantment we forgot the tired camels on their third day without water and we forgot too the sad plight of Richard. Plucky to the last, he refused to ride a camel and rest his spent frame; instead he tottered along with water bottle in hand and made us believe he was stronger than he was. It was nearly dusk. The sun blazed in a red fireball of dismissal behind us and our shadows lengthened eerily ahead as our feet tried to overtake them. Finally, we reached a sheer ridge. The mountain had gone. In front of us lay a steep descent into a flat valley bottom with high dunes in the far distance surrounding it. Clearly the sand hills were not something of the past. Yet the gleeful pleasure we took in sliding down 300 feet through soft sand which rose in disturbed clouds about us eclipsed our thoughts of the next leg. We reached the bottom and lay down with delirious satisfaction, hot and half-clothed, our skin thickly covered in layers of sand and our bodies weary with fatigue as we looked up at the last of the camels descending precariously in enveloping sprays of sand. My mouth was so dry that it felt like the inside of a cardboard box.

Only Richard stayed at the last crest, unable to move any further. We watched him but none of us had the energy to go back. He would not expect it. He was gathering his last ounce of strength for the final approach to the camp. Our first priority was to find water and several of us dug with determination. After six feet the sand grew moist and we left the Uyghurs to finish the rest. It was nearly dark by the time Richard arrived. We immediately put him into his sleeping bag and Carolyn dosed him with antibiotics. We tried forcing him to eat but he was too far gone and too weak. He lay there with his thin bearded face sticking out of the top of his bag, his mop of tousled dark hair nearly grey with sand. After a while his spirits rallied and he smiled at our remarks about the order of service for his funeral if he didn't manage to live through the night. Privately, however, I was anxious about his condition, for I knew the next day would be no easier.

With all our attention centred on Richard we did not notice the absence of the camel handlers. Long after dark they returned from the hills we had traversed, shovels over their shoulders, and sat together around their own small fire. I asked Guo where they had been.

'Looking for gold,' he replied.

'Why is that?'

'You see, the camel handlers believe there is gold in these hills according to the legends. They also believe you are not travelling through the desert just because it is there to be crossed. They came with you because they think you are searching for treasure and lost cities, and that you will lead us to them. That is why they are here.'

I walked over to the Uyghurs and asked them how the water hole was looking. They assured me it was fine and then they laid out on the ground their collection of many coloured stones from their recent foray into the hills. More interestingly, Abdul Rasheed proudly showed me an ancient-looking camel saddle that he had found. It consisted of two inverted v-shaped struts about twelve inches apart joined by flat pieces of wood at the bottom. The wood was parched from years of sun and scouring by windborne sand. Underneath the saddle, hessian padding of antiquated weave still showed some colour which would once have been highly decorative. I was fascinated by the find: either it indicated the site of an ancient dwelling in the area or it confirmed the theory that an old trading route existed along the line of the Mazartagh hills. As I turned to go, Esa Polta told me that the water hole they had started digging was no good. 'Too salty,' he said, 'the camels will get ill and die if they drink from it.'

He added in a quiet and unemotional voice, 'Tomorrow, half the camels will die anyway if we do not find water.' It was said as simply as that. Mulling over our situation – camels near to death, Richard with amoebic dysentery, a gruelling day ahead when the chances of finding water were unknown, and a team of camel handlers seemingly oblivious to our plight yet still prospecting for gold in the hills – I returned to where Rupert had set up the Ultralite for a prearranged link to England. We stood together in the darkness with the Ultralite's noisy generator churning away and waited for the satellite telephone to ring. When it did we both nearly jumped with amazement and scrambled over to the black box to reach the handset. Rupert picked it up. 'Hello,' then, after a brief pause, 'Taklamakan.' It was too much: the ridiculousness of the situation brought peels of laughter from everyone as we saw the funny side of answering the only telephone in the entire desert by its name. It was Tina saying that *The Sunday Times* wanted to run a story on our progress. She was speaking from home and was rushing off on the morning school run with the children. She sounded so normal, it was as though we were talking to each other from just down the road. The conversation was brief and I could not, and did not, convey the reality of our situation.

The mood of the caravan the following day was less confident than before and more reserved. We knew that water had to be found for the camels, but where? As fate would have it we experienced the hottest day of the crossing, the temperature reaching 115° Fahrenheit without the comfort of any wind amid the lower lying dunes. The handlers became irritated and took to venting their frustration by beating the camels when the ropes snapped or the long-suffering beasts went too slowly. Rupert and I walked side by side at the front. The heat was overwhelming. I looked back and noted how the heads of the camels had gone down and their humps had withered through malnutrition and lack of water. The usual song of the Uyghur handlers had been replaced by the bellow of complaining and distraught animals. The eight camels in the last train of the caravan concerned me the most. That morning the handlers had deliberately loaded them with the heaviest items and they visibly struggled to keep up. One of them had gone blind in the sand mountains and stumbled along in his sad and lonely darkness.

They had been loaded that way because they were the weakest and the handlers expected them to be the first to die: until they did so they were being worked to the limit in order to take the weight off the others who had a better chance of survival.

Richard rode a camel for much of the day and, thankfully, his strength and condition improved marginally. The afternoon was so hot that I found myself regularly praying for a breeze to cool us. It came at intervals. We plodded wearily on for twelve punishing miles with the caravan stretched out over two miles, that being the distance between the front and rear camels. Mid-afternoon we sighted the next feature of the mountain line and headed towards it. Its craggy rock outcrop rose from the sharp incline of the drifted sands on its leeward side like the super-structure of a vast battleship.

'Loestagh,' said Emir, who walked beside me. I studied his impassive face and wondered how he could possibly have known the name of the feature. 'Loestagh,' he repeated, inter-preting my silence as deafness, and he jutted his chin in its direction in case I had not noticed. I was reminded of my Bedu in the Middle East and their uncanny knack of navigating without the use of modern maps by merely relying on the descriptions of the desert from the stories of their forefathers, even when they were hundreds of miles away from their famil-iar patch of desert in a place entirely new to them. How was it, then, that Emir knew those names and spoke of them with the confidence of a man who passes the same landmark every day on his way to work?

After a while Rupert spotted an area of vegetation, small clumps of green tamarisk and camel thorn which indicated there could be water. I halted the front of the caravan and sent him ahead with Kirim to dig a test hole while the remainder caught up. The last camels were half an hour behind with three of the Chinese team, Guo, Zhang Bohua and Qiu Lei. Rupert flashed me with his signalling mirror and I switched on my Motorola radio, a standard procedure we had adopted for saving our batteries.

'Looks quite promising', he said, 'there may be a chance of finding water here.'

'Put Kirim on the set and I will get Esa Polta to talk to him and make a decision,' I replied. I showed Esa how to use the radio and he beamed with delight and incredulity on hearing Kirim's voice. It was the first time in their lives that they had ever used such equipment. They talked for a while and Esa told me that Kirim was hopeful of finding water. When we moved on and eventually joined Rupert, he described how Kirim and Rosa had rolled about with laughter after Esa spoke with them. Rupert's translation of the conversation went something like this.

'Esa, we may have a good spot for water here.'

'Well stop waffling and start digging, you lazy sods!' was the gist of Esa's reply.

We all took turns digging. It was the largest hole we had dug in the hope of collecting as much water as possible to allow the camels a long drink. As the sand grew moister the smell of it drew the camels away from their meagre grazing and they restlessly gathered around the dark stain of the spoil from the hole in the hope of early salvation. Finally, Emir scooped out a handful and tasted it. We looked on anxiously and prayed it would not be too salty. Had it been I would have packed everything up and continued east in the hope of chancing upon another site.

'*Yukshee! Ella yukshee!*' he said, a big smile spreading across his otherwise impassive face. We rejoiced: that night the camels would drink. We had survived yet another ordeal. While the handlers watered the animals in twos and threes from a trough they had improvised by cutting in half one of the damaged tin containers, I gathered the British and Chinese teams together and instructed them to throw out all surplus food, grain and equipment. I estimated that we needed ten days' supplies until Mazartagh – the rest was excess baggage for the camels who were already showing signs of tiredness. If we wished to travel faster then their loads needed reducing.

That night I wrote my diary by the light of the full moon that touched us with its primitive glow and cast us in divine roles. I often looked at the contrast of its dark blue, crimson and grey blemishes against the brilliant white of its surface area and thought of my family, knowing that they too were gazing at the full moon and praying for my safe return. When I did, three months later, my 4-year-old, Jack, told me how he had moved his bed so as to be able to look out at the moon and think of me underneath its radiance in the desert. It was a powerful medium of communication.

The evenings were the best time of the day; we talked around the camp fire, shared thoughts and anxieties, and laughed at each other's jokes. That night the mood was particularly good: we still had enough daily drinking water for two litres per person (no reserve) and one litre for cooking, sufficient for each of us to reach Mazartagh, and we just needed to find at least two more water sites for the camels to see them through. Also, Richard was on much better form and his unselfish display of courage and endurance served as an example to us all. Certainly he had never expected to walk for almost forty miles with amoebic dysentery on three litres of water a day across a hostile desert in such temperatures.

My knee was still painful and required twice daily pain-killers and anti-inflammatory tablets, yet it was much stronger and I felt confident it might just hold out. But we still had nearly 620 miles left to go, two months of unknown desert, a depressingly long distance after the conditions we had experienced. I deliberately avoided unrolling the entire map.

My diary completed, I lay on my back with the sleeping bag only half zipped up and followed the trace of a shooting star. I made a wish that the expedition would be guided safely through the Taklamakan. I knew the sand mountains had been but one test; more dangers lay ahead as we continued to pit ourselves against the desert's secrets. I was reconciled to losing some of the camels to achieve our quest but I feared the consequences on my conscience of losing a human life, whether by accident or through lack of water. The team had knitted together well and traits of individualism had been unknowingly compromised in the interests of the whole. The challenge we faced imbued us with tremendous strength and solidarity, as we increasingly saw ourselves battling against two enemies, the desert and time: both were inextricably linked opponents of our small caravan. Later

I saw another shooting star and made a second wish for the health and happiness of my family. It left me feeling introspective and insecure; before I went off to sleep I thought finally about my father. I touched the comfort of his old silk cravat which I wore around my neck and wondered whether he was watching over me. Even knowing there was no answer to that, except my own needs and beliefs, gave me added strength as I turned over and blocked out the many uncertainties of our quest.

Over the next four days we covered sixty miles across the varied landscape of a flat pebbled plain with low, interlocking belts of dunes that merged with sand hills against steeper rocky outcrops of the Loestagh and Gutentag mountains. As we were on the leeward side of those hills we were deprived of the prevailing north-easterly breeze and the days were unbearably hot. During the lunch breaks we sat wearily in small groups and silently ate the unappetizing biscuits, sausagemeat and Chinese congee; sometimes we shared a tin of spam, a rare treat.

The flatter ground enabled us to go faster but brought new problems for our feet. Large blisters developed in places where before there had been none, and a few of us, especially Keith and myself, hobbled along in some discomfort. The kinder terrain and the lightening of the camels' loads after our rationalization of provisions gave the injured or tired more opportunity for a ride. Some days my knee was particularly painful and I didn't feel at all guilty in selecting a suitable mount. I enjoyed those breaks, seated high astride a camel whose gentle motion, combined with the dry heat and the drone of Lucien's singing, invariably made me nod off, only to wake with a start and clutch at the saddle to prevent myself from falling. Rupert and Carolyn refused to ride. They became quite irritated when I suggested it: both had firmly set their sights on walking the entire way across the Taklamakan. I could not see the logic in that – the desert was there to be crossed and no one had ever said it should be done on foot alone. When they finally achieved their goal I had nothing but admiration and respect for them. It was a truly remarkable feat.

One of the finest sights was Esa, the 'King of Mongolia', mounted on his chosen camel. He cut a splendid figure with his broad shoulders, straight back, long white beard and dark blue padded jacket tied by a length of rope around his waist. On his head he always wore a battered sombrero. Around the rim were printed in blue the words 'World Cup'. Once he went off at an unprompted gallop, heading directly for the only poplar tree on the plain. We watched in horror as he crashed into its lower branches, expecting to see the grand old man crucified, and were amazed when he came out the other side, still mounted, but covered in broken foliage.

Five days out of the sand mountains, when Rupert was at the front selecting the best route through some high dunes, he came to the crest, turned and shouted to us below, 'Vegetation! Vegetation!' We scrambled through the deep sand to his vantage point and gazed across to the valley below where a smattering of green trees and bushes stretched before us, the dunes on the far side rising in ridges behind. It was a remarkable feast for our eyes which had been deprived of such colour for so long. '*Al Hamdulliah!*' (Praise be to God) we shouted, and the camel handlers added their shouts of praise before breaking into song. To us the valley became the Promised Land; the land of milk and honey we called it. That night we knew the camels would drink for the first time in two days. We came down the last dune into the valley bottom and relished moving between the greenery which, to our deprived senses, seemed like a forest. In all probability it was a forest, an ancient one, which survived above an equally ancient river bed deep below. The trunks of the trees were wide and deeply gnarled by years of exposure; I wished they could have talked and told their story. There were also large cones of sand nearly twenty feet high covered by the roots of countless tamarisk bushes that had been twisted into gruesome snake-like shapes.

On 4 October I heard from Barney. He sounded as if he was on the other side of the world over our crackling radio but said that he was about to head north towards Mazartagh and hoped to be there in two days. Suddenly there was great excitement at the prospect of meeting up with the support team. In spite of all the problems and hardships, things were going according to plan and I could scarcely believe that we were within days of our first resupply. With five to six days' marching left, and still carrying 400 litres of drinking water, now sufficient for 4 litres each provided there were no accidents, it looked as though we had come through the worst. Water had been an immense gamble and already five tin containers had been ditched as irreparable, leaving only eight for the remainder of the journey. Loss of water from spillage and evaporation was a constant worry. Had I covered the tin tanks with sacking and reeds for protection from direct exposure to the sun, as had Hedin, it would partially have solved the problem. But the soldering on the joints of some of the containers had ruptured and they were constantly bashed by collisions between camels or accidentally dropped by tired, weak people at the end of the day when the camels were unloaded.

My diary entry for 5 October read:

The dawn is a time of day which normally passes us by unnoticed. We are busy packing up our personal kit and preparing for the day ahead. Then the camels are ready for loading. I stood still this morning and looked across the camp towards the pale water-coloured sky with Venus still shining brightly and the silhouette of the hills to our north. At the base of a gnarled tree stump flickers the Uyghur camp fire. They move to the far side and say their prayers. Normally, they still have sand marks on their faces afterwards. Finished, they replace their dirty white prayer hats and squat about the fire; I often see them warming their bare feet right in the flames. Esa Polta had come over to our fire earlier and squatted impassively beside it. We greeted him in the traditional Muslim way. Saying nothing he produced two flat pieces of bark and removed the majority of the hot coals from our fire, putting them on one bark and covering them with the other. Satisfied, he quietly withdrew and got his own fire going. Ours nearly went out!

Bearing of 97° magnetic keeping the Mazartagh feature to our left. Walked with Rupert for two hours. The going was soft sand covered by small stones of all colours and shapes, none bigger than a thumbnail. Looking at them closely one sees a myriad of splendid tones; viewed from a distance they blend into a homogeneous rusty brown. There is a happy, contented air in the camp tonight. Progress has been good, covering 18 miles today and leaving only three or four days to Mazartagh if everything goes well. It is a tremendous accomplishment. No one has ever successfully crossed by this route before and we have taken each day at face value and tackled the problems. Richard is much improved though still weak. Rupert and I are fine now barring normal aches, pains and blisters. Keith is showing bad signs of tiredness; he may have mentally 'peaked' too early when we came over the sand mountains and sighted Hamitagh for the first time: thinking it was all over he then had no inner reserves to cope with the trials of the last few days. His feet are suffering badly in spite of having all the right equipment. He saw three small deer today, they looked like Thomson gazelles and are the first animals we have seen. Apparently they can survive on the greenery, such as there is, without water.

The dust storm that blew up two days later reminded us of another dangerous phenomenon of the desert. Because of the time of year, I didn't expect it to be serious but, nevertheless, I closed the caravan up and instructed everyone to remain with the camels in between myself at the front and Rupert at the back, both of us in contact by handheld radios.

The Chinese were sensitive to the threat of suddenly being caught in a *karaburan*, or black hurricane, that reputedly turns day into night. Whenever the caravan was stretched over too great a distance, Guo in particular would warn me that the weather might change in an instant and the expedition risked being split up and separated. He feared the legendary force and destructive power of the *karaburan* in spite of my assurances that the 'furious wind' mainly occurs in the desert before the spring and summer months. Hedin encountered one the day after he had left his two weakest camels behind, they being unable to walk any further.

Up over the dunes dashed the whirling columns of sand, down they plunged on the lee side, and careered away one after the other in a frenzied dance. The atmosphere was choked with dust and sand; it was so thick that we were unable to see the summits of the nearest dunes. All we could do was stick close together, men and animals in a clump. If you once get separated from your companions in such a storm as that, it is utterly impossible to make yourself heard by shouting, or even by rifle shots. The deafening roar of the hurricane overpowers every other sound. If you get separated from them you are bound to wander astray, and so become irretrievably lost.

A masochistic part of me hoped to experience the infamous Taklamakan sandstorm in its fullest fury. I felt I could, with some justification, later claim we had survived everything the desert could throw at us. As the storm clouds gathered, the wind howled about us and the horizon disappeared in a haze of dust particles. I began doubting my assurances to Guo and braced myself for a repeat of Hedin's experience.

Through the greater part of the middle of the day it was as dark as pitch; at other times we were environed by a dim, murky light, half yellow, half grey. Several times when the sand blast hit us full in the teeth, we were nearly suffocated. In fact, when the more violent gusts struck us, we crouched down with our faces on the ground, or pressed them against the sheltered side of a camel. Even the camels turned their backs to the wind, and stretched out their necks flat along the ground.

Though the terrain was flat that morning, thereby normally offering the tireder or sicker members of the team the chance of riding an unladen camel, I had everyone walking as a collective punishment for the Uyghurs' behaviour the night before when they had left a half-dug water hole and gone gold prospecting once more on the Mazartagh. Guo had reassured me that the camels would be watered during the night but they had not been. Whilst camp was being struck that morning I had asked Esa Polta over to explain himself. He stood there, a big man with the child-like face of an errant schoolboy taking a reprimand from the headmaster, and muttered his excuses.

'But you were showing the handlers the map,' he stated softly.

'I know, but that was just to show them the route. That did not take long.'

'Then you went off into the hills with your map.'

'Yes.'

'We thought you would lead us to an ancient site or maybe gold.'

'And?'

'Well, we followed with our shovels . . . when we came back it was dark and there was no time to finish digging the hole.'

'Why didn't you tell me? You are always complaining that the camels cannot last without water and that we must take care. Now they have to go yet another day. It is an unnecessary hardship on them when there was a good chance of finding water.'

He said nothing and averted his eyes towards the animals being couched for loading nearby. The handlers looked at me with a mixture of hostility and interest as I rebuked their chief. It was pointless continuing the conversation. The camels had not drunk and that was it. With only about two days to Mazartagh I was not unduly concerned but it was the principle that I sought to put across to them.

'Use two of the full tin containers and give it to the camels,' I instructed, 'and today no one will ride: the animals have enough to carry after two days without water.'

With the sun blotted out by the dust and the strong north-easterly wind it was sufficiently cool to need a thin sweater even as I walked. That was a novelty. Visibility was down to less than 200 yards and we went forwards blindly into a blanket of greyness. Clouds and columns of sand whirled in a mad dance across the desert and the horizon was veiled in an unbroken yellow-grey haze. The fine drift sand penetrated everywhere – into mouths, noses, ears: even our clothes became impregnated with it and we could shake off the dust that had collected in the folds by the pound. We shut our eyes and mouths tight and lowered our heads against the chill blast. I had not expected to complete the crossing without experiencing a sandstorm of some kind and again wondered if we really might face a *karaburan*.

After two hours walking I raised the support team on the radio, anticipating that they were either at Mazartagh or trying to cross the flatter part of the desert towards us as it neared the ancient river bed of the Hotan. I could not get through; either the range was too great or the atmospherics were affected by the storm. Although this tract of the desert was reasonably good going for vehicles I had no idea what it was like nearer Mazartagh or even if the vehicles had made it there up the river bed from Hotan, over 120 miles across the desert to the south. An hour later I tried again.

'Good morning, Camel, how are you today?' Barney's voice came over the high-pitched revving of the Pinzgauer engine. I could hardly believe my ears.

'Where are you?' I asked excitedly.

'Never you mind!' he answered mockingly, which I took to mean that he wanted to catch us by surprise. I tingled with anticipation: they were there, somewhere beyond the veil of dust, trying to reach us. We were about to be reunited. We had made it! The expedition plan worked. After 200 tortuous miles, crossing an ocean of desert with only a crude map for guidance and never knowing what the terrain would be like or where we would be able to dig a well for the camels, we could look forward to the comfort and security of our fellow travellers – a chance to catch up on our respective adventures and experiences, as well as a break from the relentless daily pressure of pushing forward.

The storm continued to blow and the noise blocked any sound the vehicle engines might have made; but an hour later there was a shout and I saw headlights coming out of the gloom.

'The cavalry have arrived!' screamed Richard. Over the radio came music. Music! We had heard none since Markit and now Mark in the second vehicle was playing a rousing tune into the handset of his vehicle radio. We stopped the camels and stared. The Union Jack flew defiantly above Barney's vehicle as they came towards us, horns blaring and everyone shouting and waving with excitement. I had a lump in my throat and my heart pounded with pride. The relief was enormous. The vehicles sporting the names of our sponsors and the grand title

'Joint British-Chinese Taklamakan Desert Crossing 1993' looked majestic yet incongruous beside our battered caravan of baggage camels and scruffy, bearded walkers. Suddenly they were beside us, all at once overpowering our collective senses, making us feel crude and uncomfortable with the immediacy of a world left behind. Momentarily our isolation and our affinity with the cruel landscape were eclipsed by these ugly intruders from outside.

'Eat your heart out, Sven Hedin,' shouted Keith beside me. I smiled and shook his hand.

'Well done, we did it,' I said, slapping his back affectionately. 'You betcha!'

The crossing party and support party mingled together, hugging, kissing, shaking hands and rattling off anecdotes and stories of daring about experiences that, once told, would seldom be repeated with the same spontaneity. It was a moment that no one outside that tightly knit group could possibly understand or share. The support team opened the back compartments of their vehicles and produced tea, coffee and endless bars of chocolate. We gathered around like refugees and gorged on these simple forgotten luxuries as we eagerly exchanged news. Then I noticed the Chinese and the Uyghurs. They sat in separate groups off to one side, away from what had inadvertently become a very British celebration. Suddenly they had no part in it and I felt sad for them. In spite of the many conflicts, misunderstandings and difficulties, they were still the people with whom we had lived, survived and struggled over those last fourteen days. But at that moment they were culturally excluded and alien.

The Uyghurs' position I could understand. Whether it had been an all-Chinese or an all-British reunion their very status as a less sophisticated minority people would have set them apart. But they would not have resented that. Their history and way of life had shaped their temperament and made them a humbler, yet more contented race who drew on the bonding of their own kith and kin. They had no real experience of the camaraderie of shared teamwork in a venture such as ours. Mutual backslapping was not their style.

The Chinese attitude, however, disappointed me. Even Guo, the most liberal and Westernized of the four, was long-faced and sullen, excluded from our tumultuous bout of self-congratulation. They watched us impassively, self-consciously aware of the one-sided reunion without any Chinese support team members. Their vehicles were unable to match our Pinzgauers and, even if they had, the Chinese were unwilling to enter the desert proper and preferred to remain at the resupply point. There was no national flag for them and no exchange of news with friends who had nervously monitored the struggling progress of the camel party through the desert. But their time would come. Later.

At that point it seemed a singularly British accomplishment and, considering that the plan, the funding and the leadership were ours, we felt the worthy owners of the moment. As we set off again, the vehicles going on ahead to Mazartagh, Guo, Qiu Lei and Zhang Bohua strode out at the front for the first time. United in their rejection of our mutual self-recognition of the British contribution, they struck off into the dust storm heading east-south-east. They had no compass and no map, for old Lao Zhao remained in our midst and led a camel near the head of the caravan. None of the Uyghurs followed them. It was unintentional but it completed their national humiliation and proved beyond doubt where the true force behind the crossing party lay. I let them go until they had almost disappeared from sight before sending Rupert off in hot pursuit. He brought them back and they remained silent and subdued for the remainder of the afternoon. They had tried, in their own way, to make their presence more evident but it had backfired.

We were all extremely weary and the final ten miles to Mazartagh seemed like twenty. On and on we tramped as night descended, our bodies mechanically putting one foot in front of the other as we resolutely drove ourselves to the end of the first leg. The elation of the premature and unexpected reunion had passed, leaving us more aware of our physical aches, our sore feet and our exposure to the battering of the elements. It had been a gruelling 200 miles and our bodies yearned for rest.

We had taken none, not a day, not an hour more than was necessary to maintain the daily tally over the ocean of dunes. More than anything we thought of the coming day's break at Mazartagh and the chance to collect our bodies and souls in preparation for the next leg to Tongguzbasti. There was a long, long way to go – still a further 580 miles – and we now had no illusions about it.

EIGHT

Mazartagh

The spring of 1908 saw Aurel Stein, accompanied by his faithful fox-terrier, Dash, returning westwards towards Kashgar along the southern Silk Road. In the previous five months he had rediscovered and excavated a number of ancient Buddhist sites on the eastern fringes of the Taklamakan Desert and had amassed a considerable haul of antiquities which, in time, would make their way by bullock cart through Central Asia and from there by train and steamship back to London and the British Museum. After the hardships of his journey through the long months of the Turkestan winter, with no company other than that of his native helpers, Stein was looking forward to reaching the haven of the British Consul's residence, Chinibagh, once more, and the chance to catch up on his mail and conversation with his friends, the Macartneys.

When Stein reached Hotan, however, he heard vague reports about the existence of ancient remains on the mysterious desert hill of Mazartagh. These reports aroused his curiosity and, with his thirst for further discoveries clearly unquenched, he reacted to this information by setting off at once north along the left bank of the Hotan river with the experienced Uyghur guide, Kirim Akhun, until they reached the gaunt and barren cliffs of reddish sandstone seven days later. Stein's satisfaction was great when he found that the top of the 200-foot hill overlooking the wide, sandy river bed was occupied by the ruins of a small, relatively well-preserved fort which had clearly been built to guard the route leading along the river. He then spent three long, hot days excavating in the area of the fort and found numerous ancient artefacts. Much of his digging concentrated on the rubbish tip on the east face of the fort's walls; there the refuse had been thrown down by the occupants over the years and had been preserved by the barren sandstone ridge that protected it from the moisture of the river below. Buried in the thick refuse lay Tibetan tablets and manuscripts by the hundred, along with documents in Chinese and Brahmi, and rare pieces in Uyghur and some unknown script. At night, by the light of a paraffin lamp, Stein sat for hours in his tent interpreting his finds and concluded that the fort's occupation dated to the period of the Tibetan invasions during the eighth and ninth centuries AD.

The fort was the first thing I saw when I woke on the morning of 8 October, and I immediately recognized it and the Mazartagh hill from Stein's description and the photographs in his book, *Ruins of Desert Cathay*. I lay in my sleeping bag, lit a cigarette and savoured the luxury of idleness. My knee ached appallingly and was again badly swollen with fluid as a result of the exertions of the previous two days. We had covered forty miles, not a vast distance under ordinary circumstances but a long way after everything we had been through. Our camp lay on the south-western side at the base of the rock face which towered high above, blocking out the early morning sun. For the first time on the crossing I was assailed by a sense of history; not only had Stein himself camped near or on this very spot but Tibetan warriors, Chinese delegations of officials and soldiers, traders, merchants and cameleers would all have passed by over the centuries and gazed on the same red sandstone cliffs. It was a curious, out of the way, and unlikely place but it was the first tangible piece of history in the desert that we had encountered, apart from the old camel saddle which, sadly, had been broken up by the camel handlers for firewood.

Breakfast was a treat on that serene, relaxing morning. For a change it wasn't the usual left-overs reheated from the night before complete with grit and sand; neither did we have to motivate ourselves to pack up the camp, load the camels and set the direction line for yet another day's march. For a moment we could enjoy the orderly and homely contentedness of John and Anne's domesticity as they quietly prepared coffee (real coffee!), porridge (the package, sporting a Scotsman in a kilt, was a pleasure to look at) and eggs – as many eggs as the crossing party could eat. It was our first proper breakfast since Markit (one of many firsts, including a wash of body and clothes, a drink from a can, a bottle of Chinese beer and using a knife, fork and spoon with a plate rather than the usual combination of filthy mess-tin and wooden chopsticks). The support team fussed about, washed up and did everything possible to make us comfortable. It was a brief intermission in a crossing otherwise fraught with hardship, doubts, danger and loneliness. Whilst we savoured it to the full none of us kidded ourselves about the ravages of the desert which lay ahead. Afterwards I sat in the cab of the Pinzgauer with Barney (a first seat!) and discussed the numerous and complex factors that we had to take into account on the next leg, and the remainder of the expedition.

Barney's principal problem at that point was the unresolved plan for the extraction of the vehicles at the very end. The Chinese were still dragging their feet over permission for John Thomas and a team to drive through China to Hong Kong where the vehicles and equipment would be shipped back to England. The alternative was a perilous crossing of the Khunjerab Pass in deep snow which, in any case, was normally closed by the Pakistani authorities during the worst of the winter due to regular avalanches and the impossibility of keeping the road open. If they couldn't get out to Hong Kong they would have to leave the vehicles in Xinjiang until the spring. I looked out of the vehicle as we chatted and saw a goat tied to the tailgate of the Chinese Army Kamaz truck parked nearby. I listened as it bleated pathetically in its loneliness and thought how much more noise it would be making had it known its hours were numbered; that was the Uyghurs' lunch and they would kill it just beforehand since their religion decrees that the meat must be fresh. I tried to share Barney's concern but my mind kept turning back to the desert and pondering the many difficulties that lay ahead. Planning how to get the vehicles home seemed pointless at this stage when it was possible that none of the crossing party might survive the all-devouring desert.

On the far side of the truck were a hotch-potch of white four-man tents belonging to the Chinese National TV crew who had come into the desert with the support vehicles to record the historic crossing. They were a friendly team from Beijing and had filmed our entry into the desert at Markit; then, with some drama, they had interviewed each of us in turn as we assembled for the departure, recording for posterity our thoughts at that moment and our last messages to our families. Now I learnt that we had caused a wave of media disappointment the night before by making our entry into camp at midnight in the pitch dark rather than following their plan for a triumphant arrival by daylight. After the rigours of the crossing I had been in no mood to manage the media and had pressed on regardless, intent only on getting to the campsite as quickly as possible. The film crew had opted, instead, to interview the Chinese crossing party in one of the tents and I had listened with ill-concealed frustration to their embellished stories about how they had cheated death and braved the horrors of the desert. They made out that they had done the crossing entirely by themselves. As the beer and Chinese rice wine flowed into the early morning hours, so the tales grew more fanciful. For the sake of good relations and to show a united front we played along. But I itched to tell the unedited story of the conduct of the Chinese team, especially amongst the sand mountains when they had virtually given up and would undoubtedly have turned back had it not been for us. Lao Zhao was the only one who spoke factually, disclosing his geological finds and praising the efforts and drive of the British team. My hair curled when Qiu Lei became the centre of attention and regaled the camera crew with stories of his exploits. Exploits indeed; the man was a liability without any inkling of teamwork. It was not even his right to pontificate

about my expedition when he had played no part in its concep-
tion, planning or conduct but had instead coasted along,
looking after number one. It was probably the fact that I was
very tired after all our exertions that made me feel so indignant
and so keen to see the record righted. Added to which the ide-
alist in me resented the intrusion of the media into the desert
that I had regarded as my inviolate kingdom. They were out-
siders and strangers who did not understand the rationale for
our expedition; with them they brought everything I sought to
escape from. Little things irritated me, like the bravado with
which they wore their brand-new desert boots, their chewing
gum, their clean clothes and soft, clean hands which touched
me or put a microphone in front of me as though it was their
right to own my thoughts and my spoken words.

Eventually, I left the tent in disgust and groped in the dark
for my kit among the twenty camel sacks that had been
dumped in a disorderly pile in the rush for the hospitality of
the support team. I had always known that once we were in
China their nationalist pride would take over and claim copy-
right on the expedition. It was ever going to be thus. The
British contribution would remain a footnote in the first ever
historic Taklamakan crossing: nevertheless, seeing and hearing
the reality of the Chinese twist that night had made me resent-
ful and cross. Already I wanted to be away from it all and back
in the simple and uncluttered business of the crossing.

'Have you seen Mark's find?' Barney asked, looking up from
the pile of maps of Stein's ancient sites on his lap and abruptly
bringing me back to the present.

'What is it?'

'A comb.'

'So?'

'An old comb made from wood or bone.'

'And?'

'It's probably at least twelve hundred years old.'

'That is old. Where did he find it?'

'On the east side below the fort where Stein conducted his
1908 excavations. You can still make out Stein's trenches which
suggests to me that he didn't backfill them properly to preserve

the archaeological layers. In fact his excavations, if they are his, look rather crude if one judges them against the exacting standards he claimed he maintained in his books.'

'That's terribly exciting. But there's one problem; we can't take it back to England and present it to the British Museum or the Royal Geographical Society or there will be hell to pay.'

'I know, it's a tricky one,' Barney replied. 'The Chinese are still so sensitive about the plundering of their treasures by Stein, Hedin and others that any goodwill we've gained from this venture will go straight out the window if they catch us at it.'

Before we left for China the British Museum had distanced themselves from the projects we were keen to undertake on their behalf. From our perspective it was a unique opportunity but the Museum took the view that ours was a short-term project and didn't fit into their more thorough scheme of things. Personally, I was disappointed that our British expedition to a scarcely explored part of Central Asia could serve no purpose for them. However, sensitivities run deep: curators are paranoid that the Chinese may one day demand the return of the many Stein treasures and, if that happens, who knows where it will end?

Later I climbed Mazartagh hill with Keith and Carolyn. The red sandstone rises to a height of 500 feet above the surrounding country which consists of a flat plain interspersed with small horseshoe-shaped dunes. To the east a belt of trees and bushes delineates the line of the Hotan river. I thought of Stein climbing the steep slope dressed in leather boots, trousers, shirt, tie and jacket, with a solar topee on his head. I could see him busily making observations in his notebook and letting his well-trained archaeological eye take in the site as he decided where best to place his native labourers to start digging. What a thrill he must have experienced knowing he would be the first person to attempt to unravel the secrets of the remote and long-deserted fort – piecing together the history of its occupation by Tibetan and Chinese soldiers who would never have believed, as they casually threw over the walls of the fort their broken cooking vessels, obsolete bamboo and wooden writing tablets, and other discarded implements, that one day a man of fair complexion and strange garb would dig up their cast-offs and convey them to museums on the far side of the world.

I got half-way up the scarp overlooking the river bed, which at that time of year had no trace of water whatsoever, and noticed the same collection of staffs that Stein had found with votive rags marking the supposed resting-place of a saint, from which the hill took its present name. Large shards of ancient pottery were scattered on the surface. A cool wind blew from the north-east and I savoured its unfamiliar freshness. The old fort rose above me as I poked about among the thin spoil below its mud-brick and straw walling and found a tattered piece of aged hessian with a fine weave whose colours of blue, red and brown were still perfectly preserved. Excited by the find I continued my search and uncovered a sandal made from hessian and rope, pieces of leather and some carved wood. Carolyn discovered a small splint of a wooden tablet with ancient writing which Mark did not recognize as Chinese. He thought it was probably part of a Tibetan or Uyghur tablet. I was reluctant to ignore these artefacts in spite of the earlier conversation with Barney. Instead I placed them in a plastic sample bag with a view to resolving national ownership at the end of the expedition. There were bound to be further archaeological finds and it would be better to hand them over to the Chinese together; if I changed my mind then the risk of bringing them home would be mine alone.

Barney left with the British support team the next day, 9 October, even though I had been persuaded by the camel handlers and the Chinese that two days and nights of rest were necessary before continuing. Barney was keen to pick up the extra stores he had dumped in Hotan to lighten the vehicles for their journey north to meet up with us in the desert. Then he wanted to make an attempt at reaching Dandan-uilik, another ancient site near the Silk Road between the tributaries of the rivers Hotan and Keriya. From there he planned to return to the Silk Road and collect supplies of grain, water and foodstuffs, before moving on to meet the crossing party once more at the next rendezvous, Tongguzbasti. Another part of him wanted to be independent of the Chinese support team whose urban habits had proved impossible to change. They remained behind with the journalists to see the camel party off the following morning.

With Barney went Richard: his departure was a sad loss for we had come to rely upon his wit, conversation and marvellous ability to mediate any potential conflict among the team members before it even happened. His contribution to the expedition had been great, right from the funds he raised in Hong Kong, his diplomatic handling of the Chinese and his stubborn determination crossing the sand mountains, down to his amusing vocabulary of nicknames for everyone. Never again were names like 'The King of Mongolia' (Esa Polta), 'Fagin' (Rosa), 'Calculus' (Lao Zhao) and 'Lord Blackadder [or Slackbladder] of the Taklamakan' (myself) repeated with such gusto and humour. We missed him. Yet with his departure I felt a small relief. His personality and charisma had been so strong and had had such a hold on people that my own position as leader had been less secure. I knew that: whether the others felt the same, I never asked. Richard was not the type knowingly to take over or assume the lead role but I was aware of his powers of leadership which could have won the day had there ever been a division within the team. That said, he was one of the best team members and workers I had ever come across.

His place was taken by Mark Kitto who was itching to be in the desert proper. Barney and Francis were an inseparable pair, and John and Anne were married, which had left Mark feeling the odd one out in the vehicle party. At the same time his offhand and blunt remarks had irritated Barney whose conventional military background and discipline led him to expect more respect from his subordinates. I, on the other hand, welcomed Mark's inclusion and looked upon him as a kindred spirit and ally in my still uncertain relationship with Rupert. There had been no conflicts but I was sensitive to Rupert's attitude that seemingly put my organization and leadership under the microscope. I particularly resented it since he had only joined at the last moment and had no idea how much time and effort had gone into even getting the expedition to China, let alone crossing the desert.

Keith also went with the support team. He yearned for a change of subject material after having shot camels and sand, sand and camels, dunes, dunes and more dunes, from every conceivable angle with his cameras. The Silk Road away to the south beckoned his artistry, the Pinzgauer beckoned his blistered feet, and his mind sought the creature comforts of life away from the daily hardships of the trail and the constant barrage of Army and public schoolboy humour.

One of the most unexpectedly sad farewells was saved for the morning of our own departure from Mazartagh. Esa Polta, the grand old man of 76, was going to the hospital in Hotan and thence back along the Silk Road to his home at the Seven Stars Commune in Markit. Rosa, his nephew, was being sent to take care of him and that meant we were down to four camel handlers: Lucien, Kirim, Abdul Rasheed (BP) and Emir. Esa had taken a bad fall from his camel shortly after the support party first met us west of Mazartagh. One of the vehicles came too close to his mount and the animal bucked and threw Esa savagely to the hard ground. He had lain there without moving for some time and we had feared the worst. It would not have been the dignified death amidst the splendid sand mountains that he would have wished for. Fortunately, he had only been badly winded but his right leg was injured. Carolyn thought he might have broken or cracked his femur. Even after the rest at Mazartagh it was obvious he could no longer continue. The fall had badly shaken him and he looked, for the first time, the tired old man that he really was: few grandfathers could have gone through what he had survived in two weeks.

When it came to saying our goodbyes he stood supported by a home-made crutch under his right armpit, Rosa beside him nervously twisting his Lenin cap in his hands. Esa looked at me through those big brown sorrowful eyes and I was immediately reminded of another farewell years before. Then it had been to Mohammed Musa, my Bedouin camel handler, who had ridden with me on my Lawrence of Arabia expedition. There was so much I wanted to express to Esa but words were not the right medium. Instead, I took his hand and held it for some time, gazing at his dignified face as I tried to convey a message of gratitude, respect and friendship. Then I turned to Rosa.

'Goodbye, Fagin, my old friend. No more clip-boarding around the camel sacks searching for goodies for you,' I joked.

His face was as sad as that of a boy being sent away to boarding school. For all his deviousness and cunning he had put his entire self into the expedition and did not want to be left behind. He wanted to go where we went, to share the same risks and even meet the same death if it came to that.

'Charles, *yakshee dos*, *yakshee dos*' (good friend).

'Rosa, *ella yakshee dos*' (very good friend).

I then did something completely unexpected for an Englishman. I hugged him. That hug broke my barriers of self-control and I felt a huge lump swell in my throat, my stomach knotted and my heart pounded. Tears welled in my eyes and I had to break away quickly.

'Let's go, come on then, let's go,' I shouted in a less than clear voice, picking up my walking stick and heading to the front of the caravan. The lead camels moved off. I vowed not to look back. But I did. Watching us go, Esa and Rosa stood shoulder to shoulder and their longing eyes burnt right through my soul. I cried. The tears that had been bottled up inside me since before leaving England now rolled down my cheeks. The bubble had burst after all the worry, tension, hardship and fear. The relief, afterwards, was immense.

NINE

The Chinese Prison Camp

It was a very different team which marched towards Tongguzbasti that morning of 10 October on a magnetic bearing of 95°. Not only were the four familiar faces of Richard, Keith, Esa and Rosa missing but there were also two new faces with us – Mark and another woman. She was a Chinese journalist and her name was Cheung Chan although she answered to Golden Swallow. Guo had implored me to take her along just for the next leg in order to raise the profile of the expedition with the Chinese media. Initially I had been firmly against it; after all she would be eating our rations and her additional kit would have to be carried by one of the camels, for which I had already budgeted and paid on a planned head-count. She was also an extra responsibility, another life that I would have to take into account in the decision-making, even though I did not expect the dunes to be as high and difficult to cross as the ones before. Partly because there was less apparent danger on the next leg, and partly as a gesture to Guo, who had supported me, I eventually gave in. I also knew that the Chinese authorities had it in their power to cancel the expedition at any point. If that happened at Tongguzbasti, the last definite place where they knew they would be able to contact us through the Chinese element of the back-up team, it would be a bitter blow. Currying favour at that stage, I reckoned, would be a sound tactic, and good coverage in the Chinese media later would also help.

I believed the desert would be less dangerous on the next leg because I had read Stein's descriptions of the area around Dandan-uilik, the ancient site that lies roughly half-way between the old fort at Mazartagh and Tongguzbasti, about sixty miles south of my planned traverse. It was Stein's descriptions, too, that led Barney to believe he could reach Dandan-uilik by vehicle across the dunes. Subsequently he was to be proved wrong: the desert would not simply lie down and submit to such convenience. Proof of that made us in the crossing party feel more isolated than ever, for we now knew that, in spite of hopes and boasts to the contrary, no vehicle could ever enter sufficiently far into the desert to where we were, over 150 miles north of the Silk Road, and rescue us in an emergency. The only possible place was Tongguzbasti: after that it was mere conjecture.

Golden Swallow did not look much of an explorer as we left the remains of the camp behind. She wore tight blue jeans, a blue jean jacket, Chinese Army desert boots and a splendid straw hat with an orange and white spotted ribbon around the band. She was also extremely attractive. In my shabby green shorts, now patched on the backside, and filthy, torn Army shirt I must have looked a very different sight. But I was comfortable and so, presumably, was she, at least for the time being. Carolyn's reaction at no longer being the only female was going to be more interesting.

The changes weren't all on the human side, for we had lost one camel which had roamed off during our last night at Mazartagh. The Uyghurs searched for four hours without success. Tracks led to the south but there was no telling how far they went and I decided to abandon the camel to its fate. It had been one of the weaker camels and I often wondered in the weeks that followed whether it survived. Of the remaining twenty-nine, eight were weak, thin and suffering from diarrhoea in spite of their two-day rest and good grazing along the Hotan river. One of the largest camels had a deep wound the size of an open hand on its hind quarters. The flesh moved about inside as it walked, causing blood and pus to ooze to the surface and dribble down the animal's flank. Maggots appeared from between the rotting flesh and fell squirming on to the sand. Fortunately, ten fresh camels were due to be supplied at Tongguzbasti and all of them would be needed for the remainder of the trip. The blind camel was now no more than a passenger. The poor beast crashed into poplars and low bushes as we crossed the two-mile-wide valley adjacent to the dried-up river bed of the Hotan. The dead, gnarled tree trunks, their naked branches outstretched above the grey soil, made it depressing landscape to walk through. It was as desolate and ugly as a black-and-white photograph of a shell-blasted wood in Flanders during the First World War.

Finally, after two hours, we struck the dunes adjacent to the valley, and the areas of scrub were left behind. It was good to be back among their soft yellow contours and as we entered their embrace I welcomed them as friends. Soon, we were completely enveloped, leaving the dunes to do with us as they would. That evening we camped early after only eight miles. Golden Swallow had walked surprisingly well and showed no signs of fatigue. Mark, in contrast, was suffering from slight dehydration and was regretting the softening effect on his constitution of a month in the support vehicle. For the first time the atmosphere around the camp was one of unity. The old mutual suspicions between the three cultural groupings had been buried. The contrast with the support teams at Mazartagh had reinforced our common interests and purpose. Now we were back in our solitary world in a routine which only we understood and which we had learned to cherish. The desert was no longer our enemy; it was our escape and our sanctuary. It held no more surprises, we thought, and the confidence engendered by the successful crossing from Markit to Mazartagh was visible in us. No one had done that before; the demon of Sven Hedin's failure in the grips of the desert had been laid to rest, at least for the time being. I faced the unknown ahead with new-found confidence and pride. The haunting spectre of the destructiveness and unfriendliness of the desert was held temporarily at bay. Indeed, to my eyes, the desert ocean was becoming invested with a fascinating beauty; its silence, its unbroken stillness, exercised a magic charm over me. It was a grand, a majestic sight. 'Onwards! Onwards!' whispered the desert wind. 'Onwards! Onwards!' vibrated the camels' bells.

Surprisingly, the camel handlers did not appear to miss Esa Polta. Under the new leadership of Kirim they behaved and performed as a team and seemed happy without the watchful gaze of an elder. In some ways they may have felt relief that Esa Polta had got out of the desert alive whilst he had the chance. Even before his accident the hardships of the journey had told on him: he had slowed considerably and I knew that he would not have withstood the mental and physical trials of the weeks ahead. I too had been relieved. The morale of the Chinese was also high; in fact they were positively light-hearted. Whether this was because they wanted to prove themselves real men in front of the delicate beauty of Golden Swallow, or whether it derived from a new-found inner confidence having survived the sand mountains, I never really established. I suspect it was a combination of many things.

The camel handlers had had the presence of mind to collect some loads of wood from the river bed in the morning which were lashed in bundles on the sides of the camels. After the evening meal we sat in a companionable circle around the camp fire as the flames danced in the breeze, with the cold night air on our backs and the smell of wood smoke on our clothes. It was deeply satisfying. We were a ragged-looking lot, a bunch of scruffy, determined individuals each engrossed in our own thoughts as we lapsed into periods of silence, hypnotized by the fire and savouring its primitive attraction. Behind us roamed the camels amid the gentle, rolling dunes as they searched in vain for grazing. Later, before going to bed, the handlers would round them up and bring them close to the camp, tying them together in fives or sixes and immobilizing the lead camel to prevent them wandering. We could not afford to lose any more. There was no need to water them as each had drunk its fill from a small pool of stagnant water at Mazartagh. Tomorrow, however, we would need to search for a place to dig a well.

Lao Zhao recounted the story of why the Chinese are God's chosen race as he sat cross-legged, hands outstretched towards the flames, with the ever-present cigarette between his ugly black and yellow twisted teeth – they looked as though his Creator had thrown them all into his mouth as an afterthought. He told his story in Chinese which Mark then translated for us. It went like this:

> God was sitting one day making models of man from clay. He eventually made three and put them in the oven to bake. One he placed at the back, one in the middle and one at the front near the oven door. He left them for a while and then opened the door and took them out. Well, the one nearest the door was too far from the heat and was a pink colour so God threw him away in disgust and he landed in Europe. The one in the middle had been too close to the heat and was black. God took him out, threw him in the air, and he landed in Africa. Then God reached right to the back of the oven and took out the third model which had turned a crisp yellow. 'Ah!' said God, 'Just right,' and carefully placed him in China.

The weather began to change and already the days were cooler, the average temperature having dropped to 80° Fahrenheit. This made a difference to our water consumption. We now needed only one and a half litres a day for drinking as opposed to the three litres of a fortnight before. Our bodies, too, had acclimatized – we had become used to walking for eight hours with the minimum of water. By contrast, Mark was drinking at least three litres and the back of his shirt was permanently wet with sweat. Our progress was good, maintaining a daily average of twelve to fourteen miles through dunes no higher than 200 feet at the most. After three days we were over halfway to Tongguzbasti, our tails were up, and everything was going smoothly. Then on the evening of 12 October, after managing to get through to the support team on our crackling radio for the first time since leaving Mazartagh (an achievement which elated Mark because he had given Francis in the support team only the most elementary training as the replacement operator in the run-up to the Mazartagh resupply), we heard the bad news.

'Hello, Bella, this is Camel, radio check, over.' Mark's voice carried across the sand from the site he had chosen part of the way up a small dune where the radio wave could be bounced high into the ionosphere without obstruction.

'Bella, okay, you came through first time and receiving you loud and clear, over.'

'Camel, roger, our position is 38° 23.41'N and 81° 27.42'E, Desert Camp 15. We estimate reaching Tongguz in two days.'

'Bella, that's excellent, well done, but we have a slight problem here,' replied Francis in a tone which concealed a massive understatement. 'Our Bella vehicle got bogged in right up to the cab two days ago trying to reach Dandan-uilik.'

'Camel, can't you dig it out?' I heard Mark ask. By then I was heading across to where he lay by the radio. I then heard Francis say, 'Bella, no, we are not stuck in a sand dune. We are in waterlogged sand near the Keriya river bed.'

Mark looked at me blankly and handed over the handset. I asked to speak to Barney, an evening procedure we had established once the two radio operators had done their routine business. In between the sounds of static and interference he explained the events leading to the incident.

After leaving us at Mazartagh on 9 October, he had returned to Hotan, dropped Richard at the small airstrip and picked up the expedition artist, Paul Treasure, and Krishna Guha (a Cambridge graduate who was to join the support party and study the ancient sites). They had flown together from Urumqi in a rickety aircraft which had scared them out of their wits. He had then headed east to Yutian and had driven up the left bank of the Keriya river bed with the intention of penetrating about sixty miles north before turning due west, at which point he would be on the same latitude as the ancient site of Dandan-uilik. John Thomas was confident that, if all the unnecessary stores were then dumped and the sand tyres deflated, the vehicles would be able to cross the low dunes and reach the site, which lay thirty miles to the west. This was the route which Stein had chosen in 1901 and, judging from his descriptions, Barney and John had calculated that the vehicles would have little difficulty in getting through providing they stuck together. One vehicle was equipped at the front with a winch and also carried rolls of rectangular wire meshing with black plastic coating which John had managed to acquire in Wales, apparently from the friend of a friend in the Special Air Service. These rolls of tracking were for laying on soft sand in front of the vehicles to improve the grip of the tyres. But neither winch nor specialist tracking could help the Bella vehicle driven that day by Francis which followed in John's tracks. For eighty miles John had driven close to the river where the going was flat and had just crossed an unstable patch when he sensed that it would not stand the weight of another 3-ton vehicle. He reached for the radio to warn the Bella vehicle but Francis was driving too fast and too close behind him for the warning to be given. John just had time to glance in his side mirror and see Francis's vehicle wobble unsteadily on the surface of the sand before the surface broke and Bella plunged nose first into the mire. According to John, Barney and Francis initially sat in the cab in a state of shock before taking in what had happened.

'Get out, you silly buggers!' he screamed in a high-pitched Welsh accent. 'Get out of the vehicle and start chucking the equipment before everything is lost.'

The vehicle sank by the front at an alarming rate. In a frenzy, Barney and Francis scrambled on to the roof and tried undoing the rear doors to get at the precious radio and satellite communications equipment.

'Throw me your line,' Barney shouted to John.

'No, can't do that or my vehicle will join yours.'

'Don't be daft. Turn your vehicle around and use the winch.'

'My vehicle is not moving from here, Barney. I'll bring it no closer.'

In the heat of the crisis a big argument developed. John could not be persuaded to risk his vehicle and, as it turned out, he was right: the loss of one vehicle would have severe repercussions on the entire expedition, but the loss of two would end our chances altogether.

The vehicle began to settle on an even keel while everyone waded up to their thighs in the sucking mud and sand trying to save as much equipment as possible. Once that was done they sat down despondently and looked at Bella, now buried to the height of the cab windows. By nightfall, Barney had resigned himself to seeing an £80,000 vehicle loaned by our Austrian sponsors finally coming to the end of its life in a sandy bog in the middle of nowhere.

As dawn broke the following day, the support team were astonished to see Bella in much the same position as she had been when they went to sleep. For some reason the vehicle had not disappeared completely overnight as they had expected and this gave Barney renewed hope. He now recalled having driven past some run-down concrete barracks on the previous day's journey, roughly twenty-five miles further back. Perhaps it was deserted, but if they were lucky it might be an army camp. The question then was, would they be prepared to help? He consulted Xia Xia, their Chinese interpreter.

'Barney,' Xia said in his monotone, robotic voice, 'It is a *laogai*.'

'A *laogai*?'

'Yes.'

'What is that?'

There was a long pause, and then Xia replied, 'It is a Chinese farming community.'

What he meant – although he was certainly not going to admit it – was that it was a prison camp, the Chinese equivalent of a Russian *gulag*.

Laogai still existed in China, a hangover from the wilderness years of the Cultural Revolution when hundreds of thousands of people disappeared to these prison camps in far-off places for the most trivial crimes. Officially they were a thing of the past and China worked hard to maintain that line at a time when its human rights record was under scrutiny by the West. But they did exist; all that was missing was the evidence that Western intelligence sources and journalists had been unable to find.

Carefully retracing their tracks in John's vehicle, the team came across the *laogai*, just as Xia had predicted. Surrounded on all sides by the desert was a high-walled camp complete with watch-towers occupied by armed guards It looked, to all intents and purposes, like the setting for a film. Prisoners with irons around their legs were working the worthless grey soil irrigated by canals from the river, and a vague tinge of greenery was testament to their labours. The scene had the most austere and desolate hopelessness about it. How many innocent people had been sent to die in such a place over the years without their families ever knowing?

Unsure of what might happen, they approached the front gate and the two guards armed with AK47 assault rifles who barred the way. Barney later remarked on the extraordinary indifference with which the guards then greeted them. Their arrival aroused no curiosity whatsoever, as if such visits were simply routine. Nor were they prepared for what happened next. With the utmost civility, one member of the guard ushered them inside and took them to the office of the Governor of the prison. By this time Xia was very ill at ease and Barney was not confident that the translations were running true to form. Xia's discomfort increased when the Governor later took it upon himself to give his unexpected visitors a grand tour of his little empire in the desert. By this time Barney was beginning to realize the reality and awkwardness of his position. He was, after all, a serving officer in the British Army and there he was being shown the complete layout of an extremely sensitive part of China's history, and its present. The Governor proudly took him up a watch-tower equipped with a machine gun and drums of spare ammunition neatly stacked and ready at hand. Under the muzzle of the weapon the prisoners worked in the open. There was a loud blast of a whistle and the prisoners were rounded up promptly and herded into their cells. The Governor continued his tour of the inside where the prisoners were being manacled to their wooden bunk beds by chains and shackles. They looked half starved and their eyes were those of people who have given up all hope. The cells were tiny and cramped, each containing six prisoners in two sets of three-tier beds. In a corner was a receptacle which served as their toilet. The only light came from a small opening eight feet above the ground covered by an iron grille.

Returning to his office where tea was waiting for his guests, the Governor asked what the *laogai* could do to help. When

Barney asked for manual assistance he was astonished that the Governor readily offered to send all 200 prisoners to pull and dig Bella out of the sand.

'Do you want butozer?' asked Xia a little later in the conversation.

'Butozer? What's butozer?'

'Butozer. Butozer.'

Not for the first time since Mazartagh did Barney miss having Mark in his team. Xia was useful up to a point but it became frustrating not having complete control of the language.

'Butozer. The Governor has excellent butozer.'

With the help of a drawing Barney established that he was being offered the assistance of a bulldozer. It arrived that afternoon, an ancient Chinese-made contraption of much-rusted machinery in orange paint which belched clouds of smoke from its vertical exhaust. It was accompanied by the proud Governor and a dozen or so Party officials, so-called engineers and prison warders from the *laogai*, who chatted and smoked in small groups whilst the slow-moving machine pushed sand with its blade into the vicinity of Bella to make a firmer platform. After an hour's work it broke down. The driver, the only person who knew anything about the bulldozer and relished his standing as a specialist among the uninitiated, went back to the prison camp for spare parts. By nightfall he had not returned. Dawn the next day, the third in the saga, and Bella still wallowed comfortably like a hippopotamus in her mud bath. The driver returned and tinkered with his beloved machine which, thankfully, responded with a throaty roar and clouds of smoke from the exhaust. The work continued all day until a reasonably firm base had been prepared from which the bulldozer could pull Bella out. Barney's team watched with tense anticipation as the tow rope was attached to Bella, the slack taken up and the bulldozer took the strain. Bella moved, slightly, mud, water and sand sucked simultaneously and then there was an almighty thundercrack as the steel hawser snapped and whipped through the air. More repairs were needed and this time a longer steel tow rope was brought from the camp together with the news that the chain gang of 200 prisoners equipped with shovels and accompanied by armed guards were nearly at the site.

Day three, 13 October. Bella was still bogged down. Barney and Francis were extremely unhappy. Having resigned themselves to the vehicle's ultimate fate they wished John would not continue to pretend that there could be any other outcome. For Paul Treasure and Krishna Guha, the novelty of the expedition and some of its glamour and mystique had already begun to wear thin. Keith remained happy taking photographs and thanking each hour of the day when he was not walking or leading a camel. By now the British vehicle stuck on the edge of the Keriya river had become a major spectacle for anyone in the prison camp who was not constrained by leg irons. Barney's only solace lay in watching flights of duck and geese on the river and convincing himself that it was a beautiful and tranquil spot against the lines of yellow sand dunes on both banks.

John had taken charge of the recovery process and used Xia to translate his commands to the bulldozer driver. A final effort was made to dig around Bella and release the pressure of the mud which was sucking the vehicle down. All afternoon the bulldozer strained and pulled until finally, with a burst of cheering and excitement from the onlookers, Bella's nose came up and she started to inch forward on to the firmer sand. The vehicle, and probably the expedition, had been saved. Not wishing to take any further risks, the support team bade their liberators farewell and drove gingerly southwards back to Yutian. They had just one and a half days in which to reach the camel team at Tongguzbasti, the next resupply point.

Blissfully unaware of the real drama of the support team's experience during those three days, the camel party had meanwhile made excellent progress and were poised only two days' march from Tongguzbasti. Barney had never related the real gravity of the situation but instead consistently gave an upbeat report on the radio at the end of each day. It was only afterwards that the narrowness of their escape came out. Barney's team were later questioned at length by uniformed Party officials and the Mayor of Yutian who was in a muck sweat about the political sensitivity of the incident in his region. Xia, Barney's interpreter, looked downcast and lost a great deal of face in front of his own countrymen. He probably thought he would end up in a *laogai* after the expedition as a punishment for his betrayal.

Barney had some difficult explaining to do. Though granted permission to drive along the Silk Road, he had been forbidden to leave it until he turned off towards Tongguzbasti. He had never been given clearance to attempt a route along the Keriya river with the aim of then trying to cross the dunes towards the ancient site of Dandan-uilik. In the end he feigned innocence and pretended he had got lost, two things he did with the convincing practice of an Army officer. The Mayor deliberated long and hard. A letter was drawn up which Barney was made to sign before the support party was allowed to proceed. He was not at all clear what exactly he was signing, but it involved the payment of the equivalent of £25, presumably for the use of the bulldozer.

TEN

All Men Dream

As the support team battled to extricate their vehicle on 12 October, Guo Jin Wei and I sat shoulder to shoulder on the lip of a dune with the evening sun full in our eyes. Our seat was the highest point of a sand ridge which flattened slightly behind us before dropping steeply into a vast depression whose sides resembled the inverted cone of trickling granules in an upturned egg-timer. It was the end of a long, hot and tiring day during which we had walked over eighteen miles. I had cracked lips and a dry, sore throat. There were no more than two sips left in my water bottle.

'My last cigarette,' said Guo as he cupped his hand against the gentle breeze to light a match. He took a couple of puffs and passed it over.

'We share it,' he said. I had run out earlier in the day.

'Thanks, Guo.' I inhaled deeply, my taste buds and lungs having long ago got used to the strong and crude tobacco of the Chinese cigarettes which had been donated to the expedition. We had been given 4,000 packets of 'Silk Road', appropriately branded, which when divided between only eight smokers in the camel and support parties worked out at roughly seven packets a day each. Needless to say, we could neither carry our full quota nor would have wanted to. I felt strangely guilty about smoking under a clear sky in a virgin landscape of sand whilst undertaking such punishing, yet invigorating, daily exercise. But it remained my release and I relished the occasional opportunity of a quiet, meditative smoke. For sentimental reasons I had brought my father's old K-Woodie pipe along as a talisman. Since I was also wearing his Army shirt, tatty and torn, and had his Paisley silk cravat tied around my neck, I was a bit of a walking museum, vulnerable to the diagnosis of any psychoanalyst. Fortunately there were no such people within thousands of miles or we would all have been certified insane for embarking upon such a venture. I unscrewed the black plastic top of my water bottle and passed it to Guo.

'My last drink. We share that too.'

Guo was quite weak with fatigue and thirst. He had run out of water at midday. His lips had a couple of painful-looking bloody sores which were deeply cracked. He smiled appreciatively and quickly guzzled nearly all that remained from my bottle. We were the last two people in the caravan. I had sent Rupert and Mark ahead with the camels to find a suitable campsite and somewhere to dig for water. The camels always seemed to be on their third or fourth day without water and the party's safety lurched from one such potential crisis to another. But after three weeks in the desert we had got used to that. In some respects we had become too casual about the water situation, even though we knew full well that it would be a hit-and-miss affair and had accepted that there could never be any guarantee of finding water in a desert famed for its secrets. Perhaps we were fatalistic because we knew that, irrespective of where we were, there was no turning back; there were no known water sites on any of the routes we covered between resupplies, so the only thing to do was head towards our ultimate destination and hope to chance upon one. Digging the water hole remained the most arduous and unpopular task at the end of an exhausting day spent trudging through soft sand, up and down dunes of bewildering shapes, all the while cajoling the camels along.

We sat in silence, an Englishman and a Chinese together drawing companionship from one another, two insignificant grains of sand surrounded by the vast and forbidding emptiness of the desert. What drove us to be there, on that dune, out of reach of help, dependent only on ourselves and our camels for survival? Both of us had children and could have been enjoying the pleasure of their innocent lives instead of sitting surrounded by sand dunes as far as the eye could see. I wondered what it would be like to look down first on us in our desert wilderness and then across the world to our families at home, and how to make sense of this. What was it that had lured us to leave the comfort of home for the hazards of the desert? At the same time I wondered what it would be like to look down and observe our progress from high above and to see what obstacles and dangers lay ahead. If this had been possible it would probably have caused us to give up in despair. The fact that life does not reveal the future guarantees that we live for the moment, often ignorant of what lies ahead. I always equate life with a train as it travels along its track with branch lines leading off in all directions, never knowing where the signal boxes are or how the points are set and each branch line leading to a new adventure or experience.

The setting sun cast long shadows over the dunes we had crossed that day. Just visible in the far distance I could make out the pathway made in the sand by the passage of our caravan, a dark line which disappeared at irregular intervals as one crest after another blocked out the base of the dunes. Before long the wind would whip up the sand and conceal our tracks forever, eliminating the trail we had bravely blazed and restoring the dunes once more to their untouched splendour. Our passage was as fleeting as that: we made no impact on the desert and our passing was nothing but a tiny and insignificant blip in its long history of isolation. No one would ever know we had passed that way. The present never assumed more significance than it did then, and the future never seemed more uncertain. There we were, out of reach of any assistance. In the event of an accident or a serious illness we had no choice but to go on. Each day the scene was the same and the naked challenge ever apparent. I wondered at our resilience as we obliterated all thoughts of being anywhere else, or, for that matter, of ever giving up. I don't believe we seriously contemplated defeat. Certainly there were fraught moments of danger and uncertainty, illness, boredom and frustration, and the constant gnawing pangs of hunger and unquenchable thirst, but we had grown used to them by now and each person had found their own equilibrium.

'Just think, Guo, we have walked across all that, 270 miles from Markit. We have walked from as far as the eye can see, even as far away now as the sun looks touching the horizon.'

'We are crazy.'

'Crazy? Yes, but at least the desert has not claimed us yet.'

'Why are you doing it, then?'

'I don't know. I really don't. Sometimes I wonder that myself. I think it is because I had a dream and I wanted to act it out, that's why.'

'You are doing that.'

'We are, Guo, you and me. We are the ones who have made all this possible. Without us none of the others would be here. We wouldn't even be here together if we hadn't both believed it was possible and put so much into it.'

'You are right, my friend.'

'This is our moment, our shared triumph.' I put my arm affectionately around his shoulders and gave him a hug. Guo went shy, very shy. I studied him carefully and saw, to my surprise, that there were tears forming in his eyes.

'How do you feel?' I asked.

'Very proud,' Guo replied, 'very proud that we are making history and that no humans have ever done what we are in the process of achieving.'

'We are a good team, you and me,' he added after a long silence.

'Yes, we are. Now come on, we'd better get going and catch up with the camels otherwise they'll be miles ahead and we may not find them in the dark.'

It had been a special, shared moment, an everlasting memory. For the first time on the expedition we had touched each other's hearts and had allowed ourselves to recognize our achievement. If the ghosts of Stein and Hedin had been with us, then I believe they would have acknowledged that we were worthy heirs.

As we followed the trail of the caravan down the far side of the sand ridge and over the maze of dunes beyond, I remembered my favourite passage from Lawrence's *Seven Pillars of Wisdom*: 'All men dream: but not equally. Those who dream by night in the dusty recesses of their minds wake in the day to find that it was vanity: but the dreamers of the day are dangerous men, for they may act their dream with open eyes, to make it possible. This I did.'

It took over an hour of fast walking to catch up with the caravan. By that time, dusk had descended, giving the dunes a more sinister appearance. As I overtook the three Chinese at the rear I noticed a lot of blood running down the hind leg of a camel carrying sacks of equipment. Its load had tilted to one side and had been knocking against the animal's thigh for much of the day, causing a large open wound. At the campsite later, I assembled everyone around the injured camel.

'This is not acceptable. Because some of you are not doing your job and caring for the camels we now have another one which cannot carry baggage tomorrow.'

'There's no point lashing into us, Charles,' retorted Carolyn. 'We've been at the front all day.'

'I'm aware of that but I want to make a point to everyone.'

She did not understand and became a touch argumentative and defensive. It made me appreciate that she was under strain and had become quite tired of late. Fortunately, Rupert interceded and took her to one side, demonstrating for the first time that he might fulfil what had been Richard's role, that of diplomat and soother of souls.

It was Rupert who insisted that he and I inspect all the camels even though it was dark. I was tired and simply wanted to eat and then sleep. But he was right. Using torches we checked each of the twenty-nine animals and found that twelve had wounds of one sort or another.

'We need to do this every evening, Charles,' suggested Rupert.

'Yes, you're right.'

'I read the Imperial Camel Corp's regulations for camel handling before I left England, an old book printed during the First World War which my uncle lent me, and it stipulated that looking after camels and caring for their welfare was no different from an officer looking after his men.'

'Except that the men don't spit at you and lash out.'

'You weren't in my regiment!'

'I'm glad I wasn't in that case.'

'You wouldn't have made it anyway.' He laughed good-humouredly as we worked together. We often teased each other over the differences between my regiment, the Royal Green Jackets, and his experiences with a Parachute battalion. Rupert was happiest when the conversation was about soldiering. He had got out of the Army three years before but he remained more military than any of us and still felt aggrieved that he had left Sandhurst prematurely without reaching officer rank.

One camel had a particularly bad injury around its hump, caused by the ropes that lashed the equipment. When we removed the saddle the fur visibly danced with hundreds of white writhing maggots.

'It's enough to make you throw up, the smell is so bad,' I exclaimed in disgust as Emir ambivalently picked at the wound with his stick and flicked the maggots on to the sand. The camel was restrained by tying its legs together and then wrestled to the ground with Rupert holding its neck stretched fully forwards. Carolyn brought the medical box over and set to work, sponging the base of its hump with an iodine solution. I was impressed by the camel's pain threshold as, wearing a surgical glove, she inserted her hand under the hump itself to reveal that half of it had been eaten away. Suddenly she hit a pocket of pus and blood which literally exploded. This time the camel did react and Rupert struggled to keep its head down as it bellowed in pain.

'We may not have named the camels at Markit but I reckon this one can be known as "Maggot" from now on,' suggested Carolyn, who showed little emotion at her unpleasant task, having undoubtedly witnessed worse sights in her years as an Army nurse, especially during the Gulf War.

In fact, we had named four of the camels by then on account of their behaviour or appearance. There was 'Chambar' (the Strong One), an elegant fawn-coloured camel favoured by Kirim. 'Einstein' was a small, dark-coated male with a tuft of hair on his forehead that stuck out at an eccentric angle. 'The Blind One' spoke for itself and finally there was 'The Mad One', the camel branded with the figure 8 on its hind quarter. This was the one that always created a scene and could not be trusted with any important loads such as water or the communications equipment. 'Five named camels and twenty-four to go,' said Mark. 'By the end of the trip we'll probably have a nickname for them all, just in time to sell them off if they survive that long.'

The next day I had an unnerving experience which reminded me of the dangers of the desert. We had halted at lunchtime for fifteen minutes in an area of low undulating dunes where ancient trees half stood or lay on the surface.

'Those trees are over a thousand years old,' Lao Zhao told me, using Mark as our translator.

'How long ago does he think they died?' I asked.

'More than five hundred years,' came back the reply. 'Once the whole area was forested and big animals like deer and wild pigs were plentiful. Before then even, going back to prehistoric times, the Tarim Basin was one vast sea as big as the Mediterranean.'

The distorted stumps resembled a world after a holocaust and something about the area excited my curiosity. I studied the gnarled and disfigured remains of the petrified wood, trying to visualize possible configurations for an old settlement and seeking to identify the tell-tale pattern of house posts. The area looked very similar to Hedin's and Stein's photographs of the lost cities of the Taklamakan which they had rediscovered and excavated.

'Rupert, you and Mark take the camels on,' I instructed. 'I shan't be far behind but I want to have a nosey around here in case there is a site.' We double-checked our bearing and the safety channel for our radios.

'After the first half hour I'll call you on the blower every fifteen minutes, just in case,' Rupert called as he led the camels on ahead.

'What is it, Charles?' asked Carolyn, who had been walking near the rear. An old leg injury of hers had started playing up as a result of the constant daily mileage over difficult terrain.

'I don't know. I've just got a feeling about this place,' I replied. 'It is perfectly situated half-way between the ancient lines of the rivers Hotan and Keriya and not so far from such sites as Dandan-uilik and Karadong which were rediscovered by Hedin and Aurel Stein. It's certainly worth a quick look. Who knows, we may even find a lost settlement.'

The last of the caravan disappeared in a meandering line between the dunes and I was left alone. I carefully rechecked the bearing Rupert had taken before setting off in a northerly direction. Initially, I paced the distance from my last known spot but I soon forgot that as my enjoyment mounted with the pleasure of being alone in such a silent wilderness. A steady north-easterly breeze had blown up. After half an hour exploring the remains of the ancient forest I found nothing, so turned to begin retracing my tracks. I had walked further than I'd realized because only my more recent footprints remained visible, the rest having been covered by windborne sand. Unperturbed, I took out my compass and set a south-easterly bearing in the belief that it would take me to the caravan's tracks or at least bring the party into sight. I climbed a ridge of dunes some 200 feet high and gazed into the dust haze to the east, fully expecting to see the camels. There was nothing. For the first time I appreciated the solitude of the desert and how insignificantly small I was within it. It lay in ruffled folds of virgin sand at my feet and stretched like a white sheet in every direction. I began to feel very lonely.

'Well, Blackmore,' I said aloud to myself, 'this is a fine example you are setting. You've broken every rule in the book by separating yourself from the caravan and just look at you – equipped for nothing! Half a water bottle, a radio, a mirror, a penknife and a compass. Fat chance of survival you'll have!' It was one of my golden rules that everyone carried a small daysack containing a day's rations, essential survival aids and some form of protective clothing. Because my knee had continued to be painful I had stopped doing so myself half-way through the sand mountains and instead had attached my daysack to the side of a camel.

I tried to raise Rupert on the radio. There was no reply. Next I flashed my mirror towards the east in the rough direction of the caravan but the sun was too far south for me to get the right angle of reflection. Seeking to calm my rising panic I took to studying the ground using a technique I had been taught in the Army, dividing it into foreground, middle ground and distance and then conducting a figure-of-eight search with my eyes over each of the areas in turn. I looked through the line of dunes to detect signs of movement at the edges of their contours. Still there was nothing and I wondered how long I could survive alone.

I had no choice but to keep walking on a south-easterly bearing. The longer I waited the further away the camels would get, and I knew from experience that the speed with which they covered the ground was deceptive whenever someone was trying to catch up at the rear. Trusting my judgement I marched on the bearing for twenty minutes until I reached the top of a further dune range. I stopped and studied the ground ahead. I used the same method again for searching the ground and there, to my relief, were the tiny specks of the last camel train in the far distance. Immediately I took an accurate fix on their position in case a sandstorm suddenly blew up. I was amazed at how far they had travelled and equally surprised that Rupert had not halted beforehand, but he had obviously underestimated the distance that he had gone. Walking as fast as I could, and occasionally running on the flatter sand between the dunes, I pushed my knee to the limit in an attempt to close the gap. As I plunged down dunes and crawled up the far side the caravan would be lost to me for some while. Each time I became anxious until I caught sight of them again. After half an hour I reached the crest of a high dune and stood panting with the exertion. My mouth was parched and my lips were bloody and sore. I resisted the temptation to drink because there was still the rest of the day's journey ahead and I could hardly ask for someone else's water when it had been me who'd been so irresponsible.

Then I saw the flashing of a mirror. Bursts of bright light flickered out of the wilderness of sand as its unidentified owner tried to get the best angle of the sun. Someone had spotted me. With huge relief I switched on my radio. Until then I had not put it on for fear of using up its precious battery life.

'Hello, Charles, this is Rupert, over.'

'Charles, send, over.' I tried to sound calm and indifferent.

'We were beginning to think we weren't going to see you again. Perhaps you should be called Sven Hedin after that performance.'

I smiled and told him to continue slowly as I expected to catch up shortly. Nothing further was said about the incident when I finally rejoined them but the lesson had not been lost on us.

Early one afternoon I was walking near the front of the caravan with Mark and Lao Zhao when we crested the rise of a belt of dunes and looked down on to a vast depression about a mile long and nearly half a mile wide. Scattered around were the remains of trees. It was a strange feature, for it was neither an ancient river bed nor a natural valley between the dune hills which flanked it on all sides.

'What do you make of that, Marco?' I asked.

He shrugged. Then Lao Zhao suddenly became excited and began to talk animatedly. We descended into the bowl. There Lao Zhao began prodding the hard, sunbaked and cracked surface with his camel stick.

'He says this used to be an ancient lake,' Mark translated. 'His theory is that it is probably the long-lost water supply of Dandan-uilik which he reckons to be about three days south of here.'

The significance of the discovery was astonishing. Sven Hedin had first excavated Dandan-uilik in 1895. The mysterious city, which the oasis dwellers called simply 'Taklamakan', was almost totally buried in the sand. For Stein, who arrived on the scene five years later, the real mystery lay in the complete absence of any water supply to sustain the settlement so deep within the desert. Hedin had concluded that the Keriya river had run on a different course and that, aided by irrigation canals, it had served the city until the waters dried up and the site was abandoned in the eighth century AD. Stein dismissed that theory, although he could not adequately explain the secret of the water. Now, nearly a hundred years later, our expedition had stumbled across the answer.

The camel party reached the settlement of goat herdsmen at Tongguzbasti, the second resupply point, on 14 October. Tongguzbasti is situated 110 miles north of the Silk Road at the foot of the valley into which flows the Keriya river after its waters drain down from the Kun Lun mountains. The valley is thick with poplar trees, small pines and low scrub which cling to its width in a never-ending battle of nature against the encroaching sand dunes. In places the valley is a mile wide between the belts of dunes, in others less than a few hundred yards. There was no reason for such a settlement to exist there, and history does not record whether it had been a site of earlier occupation at the time when other Buddhist sites were at the height of their civilization. Guo Jin Wei told me there were just fifty families in Tongguzbasti and that they seldom left the immediate vicinity of the village except for a rare trip to Yutian to trade their wares and purchase provisions. At some time during the last ten years the Chinese regional government had attempted to civilize 'the lost tribe of the Taklamakan', as the people had been called, by building a school and a village hall harnessed to its own supply of electricity from a diesel generator. There were half a dozen other brick houses without glass in the windows which belonged to the richer families. Glass was obviously something of a luxury: even in Kashgar in the early 1900s it was unheard of and the Macartneys had had to make do with oiled paper in their windows at Chini-bagh instead. Otherwise, the standard 'house' was no more than a primitive hovel made from wood and thatched with poplar leaves and grass.

In spite of my navigation we had nearly missed the settlement by continuing through the dunes to the north. It was only when Emir spotted a Uyghur astride a donkey bobbing up and down between clumps of vegetation that we managed to get accurate bearings. Our guide had a deeply lined face like the bark of an old tree, extraordinarily long ears and a large hooked nose pitted with scars from chickenpox. He could have been any age from 30 to 60. On his head he wore a thick black goat's wool hat. It was his smartest item of clothing.

'*Asalam alayakum*,' (Peace be with you) called Emir, who was at the head of the caravan.

'*Alayakum asalam*,' (And upon you be Peace) muttered the man on the donkey after a long pause while he came closer. He displayed a toothless grin which looked more like a painful grimace than anything else.

'Looks like the village idiot to me' said Mark.

It was noticeable how indifferent the Uyghur was to our sudden appearance out of the desert with just about the largest single group of camels in Central Asia. His face did not betray the slightest flicker of surprise or interest at such a sight. Nor did he seem to register that a third of our company were Europeans.

'I suppose he meets people like us every week,' observed Carolyn.

The support party had still not reached the village by the time we had unloaded the camels. We had not been in radio contact with them since they had retrieved Bella from the bog. They eventually turned up in the early evening and enthralled us with the stories of their adventures on the southern Silk Road.

'Well, Barney, you've probably had a far tougher and more interesting time than we have,' I remarked. The high point of their arrival was a mail sack which Paul Treasure had brought with him from England. We eagerly gathered around Barney as he handed out letters and parcels before slipping away to a quiet corner to read. Finding a moment of privacy was a rare thing and I noticed then how each member of the crossing party quite deliberately and unconsciously sought that opportunity. One of the dangers of such ventures is continual proximity one to another. I often felt my companions could read my thoughts in the daytime, and even when I walked alone I could never totally shut them out. It was only when I lay under the stars in my sleeping bag at night that I felt free from intrusion: then I delighted in gazing up at the vastness of the sky and let my spirit and thoughts wander from this to that according to my mood.

The arrival of the two vehicles caused more of a stir than the camels and they were besieged by hordes of small children crowding around chattering and pointing excitedly as the stores were unloaded. Barney gave many of them the expedition badge which they pinned on their chests and wore with self-conscious pride as though they had been awarded an important foreign decoration. Packets of McVities' digestive biscuits became the next most prized item, handed out like liberation rations until we were in danger of seriously denuding our supplies. Inevitably, there were more touching sights. Mothers with sick children appeared in search of miraculous cures. Carolyn, who had been affectionately nicknamed 'the Camel Doctor', was continually faced with the awkward decision of how much medicine to give and to whom.

'It's a terrible thing but I simply can't set myself up as the village doctor,' she said to me, 'otherwise there won't be sufficient medical supplies for us on the trip. Just look at some of these pitiful cases. The elders I can cope with but the children's eyes are so trusting and appealing that it breaks my heart not to be able to give them more.'

'It's tough, Carolyn,' I replied, 'but once you treat one you have to treat them all. I know it goes against the grain but you'll have to turn your back. After all, what happens the day after tomorrow when we are gone?'

That night the villagers staged a colourful display of dancing and the audience turned out in their Sunday best. The dancers were young girls in bright crimson, black and turquoise dresses and they moved with gentle grace and charm. Behind them on the steps of the school veranda sat the village's four-piece band, playing antiquated local instruments. They were surprisingly sombre for such an occasion, dressed in dark traditional suits and flat black hats. The families sat in a semi-circle in the dust, the children at the front, with only the headman, a few Party officials and ourselves on the benches at the rear. I delighted in watching the animation on the faces of the children and they made me miss my three sons all the more. I had kept Tina's twenty-two page letter in my pocket for later and I longed to get away from the entertainment to read her news and stories about the children and hear how they were managing in my absence. Tongguzbasti was the last point at which we could receive letters until the end of the crossing, another two months away.

The dancing over, the headman led us into the school building where we were seated at small tables. Trays of food were brought in amid great ceremony and before too long the redoubtable *bai jiu* was produced.

'I thought these people were non-drinking Muslims,' commented Francis as the headman filled his glass for the third time in as many minutes.

'*Gambei!*' (Cheers).

'*Gambei!*' And down it went in one. Francis coughed. 'Golly, that's strong.'

By the time Francis had drunk half a dozen toasts he was away, as relaxed and unwound as any of us had ever seen him. We were dragged into the centre of the floor and thrust into the arms of local girls while the band played, or rather shrieked, in unmelodic agony, and partners half-shuffled and half-waltzed to the delight of those in the ringside seats who cheered, clapped and pointed with glee.

Incapable of another *gambei* in *bai jiu*, Barney stole outside to the vehicles and returned with two bottles of Famous Grouse.

'Scotland's revenge!' he cried as he made the Party officials down their whisky. The expression on their faces suggested it was as fine a piece of revenge as any. There was no more *gambei* after that, and Barney retired unsteadily in the knowledge that he had achieved a major coup. Avoiding the strong embraces of the now lurching headman who wanted me to dance with him, I too sought the fresh night air. As I squeezed past the packed crowd of local men at the door they held their noses. Either it was the smell of a 'long-nose' (as the Chinese call us) that offended them or they were demonstrating their religious scruples about alcohol.

The faces of the team in the morning bore testament to the evils of *bai jiu*. Francis stuck his dishevelled head out of the top of the penthouse, as John called the sleeping rack on his Pinzgauer, and groaned in self-pity. One by one they emerged.

'Did you hear that camel in the night?' asked Keith.

'No, which one?'

'The one that must have gotten loose and walked into the support team's tent.'

'Oh really?' I replied in feigned surprise. 'What happened?'

'The whole tent came crashing down on Krishna, Paul and me at about three in the morning.'

'Poor you.' I turned away to suppress a smile because I knew the 'loose camel' had actually been Mark and Rupert playing a prank on the support party.

Nine camels were changed at Tongguzbasti. The fresh ones, including, for the first time, two females, had been herded north from Yutian the day we left Markit. Of our original camels, one was completely blind and another had lost the sight of one eye, two were weak and emaciated, and three were too small for the amount of baggage that needed carrying in the later stages. In addition, 'The Mad One' went, as did 'Maggot' with the rotten hump. In their place were two distinctive white camels with coloured neck halters that made them look pretty and effeminate. The remaining eight were a cross-section of size and colouring. None looked as fit and robust as our initial batch. We were back to thirty camels. With the new arrivals came two handlers called Suleiman Musa and Abdul Rene. Suleiman was the eldest and sported a white goatee beard. He had small piggish eyes which darted about and I was quickly impressed by his manner of handling the camels. It came as no surprise to learn that he was a camel breeder and trader from a village near Yutian. Abdul, at the age of 30, was half Suleiman's vintage and looked different from the other handlers. He wore semi-Western clothes and had longer hair and a clean-shaven face except for a thin moustache, assuming an air of almost cosmopolitan sophistication. At first glance he didn't seem the sort of person capable of the work of a camel handler. But then appearances weren't everything. Lao Zhao's scrawny and bent frame, his shuffling gait and the manner in which he wore his thick glasses at an angle hardly portrayed the impression of a tough and versatile desert explorer. In a slightly different vein was the discovery we made about Kirim Yunus who had stepped into Esa Polta's shoes as head handler after Mazartagh. Only in the last hundred miles of the journey did he let it slip that he was in fact a lorry driver and had never seen, let alone handled, a camel before coming on the expedition.

ELEVEN

The Uyghurs

I envied the support party their experience at first hand of life on the Silk Road amidst the colour of the bazaars and their opportunity to study the diversified cultures of the people whose ancestors shaped the history of the region. The Uyghurs who accompanied us across the desert were but one minority tribe among many whose fortunes have been reversed and who are now under Chinese rule. A thousand years before, this Turkic tribe of nomadic herdsmen had migrated to Gansu from the Altai mountains and gradually conquered the north-east of what is now Xinjiang, establishing their capital near Turpan. By the tenth century the Uyghurs – or Eastern Turks – were masters of the entire region and controlled the trade along the northern arm of the Silk Road. A talented and adaptable people, they had absorbed cultural influences from the three religions then flourishing in Central Asia – Buddhism, Manichaeism and Nestorian Christianity – all of which had Uyghur converts at various times.

They managed to survive the terror of the Mongol invasion in the thirteenth century by co-operating with the conquerors, interbreeding with them and teaching them some of the benefits of civilization and trade. (The Mongols had no written language, for instance, and adopted the Uyghur script, which had in turn been borrowed from the Nestorians and had originated in the Near East.) By the end of the fourteenth century the Uyghurs, like their Mongol overlords, had been converted to Islam, and all the Buddhist, Manichaean and Nestorian shrines were destroyed or abandoned.

The Uyghurs were influential in China under the Mongol rule of Kublai Khan and his successors, with whom the Chinese aristocracy refused to co-operate, but paid the penalty in the fifteenth century when the Ming dynasty drove out the Mongols and the Uyghurs along with them. This also brought trade between Central Asia and China to a virtual halt, and the fortunes of the Uyghurs declined. They had a brief resurgence in the nineteenth century under Yakub Beg, who declared himself ruler of Eastern Turkestan, but he was soon routed by a Chinese army in 1877. Since that date, apart from a period in the 1930s to mid-1940s when the area came under Soviet domination, it has remained under Chinese rule, though with occasional flashes of discontent which are never far below the surface.

Chinese fears of Muslim unrest combined with a reassertion of Uyghur independence, the two obviously being interlinked, have forced the central government to adopt a more conciliatory and placatory approach to the province. The Governor at the time of our expedition, for example, was a Uyghur, although the reins of power remained firmly in the hands of Chinese Party officials who, in turn, were closely controlled by Beijing. There were Party officials, too, at every level of local government within Xinjiang Province, which is divided into its own administrative zones. These zones compounded the many difficulties Barney's team had in moving freely along the Silk Road. Between Mazartagh and Tongguzbasti they had been through three separate ones, Shache, Hotan and Yutian, each headed by its local ethnic mayor, normally a Uyghur, but with Han Chinese officials holding the key administrative positions, in particular those controlling Party policy and the Army. At Tongguzbasti it was the Mayor of Yutian who entertained us and made a tremendous fuss over our camel handlers. At the same time there were two senior Party officials there to keep an eye on our activities. No doubt, they reported back to their cohorts in Urumqi who would in turn relay the information to Beijing. It all seemed rather like George Orwell's *Nineteen*

Eighty-four. We did not feel threatened by it, nor was the atmosphere sinister, but Barney's team always thought something lurked under the surface and could never totally relax. After all, they were foreigners and soldiers travelling in a highly sensitive military region.

Kirim Yunus, our lorry driver turned camel handler, was a good example of the contradictions of the region. Although he was a practising Muslim, and a Uyghur, he nevertheless wore the plain blue trousers and jacket favoured by the Han Chinese. His face was Mongolian, pale but with rosy cheeks, and his features were almost European or Turkish. He spoke Mandarin Chinese yet he was not at one with the Chinese in our crossing party. On the contrary, he remained proudly Uyghur and just occasionally you could see the flash of defiance and independence in his otherwise gentle eyes. When he eventually told us about his life as a lorry driver we inquired further and he admitted to having spent four years as a soldier in the People's Liberation Army. Only then could I fully understand his behaviour when the Chinese, in particular Zhang Bohua, our Uyghur translator, were insensitive and heavy-handed in dealing with the Uyghurs. Kirim was a proud 37-year-old who kept his own counsel but I could see that if tomorrow there arose another Yakub Beg, then men such as Kirim would be amongst the first to support an uprising against the colonial rule of the Chinese.

The Uyghurs impressed me with their simple needs and calm acceptance of the destiny of the expedition. They had left their wives and children in Markit nearly a month before without any idea of the timetable for the crossing or any means of communicating with their families. At least we British and the Chinese knew that we were caught up in a venture that was bigger than us, and that the outside world was tracking our progress with interest. Barney's team was the primary source of news to and from London and Beijing, and occasionally the crossing party used the satellite link to relay a story to the UK press. By this means our families could keep in touch. For the Uyghurs, however, there was no rear link to the Seven Sisters Commune in Markit, and their families would not hear any news until they came home in December. The only exception was Esa Polta's premature return. However, the stories he would recount of crossing the sand mountains on the first leg to Mazartagh would undoubtedly provide them with little comfort, for such tales would only underline the dangers of the crossing and fuel fears for the safety of their loved ones.

The Uyghurs had very few personal possessions by comparison with our modern equipment. Apart from the clothes they stood in, each had a large coat, commonly a green Chinese Army one, with sleeves that were far too long for them. As I learnt later, this seemed to be a characteristic of the Uyghurs. Lady Macartney, in her book on her years at the British Consulate in Kashgar in the early 1900s, wrote that,

> The Kashgaris of both sexes wear their sleeves quite six inches below the hands, and to do anything these sleeves must be rolled up to get the hands free . . . The long sleeves had many uses, as a muff in cold weather, as a handkerchief, or a duster, and when a Kashgari wanted to show contempt, or disgust, he put his nose into the opening of the sleeve . . . To keep the hands covered was a sign of respect, and one should never show one's hands before a superior unless they were being used.

The needs of the Uyghurs were few, their minds were simple and their expectations were never as far-reaching as our own. That does not mean to say that they were simple people, though. Theirs was merely an uncluttered life – free from the pressure of time and the striving for achievement as well as the presence of modern comforts. After a few weeks in the desert we gravitated unconsciously towards their way of life and by doing so found we could treat the long days of repetition as though each was an entirely new experience without precedent. By reverting to nature we found the code for survival. After all, you would have to be a Uyghur to enjoy, after two months, the same joke about Rupert's voracious eating habits. Yet they did. Each time Rupert produced his large blue thermos mug for the evening meal the Uyghurs would burst into peals of laughter about '*loto*' (camel), as they called him, eating twice as much as anyone else in order to keep up his strength. '*Chumbar loto!*'

(the strong camel) they would exclaim, the delight at having cracked an original joke for the first time written across their faces.

Though I had not wished to take Suleiman as well as Abdul, we departed from Tongguzbasti with them both and the original four camel handlers from Markit. Golden Swallow was left behind, but Paul now joined the crossing party, for I wanted him to experience a leg of the desert crossing before it became so cold that he would be unable to sketch or paint. Keith had been keen to rejoin us and was disappointed at not being back with the camels, but he took it well and planned to return at the next resupply point 140 miles further east, providing the link-up was made. Barney and I had chosen to attempt resupply to the north of a settlement called Yawatongguz. From the map that looked the most likely spot at which his team might be able to enter the desert. But we were now moving into an area about which we had even less knowledge than we had had of the earlier stages.

Once the camels were loaded it was time to say our farewells to the support team. I felt particularly wistful as I shook Barney by the hand. The pressures of not knowing what lay ahead were difficult to bear at times and, after the comfort and rest away from the adversity of the desert, I had to brace myself to resume the mantle of responsibility and loneliness. With Barney I had found the security, strength and respite from those anxieties that comes from close friendship and understanding. In him, I detected similar emotions and strains, and I like to think that he too was able to draw on me. I knew some of the pressures that he had been under in dealing with the Chinese in the support team as well as with minor Party officials along the southern Silk Road. On top of that he was having difficulties with John Thomas who also had strong views about the way things ought to be done. He and John no longer saw eye to eye and the continual pressure of this was taking a great deal of the fun and reward out of the venture for Barney. John operated according to his own precise guidelines and did not seem to understand the impossibility of getting the Chinese to commit themselves to one thing or another. John tended to see everything as black and white, a characteristic I put down, rightly or not, to his very Welsh upbringing in the valleys. Nothing in him allowed for compromise or appreciated that most expeditions survive through long periods of grey when nothing can be guaranteed except that the plan you make seldom survives intact. John also seemed dismissive of the dangers and difficulties of the dunes in the desert, on more than one occasion claiming that his Pinzgauer vehicles could drive right across them. He may well have traversed parts of the Sahara but clearly even his expertise and vehicles had met their match in the sands of the Taklamakan. Nothing could get through that desert except human beings and pack animals.

Barney's role was infinitely more difficult than mine. The camel party was unified in one solitary aim: to make the first ever complete traverse of the desert. Nothing else mattered. Every day, every hour, every mile and every step of the way was one more that brought us closer to our ultimate objective. It burned ahead of us like a bright star and our days were filled completely with its light. Barney's team had long periods of waiting in between the resupplies when they were at odds with the Chinese element who only wanted to sit out the days in miserable hostels in the towns of the Silk Road. There was no adventure in that.

And so we left the throngs of goat herdsmen and their families at Tongguzbasti on 16 October in a cloud of fine dust as our heavily laden camels set off on the next leg. It was a crisp morning and the water containers chinked with ice as we were joined by another new arrival, Mr Winter. Once we were actually moving it felt good to be back on the march again and my personal well-being was improved by the gradual strengthening of my injured knee. We had come 300 miles in three weeks and had nearly 500 miles of empty, hitherto uncrossed desert left.

Paul walked beside me for most of the first day. I enjoyed his refreshing conversation and genuine delight in many features of the desert's landscape which I had long since taken for granted. What did hold my attention, however, was the beauty of the autumnal yellow, red and orange of the poplar trees as we meandered through the river valley heading towards the dunes. I also saw two birds not dissimilar to blackbirds and closed my eyes briefly, visualizing the woods at home. When I opened them again the romance of the landscape I was walking through struck me. In a small corner of Chinese Turkestan in October, amidst the tolling of camel bells, there we were, striding confidently between gnarled tree trunks, tramping in the grey sand and relishing the deep blue sky and warm sun that made the autumn colours dance with light. We were off to another unknown and it filled us with a great sense of purpose and adventure.

'I can walk in the woods of Hampshire at any time in the future,' I said to Paul, 'but when will I ever lead a camel caravan through these trees again?'

'Let alone the infamous Desert of Death!' he replied.

I estimated that it would take about fifteen days to reach Yawatongguz. *En route* I was determined to locate the ancient site of Niya. In doing so I was unwittingly placing an additional strain on the crossing party. We carried sufficient water and rations for only fifteen days and there were now more mouths to cater for, Paul and the extra handler. In addition, the camels were carrying heavier loads than before. The approaching cold weather necessitated taking our warm clothing and some of the tents – the Chinese had insisted upon the latter items even though we still slept in the open. I was less than happy as the tents made the camel sacks even more bulky. I also knew that the chances of hitting Niya on the nose were slight. I had only Stein's map co-ordinates to go by and could not completely trust their accuracy; we might have to search for up to two days to find any evidence of the lost settlement. That left little margin for error in the rest of the march to Yawatongguz. And even then there was no guarantee that Barney would find a suitable location for a resupply. Finally, to reach Niya, the camel party would be forced to travel along two sides of a triangle rather than maintaining the existing traverse line straight across the desert. I could only hope the extra mileage and the risks I was taking would eventually be worthwhile.

On Sunday, 17 October, less than two days out from Tongguzbasti, we made a near-fatal discovery. The water we had taken from the supposedly sweet well at the village turned out to be salty and was virtually unfit for human consumption. That evening Carolyn and Mark tested each container and jerrycan. Of all the water that we had with us, only 100 litres, left over by chance from the Mazartagh resupply, were drinkable and they would have to last all fourteen of us for fifteen days. There was no point in turning back since the well was the village's main source and we could not hope to find better. Obviously the families of the goat herdsmen were either used to drinking partially saline water or they had a means of treating it. Fortunately, the salty water was fine for cooking and the camel handlers didn't mind drinking it which meant the clean water could be shared between the nine British and Chinese. We marked the containers of unaffected water clearly and I instructed that only one litre of good water was allowed for drinking each day, the rest being taken straight from or mixed with the salty water. That way we would have enough good water to last nine days. There was nothing else we could do. In an emergency the salty water wasn't completely undrinkable and the taste could be diluted by adding orange powder from our survival packs, but it did make us extremely thirsty.

'You can leave me out of it,' offered Rupert, who said he was quite content with drinking bad water.

I was less sure. Plucky though his example was, I knew the consequences of the oversight and realized that it reduced our safety margin dramatically.

'I suppose there is one consolation,' Carolyn added. 'The weather is beginning to cool and our daily intake is already falling. Three weeks ago in the sand mountains we would have killed for a few extra litres!'

As with many of the practical problems we faced the team took the news in their stride and with humour. It was the little things that irritated and often grew out of all proportion. Carolyn was never at her best in the mornings and liked to be quiet. By contrast, Rupert was larger than life, back-slapping his companions and relishing his status as the work-horse of the party. His strength and energy seemed limitless. One morning he bounced across the sand like a cartoon character and seized Carolyn by the waist.

' 'Allo darling, fancy a bit this morning, do we?'

This was obviously meant in friendship and Carolyn would have taken it in better humour had Rupert not said something similar every morning for twenty-five days. In a flash she struck him on the side of the head.

'Bugger off, Rupert, you're a filthy pig and a bore.'

Rupert did bugger off. What is more he ignored Carolyn for the next week and their relationship deteriorated abruptly. I tried to mediate but Rupert maintained his distance. That one incident drove him into his shell and he excluded all except Mark from his normal banter and conversation. Neither did Rupert particularly welcome Paul in the team. He did not make it obvious but I could sense his reservations and the distance he put between them. Part of the difficulty was the routine we had evolved and the strength we drew from our isolation. It seemed as though we had never done anything other than walk across the desert with our strange collection of camels, Uyghurs and Chinese. Each of us had developed a protective layer which we carried with us. It enabled us to cope, and by coping we were able to withstand the constant doubts over our chances of survival, and that of the camels, as we tackled the endless sea of sand dunes stretching for hundreds of miles around us. Paul's presence merely added a new factor that Rupert had to accommodate in an equation that he had already worked out. For my part, I welcomed Paul's freshness, as did Carolyn and Mark. His observations put a different perspective on things. But because he did not share Rupert's Army sense of humour, and because he took much artistic delight in his surroundings, Rupert was unable to relate to him easily.

I felt his resentment one evening at the end of a day when we had tramped through high dunes against a strong north-easterly wind. A number of camel loads had slipped off and the ropes between the animals had repeatedly broken. It was a day of bad tempers, delays and utter exhaustion at facing the

monotony of the same scenes and the same problems. We had
covered seven miles, a depressingly short distance, and our
overriding feeling was of the need to get the crossing over and
done with. The challenge and danger of the sand mountains
on the first leg were behind us. We were now familiar with
our environment, and its difficulties had lost their magnitude.
In short, the team had become complacent, and the sheer
grind and daily slog of loading and unloading camels, driving
them up and down dunes, living in sand, eating sand and
coping with the child-like mentality of the Uyghurs and the
Chinese had started to wear us down. Oblivious to this, and
excited by the natural beauty of his surroundings, Paul had
collected some of the thin reeds we had camped beside in a
depression between the dunes and had made them into a
desert sculpture. As the evening routine unfolded, with Mark
and Rupert trying to reach Barney on the HF radio and
Carolyn attending to injured camels, Paul happily built his
sculpture and then sat on a far dune and sketched the evening
camp scene. It was what he was there for and I had deliberately stated that he was not to do any of the work but was to
concentrate instead on capturing the expedition on canvas.
Rupert saw it differently. As far as he was concerned every
pair of hands was there to work; if there wasn't the work then
the pair of hands should stay with their owner on the Silk
Road.

The camel problem was more serious. One of the two
females we had picked up at Tongguzbasti had maggots coming
out of her sphincter. The sight was not one for those with weak
stomachs as we picked them out with a stick.

'I can't keep using our precious medical supplies on these
animals otherwise we'll have none for ourselves,' Carolyn muttered as she cleaned between the buttocks. The indifference of
the handlers to the condition of their animals irritated me. It
seemed that Rupert and I had constantly to be supervising the
loading of the baggage on to the right camels in order to enable
the injured ones to recover. In the evenings it was us who took
the initiative and checked their wounds and Carolyn who then
treated them. At the day's end, with a water hole to dig, it was

another long and tiring task. The camels' condition was exacerbated by the amount of weight they had lost and the paucity of the padding in their saddles. These had been packed with dried reeds which had gradually become flattened and crushed with use. On some saddles the padding had virtually disappeared, causing the baggage to dig deeply into the animal's protruding bones.

Suleiman, at least, had taken the lead and got the other handlers busy packing fresh reeds into the padding whenever we came across them. In this respect he showed his better understanding of camel husbandry. He had, however, caused chaos since Tongguzbasti by redesigning the technique for loading and lashing that we had become familiar with since Markit. The net result was a longer loading time in the morning as Suleiman shuffled busily from couched camel to couched camel, supervising his new system. This added another irritant.

One person who remained completely detached from the mounting tension and the daily problems was Lao Zhao. He amused me greatly. One morning, when I had said people could ride the unladen camels since the dunes were small, Lao Zhao trotted past Mark, who was on foot, and remarked to him, 'Life's a bitch. When I walk my legs ache and when I ride my arse aches!' Nothing dissolved his steadfastness and sense of humour, and he remained above the small conflicts between the ethnic groups. He was also a delight to watch. In the evenings when there was firewood to fetch, if we were lucky, there was Lao Zhao, cigarette in mouth, blue and white Volkswagen baseball hat (origin unknown) askew on his head, glasses at a jaunty angle, shirt tails hanging out, in a threadbare brown sweater with holes in it, black baggy Chinese workers' trousers and green plimsolls with the laces undone. Oblivious to his personal appearance, he would totter off with a camel rope and return dragging a welcome pile of wood across the sand. He was in a world of his own, quietly going about his business with no fuss. If we had all had his approach then life in the crossing party would have been easier. On the other hand, one of the strengths of the crossing team was its mix of different people and cultures.

Mark got on well with Lao Zhao and they were forever sharing stories. It was through Mark that I picked up for the first time the geological discoveries which 'Calculus' had made on the crossing to Mazartagh. Typically he would find something or make an observation as we slowly travelled along but would never think to tell us. One of the most interesting was his conviction that the line of the Mazartagh hills, with its named features of Hamitagh, Loestagh and Gutentag, was the rim of an extinct volcano, which accounted for the fine black-pebbled desert at its baseline and the semi-precious stones that littered the ground.

I enjoyed talking to Mark and sharing his love of the Chinese language and people.

'What will you do when you leave the Army?' I asked him one day.

'Work in China, I hope.'

'Really? Don't you find it a somewhat soul-destroying place?'

'Yes!'

'Then why live here?'

'I don't know. It's something to do with the fact that I do hate it so much which attracts me.'

Seated in the sand at the end of an evening meal, the stars bright in the sky and the thin slither of a new moon rising just above the dark lines of the sand dunes, Mark told us a Chinese fable. It concerned a stonemason who was chipping away at the rock near the base of a large mountain. The work was back-breaking and poorly paid. He happened to look up from his labours one day and saw a merchant riding past, going to the nearby town. With all his heart the stonemason wished he could be that merchant, when suddenly he was transformed into one. As a merchant he reached the town and was busy selling his wares when he spied a smart official, surrounded by his retinue of bearers and slaves, being carried in a sedan chair, its blinds down against the sun. The merchant envied the official and the next moment found himself in the chair going on a long and uncomfortable journey. The sun nearly cooked him in his carriage and as he jolted over the roads he wished he could be the sun, bringing drought and famine as well as making all important officials hot and uncomfortable.

Now transformed into the sun, he decides to take it out on some minor province but just as he is about to deliver the blast of a furnace, a cloud gets in the way.

'Damn that cloud,' says the sun, then he retreats and admires it scudding past below. 'As a cloud I would have the power not only to block out the sun but also to wreak havoc with floods and deluges.'

So off he goes as a cloud. Just as he is about to wash away a mountain a breeze gets up which blows him out of the way.

'I see,' says the cloud, 'the wind is really the boss because it can move the cloud around which also blocks the sun. Now maybe if I was the wind I could whiz around the world and cause far more damage.'

So off he goes as the wind and blasts across the open countryside until suddenly he hits a mountain. Annoyed, he decides he should really be a mountain after all with the power to stop the wind which moves the clouds which blocks the sun.

'A mountain is what I should be.'

So the wind becomes the mountain and sits there solid and impassive, enjoying the ultimate position. Then, when the wind dies down, the mountain makes out a faint chipping sound. He ignores it and continues to relish his vantage point. But the chipping persists and the sound grows louder as the wind gusts up the mountainside. This time he looks down and there, at the very base, he spots someone working. It is a stone-mason.

TWELVE

Water Crisis

Late in the afternoon on our fourth day out from Tongguzbasti, 19 October, I crested the top of a high sand mountain and stood there panting with exertion. The sand was very soft and my feet sank in to my ankles. The air was still and the temperature was 88° Fahrenheit. I longed for the end of the day and with it the cool night and a brief respite from the weariness of long marches across the sea of dunes. I was thirsty and the salty tang of the water in my bottle only made worse that continual craving for clean, sparkling drinking water in abundance. The sensation never left me even though I had learnt the satisfaction which comes from conquering hardship and the pleasure which springs from abstinence. I spat to try and cleanse my mouth of the grit which was always there; it crunched between my teeth so much that I was sure it would remove all the enamel by the end of the crossing. I tried spitting again but there was no saliva left and my tongue stuck to the roof of my mouth.

I was pleased with our progress, which had been better than expected, and I estimated we would be able to knock two days off the crossing time to the ancient site of Niya, if we could find it. That was two more days in the bank as a reserve against harder times or, better still, two days off the aggregate duration of the crossing. There was no longer any pretence of wanting to spend more days than necessary in the desert. The stark reality of daily survival had eclipsed any notions of an old-fashioned, more leisurely style of exploration: this was a brute struggle against the invisible hand of disaster that patiently waited to grasp our struggling caravan.

I rammed my stick into the dune, the sand yielding fully one foot before it could go no further without more pressure, removed my jungle hat and put it on top. It reminded me of a soldier marking the spot of a fallen comrade on the battlefield. Sitting down on the hot sand I took off my boots and aired my blistered, sand-encrusted and sweating feet. I wriggled my toes in the sand and decided to walk barefoot for a while and air the painful sores on my heels, outer soles and two smallest toes, caused by swollen feet and accumulated sand inside each boot. I was struck by the essential helplessness of our situation – day after day bashing against the lie of the dunes, keeping the camels together and moving, looking at the same scene for hours at a time, and never knowing whether we might be lucky and find somewhere to dig a well. What reckless but brave people we were. Why should we be spared a fatality? I had no illusion that we might not be.

I studied the greyish-yellow colours of the sand against the blue sky, the long precise lines of the sides of the dunes which rose to an apex at the crest, the saddles between them and the deep but gentle depressions that looked so pure and untouched. Here and there little sand spouts drifted towards me, their upper ends slightly bent over in the direction of the wind currents from which they had been formed. It was a tranquil scene and I marvelled at its magnificence. No one had seen it before: it was mine. I was its conqueror and my footsteps would strip the virginity from the ruffled layers of sand that stretched unbroken and pure in front of me. After twenty-six days in the desert I was still assailed and entranced by its beauty, and filled with a great contentment. The desert had already claimed me. At times like this I forgot my anxieties over the plan, my problems within the crossing party and my responsibility for the expedition's success. Being at the front of the caravan enabled me to escape into my own world and I selfishly sought the gratification of those moments.

The silence assaulted me. Never before, never again, would I experience such silence amidst an empty waste, nor could I hope to find the peace that comes with such solitude. There I was, further from the outside world than at any time in my life.

I looked up from the sand and stared. A mistake, surely? I looked a second time but concentrated now on interpreting the image I believed I had seen in the middle distance. Yes, it was. I had seen a tree. I blinked, waiting for the mirage to go, but it remained – a tall lollipop-shaped deciduous tree with bright yellow flaming leaves standing as a solitary sentinel amidst the wilderness of the sand. It looked so completely out of context. It was nothing short of miraculous. Hoping the others would not catch up with me, I set off at a fast pace. I wanted to be alone when I reached the tree, to sit beneath its yellow leaves and watch as one, maybe two, of them finally surrendered their hold and drifted down to the void of the warm sand beneath. But, just as I struck out, the head of the first camel train reached me and the spell was broken. My tree was theirs and it was photographed and admired by everyone. Its splendid isolation had ended. More importantly, however, the living tree was a sign that there should be water somewhere in the area. It was the second day that we had not found water for the camels and, unlike the early days in the sand mountains, they were not coping well. I suspected that, like ours, their reserves were much diminished.

None of us was prepared for the sight which unfolded in front of us two hours later after traversing a labyrinth of dunes 100 feet high in places. Ahead was another ridge of sand hills that rose to nearly 800 feet and we coaxed the long line of camels up its westernmost side in a tortuous and twisting route, forever seeking the sloping plain between the crests and the depressions until we reached the top. Below, before the next ridge of sand hills, lay a flatter valley of low dune belts about two miles wide. But it wasn't that which excited us. There in the centre of the linear depression lay a line of trees about half a mile long, sparsely spread at the northern and southern ends and reasonably dense at the mid-point.

'Well, bugger me with a camel stick if that's not an ancient forest,' exclaimed Mark.

'Incredible, absolutely incredible,' remarked Paul again and again, with slightly more refinement.

It was an extraordinary and unexpected phenomenon to find in the middle of a waterless desert, sheltering below the level of the dunes like a secret oasis. Its discovery meant the prospect of a well for the camels, but my excitement went beyond that.

'I think there may be an ancient site there, Charles,' said Guo Jin Wei, who stood beside me and seemed to read my thoughts.

It certainly looked as though there could be. I could not imagine that Stein, Hedin or any of the other early explorers had chanced upon so remote a place since it was far off their direct routes from the periphery of the desert to the ancient sites they were after. With high expectations we led the camels down the steep easterly side of the sand hill towards the valley bottom. It took a further hour before we reached the edge of the forest.

'*Cha! Cha! Dut! Dut! Dut!*' urged the handlers as they coaxed the camels along. Lucien started singing and I held back to capture the scene in my memory – the vastness of the lunar landscape, the clouds of sand that rose as the camels slid down the steep slopes, the team members all working the line of the caravan, ensuring none of the camels came to grief and damaged the valuable water containers, and the remarkable contrast of the brown, green and yellow of the trees in the far distance that reached out to us like a safe haven, all set against a backdrop of the shadows of the small dunes in the valley that resembled hundreds of little pyramids of Egypt laid out together. The valley must have formed an ancient river bed and the possibility of rediscovering one of the lost cities of the Taklamakan filled me with purpose.

'*Tograk!*' (trees) '*Tograk!*' shouted the camel handlers.

'*Al Hamdulliah,*' (Praise be to God) we chorused in unison.

I had to pinch myself to appreciate the spectacle that I was witnessing. It was a privilege to be exploring a small part of the world hitherto untouched by man in its present state. Had anyone ever lived along the edge of the ancient river bed then it would have been more than a thousand years ago, before everything changed. Our quest, however, turned out to be bitterly disappointing. I sent water parties in all directions from the centre of the ancient forest but there was nothing, no sign of any surface water. And at every spot they dug it was the same story: fine, grey sand with traces of amica like the residual dust from a volcanic eruption.

'There are people watching us,' said Guo Jin Wei.

'Why do you say that?' I asked.

'We Chinese can feel these things. I tell you there are spirits looking at us here. We all can feel it.'

I studied his face closely. There was no sign of humour. He was deadly serious.

'I also hear voices. There are voices all around us.'

Despite the fact that dusk was setting in I consulted with Guo and we both agreed to push on past the next sand ridge. If we could find somewhere to dig for water then at least the camels would drink in the morning. I could tell from their expressions and lethargy that everyone wanted to remain in the area of the trees and rest. It was an easier option and held a personal appeal, for my knee had begun to play up and was quite painful and swollen. But it didn't resolve our dilemma.

'We'll carry on,' I said. 'At least there cannot be any less chance of finding water over the next belt of dunes than there was here.'

Wearily, the lead ropes of the camels were picked up and the animals urged to their feet by a mixture of oaths, kicking and pulling. They bellowed in protest and many of them looked as exhausted as the rest of us. Their heads were down and they had that languid air of long-suffering about them. As we left the last disfigured tree stump behind and ascended the soft and quickly cooling sand of the first dune, I looked back sadly at the forest and regretted many things apart from the absence of water. I regretted most that the pressure of time and the quest for water constantly drove us desperately onwards, pushing us to the limit and preventing us from stopping to savour the uniqueness of our surroundings. Had water not been an issue I would have camped for at least a day in the forest. Paul could have sketched to his heart's content and we could have studied the vegetation and taken samples of this miracle in the midst of the desert which surely had never been seen by man before. We found no water that night. Neither was there anywhere to dig the following day.

My diary entry for 20 October read:

Desert Camp 22 (38° 00.00′N, 82° 41.10′E)
We have a serious problem. A total of only 375 litres of water remains (of which less than 70 litres is uncontaminated) and the camels have not drunk for three days. There is no sign of a possible water site anywhere. We have been for two days now in the midst of one of the most desolate dust bowls. The desert here is dead apart from the extraordinary phenomenon of the ancient forest yesterday. Did we imagine it? On my calculations, by giving nearly half of our contaminated water to the camels in the morning (five litres each) we might just have enough to reach Yawatongguz which is six or seven days east of here. It will mean we can no longer be choosy over the clean water and we'll have to reduce our intake to only a litre a day of everything but it takes no account of spillage, evaporation or an accident. The alternatives are to try and locate the Niya site, which is about a day away, and hopefully water, or we abort and turn south to try and find water where the dunes are lower. How far south we would have to go is unclear. My map holds no clues.

I was haunted by Stein's account of his journey into the desert from Minfeng, above the Silk Road, along an ancient river bed which had long ago dried up, and by his descriptions of the terrain and its utter lack of water. Stein had even sent all his camels back once he discovered the ancient settlement as there was nowhere for his helpers to dig for water. Barney's observation – 'You do realize Stein never found water at Niya, don't you?' – rang in my ears. Suddenly it all came back as the grim reality of our situation sank in.

We had two options, neither of them encouraging. The risks associated with going east direct to Yawatongguz were quite high. We could easily run out of water and there was every chance that the six weakest camels would die before we got there. Similarly, heading south in search of water was not a simple option either. The chances of reaching a water site in less time than it took to get to the planned resupply north of Yawatongguz were slim. None of these factors allowed for a search for the Niya site nor for the time we would want to spend surveying it. Missing out on that opportunity would be a considerable blow. The options were discussed at length. Before making the final decision I wanted to be certain that everyone had had their say and that all avenues had been properly explored.

'The expedition has been going so well that none of us has dared say it,' commented Carolyn as we worked out the amount of water left, 'but something like this was always waiting to happen.'

'Well,' I replied, 'I take the blame for the situation. I made two classic errors. First, I assumed that there would be water at Niya. Had I cross-checked my Stein research, like Barney did, I would have known that that wasn't the case.'

'Hardly surprising, when you look around us,' remarked Carolyn, 'the landscape is like the Valley of Death – dead, petrified stumps of trees dotted all over the place like a graveyard. Every dune we crested today I was sure we'd find somewhere to dig for water but the absolute desolation and barrenness of the area is beyond description.'

'What was your second mistake, then?' questioned Paul.

'Three days ago we could have dug for water. We didn't. There was no excuse for it and as the camels were reasonably fresh and well-watered from Tongguzbasti I took the easy way out. Had we done so then at least they would have gone without for less time and we would also have carried some spare in the containers.'

'That's the sort of mistake that could cost lives.'

'Yes. To give him credit, Rupert did suggest we dig for water on the basis that we didn't know what lay ahead but I ignored his advice.'

'To be fair, Charles,' interrupted Carolyn, 'we have been lucky in the past and I suppose we've all allowed ourselves to become lulled into a false sense of security. Any complacency is as much our fault as yours; after all, our lives are on the line as well!'

I gave instructions that our water intake was to be restricted to only one litre a day per person with one litre each for communal cooking split between the mornings and the evenings. It worked out as twenty-eight litres a day between us. On that basis we could afford to give the camels half of our remaining water before they reached the point of no return. If they went down we'd had it. Rupert and Zhang Bohua were made responsible for filling everyone's water bottles to avoid any temptation to cheat, starting with the remaining clean water first. I had seen how people behaved in times of stress and crisis and wanted no grounds for potential conflict: in the desert, all coverings of pretence are stripped away and basic truths emerge.

More immediately, the plight of the camels was a major concern. For the expedition to succeed they had to remain fit enough to carry the baggage. It was no good just the humans keeping going. It is true that camels can normally survive by watering at very infrequent intervals, but that is when they are not working: the plain fact is that the more work you ask a camel to do the more water he requires. And under the conditions of our marches in the Taklamakan, and the heavy loads the camels carried each day, they were being severely tested. As fate would have it the day had been particularly hot, 90° Fahrenheit, and there had been little wind. The effect on everyone was crushing. Before we found a campsite we traversed a high range of sand dunes and two camels from separate trains collapsed at the top, going down hard on their forelegs, bellowing and snarling in frustration, weakness and confusion. No amount of persuasion, verbal or physical, could move them. They refused to get up. They perched there at the lip of the dune like grounded ships and gazed uncomprehendingly at us through large, mournful brown eyes. I felt sorry for them. In the end we unloaded their baggage and distributed it among the stronger ones before managing to coax them to their shaky feet.

'Tomorrow these camels die,' said Kirim, matter of factly and without a trace of emotion. I had noticed how much the hind legs of the camels had been trembling recently with the strain of clambering up the soft, crumbling dunes. I knew we were

15. The author wearing the coveted silk cravat that had belonged to his father. Behind is the tell-tale white salt crust that indicated there was a place to dig a water-hole for the camels. It was discovered the day the handlers predicted that eight weak camels would die if we found no water by nightfall

16. Rupert Burton who was nicknamed *loto* (camel) by the Uyghurs on account of his physical strength and endurance. He has just been the victim of a camel's regurgitated breakfast

17. Carolyn Ellis ('camel doc') earned the respect of the Chinese for her indomitable spirit and staying power. She and Rupert Burton were the only two to walk the entire route without once riding a camel

18. Keith Sutter was the expedition photographer and the only American in the party. He grew very close to the 'eccentric Brits', as he called us

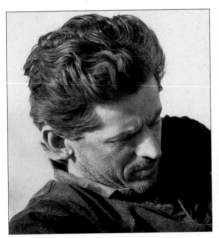

19. Richard Graham (known as 'Bright Little Bean' by the Chinese) had a remarkable ability to knit together the British, the Chinese and the Uyghurs. He was very ill with amoebic dysentery in the sand mountains and we worried about him surviving

20. Mark Kitto ('Kipper') replaced Richard at Mazartagh as the Chinese interpreter and assisted Rupert with the communications equipment

21. Guo Jin Wei talks to the Silk Road party on the radio. He was the leader of the Chinese team, and without his support in China the expedition would never have got off the ground

22. Lao Zhao ('Calculus') a 56-year-old government scientist with an impressive knowledge of the desert. 'Life's a bitch,' he once said. 'When I ride a camel my backside aches, when I walk my legs ache'

23. The Uyghur camel handlers on the first day in Markit. *From left to right:* Kirim, Emir, Lucien, Esa Polta, Rosa and Abdul Rasheed. They believed our expedition was searching for gold and that we would lead them to the fabled 'lost cities' of the Taklamakan

24. (*left*) Esa Polta, our 76-year-old head camel handler, nicknamed 'the King of Mongolia'. He was evacuated at the first resupply after a bad fall from his camel

25. (*below*) Lucien who sang the haunting song of the camel handlers about travelling across the ocean of sand without water

26. (*left centre*) Abdul Rasheed ('BP' or 'Dopey')

27. (*left below*) Suleiman joined the crossing party with nine replacement camels at Tongguzbasti. He was the most experienced handler. Later in the journey the others admitted they had never worked with camels before

. Barney White-Spunner
d the Silk Road party and
d a hard job coping with
hinese officialdom

. Francis Seymour relaxes
1 the Silk Road. He drove
1e of the Pinzgauer
hicles (Bella)

30. The Silk Road party with their Pinzgauer vehicles (Thomas and Bella). *Left to right*: *(standing)* Krishna Guha and John Thomas; *(seated)* Anne Thomas, Francis Seymour, Barney White-Spunner, the leader of the Chinese support team, and Xia Xia, the interpreter

31. Kirim leading the camels. Two went blind during the crossing, one gave birth to still-born calf, one wandered off never to be seen again, and one we had to kill rathe than abandon it to a slow death

2. Rupert and Lucien loading the camel known as Einstein. Loading thirty camels took two hours each morning and was hard work, especially when we had dysentery

3. The ancient site at Niya with the preserved timbers and rattan walls of a house that was abandoned in the third century AD. We found pottery, glass, beads and animal bones scattered about

34. Each day the scene was always the same, with dunes stretching to the horizon on all sides. It was a struggle for survival as we sought to escape our desert prison

stretching them to the very limit and at any moment they could simply collapse. There was a marvellous passage I was reminded of in the only handbook I had found on camel husbandry, a War Office publication dated 1908 which blandly read 'Patient to a degree, enduring hunger, thirst and pain with a stoical courage beyond all others, the first sign a camel may give that he is being asked to do the impossible is to drop down dead.'

The mounting pressure of the situation began to affect me. I was annoyed by my errors of judgement and frustrated by our painfully slow progress through the maze of soft dunes. They boxed us in and forced us to make long detours around their crescent shapes. As I stood on a vantage point with the sun behind me I thought how vulnerable we were. We had no right to assume we could conquer such a formidable obstacle of nature. Why should the desert be kind and allow us to chance upon a site for water every few days? By not doing so now, it was attacking the weakest part of my plan.

Selecting the next stage on a bearing of 114° magnetic I looked up to see Mark and Rupert away to my south on a separate saddle between two deep depressions. Half the caravan followed their tracks. The other half were stretched out half a mile behind me.

'Are you two taking the piss or what?' I shouted at them.

They looked at me blankly and then at each other. I could sense rather than hear them saying to themselves, 'Oh dear! Looks like Slackbladder is about to get upset. Play along with it and let him have his say.'

'What do you mean?' Mark called back innocently.

'What I mean is this,' I screamed across the distance that separated us, 'there must be one direction-finder and route-selector, and one only. If you two keep wandering off, waffling away to each other and choosing your own route, then the rest of the caravan falls into chaos.'

I saw Mark shrug his shoulders and once again sensed rather than heard Rupert say to him, 'I can't think what the dear little chap is getting all worked up about.'

Their completely relaxed and indifferent approach irritated me still further. With their camel sticks they looked to all intents and purposes as though they were going for a walk in a London park. I finally snapped.

'Stop winky-wanking around and get back on my direction line!'

'Winky-wanking?' Mark repeated, 'What on earth's that?' before both of them burst into laughter.

Fortunately, I joined in. If nothing else my outburst released the tension, and from then on the term winky-wanking was used to refer to someone who took a meandering route rather than a straight line. The incident was good for me; the imperturbable spirits of Mark and Rupert brought our situation into perspective and reminded me that, no matter how bad things looked, a sense of humour and, especially, an ability to laugh at oneself, were essential. Nothing was going to shake their stoicism; neither could they treat the seriousness of our situation with anything other than resolute fatalism. They lived for the moment; tomorrow's anxieties were far away. It was sensible escapism and, without it, there is no doubt we would not have forged ahead as each day took us deeper into the wilderness.

THIRTEEN

Discovering an Ancient Site

I left the campsite early the following morning, 21 October, and walked for some distance on my own. I wanted to savour the splendour of complete isolation. At the same time, the co-ordinates I had from Stein's map indicated that we should already be near the north-west corner of the sand-covered ruins of Niya. There was the possibility that, amidst the numerous gaunt and twisted tree stumps, I might chance upon the tell-tale house posts that would indicate the site of an ancient building. I walked amidst belts of steep, conical sand-knolls, each rising fifteen to thirty feet and all covered on their tops with tangled masses of living and dead tamarisks. As I went I pondered my decision of the night before. Having finally got through to Barney on the radio, we established that he had anticipated the gravity of our situation. By pure luck he was poised at the only place in the crossing where he stood a slim chance of striking northwards into the desert along the flatter ground of the former river course of the Niya valley. Knowing that we courted potential disaster whether we continued east or headed south, he agreed to risk his vehicles and attempt to reach us. Everything that was surplus to immediate require-ments was stripped out of the vehicles to lessen their load and improve their chances in the soft sand; everything, that is, except for a vital 150 litres of water which were crucial to our survival. We had decided to take a gamble. The camel party would head south as far as possible while Barney would come north: if the vehicles got stuck, or for some reason didn't make it, the success of the expedition would be jeopardized and we risked losing valuable time and even more valuable water.

I climbed to the top of a conical hillock formed over the course of centuries by the constant accumulation of drift sand around a tamarisk. It was 7.15 a.m. I took out my diary and wrote:

> Around me is an amazing panorama as I search, alas in vain, for some sign of the ancient Niya site. Far to the east are undulating low dunes with the high sand mountains silhouetted against the sunrise on the horizon. The shadows make the dunes resemble dark bunkers. Looking to the south, the sun is just catching and illuminating the sand ocean and the expanse of desert is indescribably huge. It is awesome. Towards the west where we camped, the sun picks out the ancient disfigured trees like white, grey and silver sticks merged together, forming the impression of a forest laid bare, devastated and uprooted for thousands of years. I so badly want to find signs of Niya but there are none here. I keep willing the spirit of Sir Aurel Stein, saying, 'Come on, tell me where it is. Where did you dig?'

Somewhere, out there in the vastness of the sands, lay the treasures of Niya which Stein excavated in January 1901. He uncovered a wealth of wooden tablets enscribed with Kharosthi characters, a script which came from India and belonged to the period when the Indo-Scythian kings ruled over the Punjab and the region west of the Indus in the first three centuries of the first millennium. His discoveries justified the conclusion that the Kharosthi script had been transplanted, along with an early form of Indian speech, from the extreme north-west of India and brought into use in the territories of ancient Khotan along the Silk Road.

The sun was high in the sky and the landscape drained of colour in the bright light by the time I returned to camp. In my absence the loading had taken an age because the camels were desperately tired and thirsty, rebelliously kicking and shaking off their loads in protest against our harsh treatment. Each carrying our meagre water ration, we set off on a bearing of 172° magnetic, hoping that, somewhere twenty miles in that direction, Barney was overcoming the dunes and driving towards us. The knowledge that he was there helped. But I still feared that both teams might be heading towards an unidentifiable goal and end up missing each other.

The heat was oppressive and I sweated freely. I dared not risk drinking from my one water bottle until midday and had made a secret pact with myself not to do so, but the temptation was nearly overwhelming as the hard toil across the lie of the dunes soon drained me. The 'Valley of Death', Carolyn named it: it had that lingering air which carries every portent of a disaster waiting to happen. Lucien did not sing that morning. If he didn't then none of the other handlers would. It was as if we had all stepped over that line between tiredness and exhaustion. The prospect of another few hundred miles of the unknown became daunting. Everyone clung to the hope that the emergency rendezvous with Barney could be made.

I walked a mile ahead and off to one side in order to maximize our chances of finding signs of ancient buildings. At one point I climbed a high sand dune and enjoyed seeing the small, ant-like figures of the caravan led by Rupert winding their way through the dunes with the bleached and splintered trunks of ancient trees scattered everywhere. As we drew within range of the hand-held radios it was an immense relief to hear Barney on the air, and we exchanged the co-ordinates of our respective positions. By this means, and by altering our heading each time, he was able to talk us into the valley bottom between two high flanking dune hills where his vehicles lay.

'We've got you visual now, can you see us?' came Krishna's voice over the radio.

Krishna had been sent by Barney to scout ahead with binoculars. The valley was hot and windless, and the brightness of the sand made it nearly impossible to see without sunglasses. We stretched our legs further in anticipation of the reunion and soon Rupert, Mark and I were far ahead of the camels.

Suddenly there they were! The vehicles looked tiny in the vast open landscape. And there, walking towards us, was Anne, bearing a rare gift of bottles of drink.

'Now this girl is unbelievable,' chorused Mark and Rupert together as they emptied the contents in one gulp.

'I kept them specially for you,' said Anne. She was wonderfully protective towards the crossing party and always ensured that we got the best of the rations at the resupplies.

'If it hadn't been for me the others would have drunk them by now,' she added in her delightful Welsh accent, 'we were that hot and have barely enough water for ourselves, seeing that you boys are taking it all!'

We halted with the support team for just over an hour. The valley was stiflingly hot and I felt light-headed and tired. All I wanted to do was seek the comfort and shade of a vehicle and opt out for a while. It was a dangerous mood and I had to snap myself out of it. With the vital water transferred to our containers we struck out in a north-easterly direction for Niya straight up a vast sand hill. Below us, like the camp of an expeditionary force, were Barney's team with the Union Jack flying above the Bella vehicle. It was a stirring sight. But, in our negligence, brought on by lethargy, we had decanted the 150 litres of clean water from the support team's jerrycans into our tin containers without thinking. All we had done was dilute the salty water from Tongguzbasti. Half of our supply had been given to the camels and we might have to give them more in the days ahead. We were now only marginally better off.

'Look at them go,' said John to Francis. They watched the camels being dwarfed by the dunes as the long line of the caravan snaked its way over the sand mountain pass.

'Do you think they'll make it?'

'Who knows? They looked pretty rough, and I'm certain of one thing.'

'What's that?'

'I'm glad I'm not in their shoes, they're only just half-way across.'

We left Paul behind. I had not wanted to risk taking him further in case anything went wrong. It was one life less to worry about. Keith had expected to change with Paul and he was very disappointed.

'Sorry, boys, it's the only way,' I said, trying to console them.

'It's an extra mouth to water and every litre adds up. If Barney had the room in his vehicles I would also have left behind a camel handler and a member of the Chinese team.'

Before leaving, John and I had a long conversation about the likely location of the Niya site. I trusted John's sense of direction which was far better than Barney's. John had his own characteristically precise calculations.

'Head more north-east than east is my advice,' he said, 'and keep going for a day like that even though you will be tempted to veer away.' I took his advice. It was as well that I did. After three hours I came across a small fragment of pottery in the sand at the base of a tamarisk hillock.

'What is it, Charles?' inquired Mark who had come up behind me and wondered why I was looking so furtive.

'Pottery,' I replied, 'pottery! We've made our first discovery!' and my heart raced with excitement. One shard was sufficient evidence to suggest an ancient site somewhere out there. I was behaving furtively because the Chinese were watching our every move. The fact we had wanted to go anywhere near Niya had caused Guo Jin Wei difficulties from the very beginning.

'You must have permission first to visit the site,' he had told me many times.

'But Guo, who is going to know out here? The last person to excavate the site was probably Stein himself nearly a hundred years ago, and you can't tell me we are just going to walk straight on by and ignore it.'

I was being economical with the truth because Niya had been the target of significant internationally sponsored archaeological excavations in the last ten years, particularly by Chinese and Japanese teams. Due to its outstanding reputation for fine Buddhist artefacts dating from before the third century it had become hallowed ground. All approaches to the site, however, had been directly from the south, a journey of at least five days by camel from Minfeng.

'No one in history has ever approached the site from the west as part of a complete desert crossing, Guo,' I continued, 'so imagine what we may find. You will be famous! Guo Jin Wei, the great Chinese explorer who crossed the "Desert of Death" and rediscovered another area of ancient Niya!'

'Okay, okay! But no digging and no taking any remains.'

'I promise.'

'Because if you do then I will be in big trouble with the authorities when we get back to Urumqi.'

I knew where the source of that trouble would come from – Qiu Lei, our ever-vigilant political agent.

As Rupert came up I told him to continue leading the caravan on a bearing of 80° magnetic until he found a suitable campsite within two hours. Mark and I planned to detach ourselves from the team and conduct a proper search of the area. First, however, remembering my own experience before Tongguzbasti, I checked that we were properly equipped in the event that anything went wrong.

The next hour resembled a treasure hunt. There were plenty of pottery shards scattered over the surface, particularly in the depressions between the leeward and windward sides of the dunes where the wind had scoured the sand away to the bare ground beneath, and around the bases of the hillocks of tamarisk cones which were closely packed together. It was tantalizing yet frustrating. There was not a single configuration of bleached and splintered wood that resembled an ancient house.

'Charles, this is Rupert, over.' His voice suddenly boomed from my hand-held radio.

'Send, over.'

'I've walked into a house. In fact, not a house but a bloody great block of flats.'

'I'm not with you, say again, over.'

'I've found three houses – *houses!*' he said, emphasizing the last word.

I looked at Mark in amazement.

'He must be taking the mickey,' Mark remarked, 'Rupert wouldn't know what an ancient house looked like even if he walked straight through the door.'

'Rupert, can you be more specific?' I asked.

He described how he had been leading at the front of the caravan with Carolyn when they skirted the side of a high tamarisk hillock before ascending an area of dunes. As they reached the highest point he glanced north and noticed a bowl-shaped valley with dunes on the far side. In the middle lay a flat-topped hillock with upright timbers on it. Never having seen anything like it in the desert before Rupert altered direction and took a short detour into the valley he was about to bypass.

'And there it was. Not just wooden posts but complete with walls and pottery scattered all over the place. I then took a quick recce and came across two others. But you need to get here sharpish as the Chinese are crawling all over them. Guo has decided we should camp here as well.'

'So much for Guo wanting to keep a low profile on Niya,' I remarked. 'Anyway, Rumper, that's brilliant work and maybe one day the British Museum will name them Rupert's Dwellings 1 to 3 in your honour!'

Mark and I followed the camel trail and caught up in less than half an hour of hard walking. The first dwelling was exactly as Rupert had described it, perched on the elevated plateau of a twenty-foot mound of loess soil that had survived centuries of erosion. The Chinese had retired to the camp and I stood in the arena-shaped depression on my own while behind me Mark filmed with the ciné camera. Almost breathlessly I climbed the side of the mound, carefully avoiding vast quantities of pottery and bones strewn everywhere, and eventually stood at the side of the building.

The layout of the rooms was immediately apparent from the substantial timber uprights in each corner and the smaller 4-inch-wide stakes between them to which were fastened rattan woven walls in a criss-cross configuration. The rattan survived intact to a height of about 18 inches. The building was 40 feet long and 20 feet wide, and contained three main rooms. The roofing had long since gone. At the northernmost end was what may have been a courtyard; in its centre stood the trunk of a sizeable mulberry tree. The foundations of the building were made from long timbers, 7 inches by 6 inches across, with grooves carved at 2-foot intervals for the vertical timber joints of the walling. The quality of the craftsmanship surprised me and the joints of the timbers looked as though they could have been made by modern tools.

Nothing could replace the elation of that moment – standing there in a building which had probably been inhabited until the third century AD, the date Stein had fixed from his excavations of the main site. It was a joyful sensation to pick up peach stones and handle green beads and pottery of a civilization that had flourished at the time of Imperial Rome.

I went from one building to another in a state of exhilaration. After twenty-nine days in the desert and 400 miles we had finally rediscovered one of the mysterious lost settlements of the Taklamakan. I used every minute of the last two hours of daylight to make a comprehensive survey and in doing so discovered three further dwellings and the remains of an enclosure made of thickly packed rushes that surrounded an orchard of ancient fruit trees. There could be little doubt that the ruins belonged to a widely scattered agricultural settlement on the fringes of the main Niya site which would have existed in the third century AD and was abandoned when Chinese supremacy in the Tarim Basin came to an end towards the close of that century.

Adjoining House 3, as I named it, was a simpler structure which would have accommodated animals. To the side was a compost heap of innumerable layers containing pottery fragments, fruit stones, charcoal, straw, animal bones and animal stools.

'Just look at that,' said Mark, picking out a particularly large stool, 'a seventeen-hundred-year-old lump of cow dung!'

There was too much to take in at once. The evidence of occupation lay all around and it was impossible not to step on the curious mementos of life long departed. Carolyn made some of the finest finds – beads and small pieces of a delicate blue glass. The best I could accomplish was to sketch each dwelling and pace the measurements of the rooms. I longed to spend a couple of days camped here in order to conduct more detailed studies but the pressing problem of water and the health of the camels prevented that. In any case, it was not our right to conduct excavations, neither were we equipped or trained to do so. From my brief observations of the layout of the site, which covered approximately a kilometre square, I concluded that it had never been excavated. This was one area that Stein had not discovered and the surety of that knowledge thrilled me beyond all measure. We were probably the first people to enter the site in seventeen centuries.

The discovery of the site was one of the most uplifting moments of the expedition. If Rupert had gone just one dune to the side then he would have missed it. All thoughts of the water problem paled into insignificance by comparison with our discovery. That evening, as we settled around a camp fire of petrified timbers (not taken from the buildings, I hasten to add), I felt a warm glow inside. Under the half moon and the bright stars I gazed across at the former dwellings and wondered who had lived and died there and what spirits, if any, still roamed those silent witnesses of ancient habitation. Emir produced a string of round, black beads with rectangular orange and yellow ones at alternate intervals and said he had found them somewhere on the site. Abdul then showed us a perfectly preserved wine jug some eighteen inches high with a fine handle and curved spout. Nothing like that had been visible to us on the surface and we did not solve the mystery of their appearance until the following day when Mark and I deliberately stayed at the rear of the caravan in order to scout around further. We were rewarded in this and came across another more substantial dwelling to the east of the site we had discovered the day before. We were not, however, the first people there. In each corner of the rooms and at certain places adjacent to the walls by the doorways were large holes that had been freshly dug.

'So this is where the Uyghurs found their booty,' I said to Mark.

'Yes, obviously. It makes you wonder what else they may have discovered.'

'Isn't it interesting where they have dug? I bet they did so knowing where they hide their own precious possessions in their houses. Habits don't change and, after all, before there were banks everyone kept their treasures hidden somewhere in the home. All they have done is apply the same logic.'

Before we departed that morning I went back to the site whilst the others were having breakfast and making preparations for loading the camels. I stood in the middle of the rooms of House 1 and watched the sun as it rose gently above the dunes, its light touching the valley as it shortened and then finally dissolved the shadows. The peace was total. I wondered again about the people who had lived in that room seventeen hundred years before; how tall were they? What did they wear? At that time of morning one of the family would have been down by the fence I had just walked through, shooing the goats out of the orchard. In the back of the house where the kitchen area would once have been, now strewn with broken cooking pots and lumps of charcoal, the woman of the house would be rekindling the fire and putting the large cooking pot over the clay oven. Children would be playing in the dirt with their beads. Their father would be leaving through the doorway beside me and crossing the fields to his cattle, giving them some straw from the rick adjoining the house. Who were they? How many babies were born within the remains of those rattan walls and how many aged grandparents finally let go their hold on life?

As the sun rose higher and enhanced the colours of the desert, it resembled an open sea of yellow dunes with nothing to break its wavy monotony but the bleached trunks of trees and the tamarisk hillocks. It was hard to believe that in the valley where the ruins of the dwellings survived, there would once have been irrigated canals, lush fields, wild flowers, bird song, animals grazing and abundant fruit trees. What had it all been for? I asked myself. I was glad I had made a pilgrimage and glad that I had spent time in the memory of those who had lived and died in this now barren wasteland.

FOURTEEN

The Chinese

It was interesting noting the changes in the Chinese team after a month. Guo Jin Wei had developed a more confident style of leadership and was quick to pick up minor aspects of camel husbandry and the workings of the Uyghurs. When he saw mistakes being made he put them right immediately. That enabled me to step back from the detail which in turn allowed Guo and Rupert to take the lead in organizing the caravan. I made a deliberate effort to consult with Guo on all decisions which were eventually made jointly. There was no longer an atmosphere of stand-off between the British and the Chinese, and I no longer felt protective, and therefore undoubtedly arrogant, about my plan for the crossing and my role in cracking the whip to get things done. Since those tortuously hot days struggling over the sand mountains, Guo had developed a robustness and a strength of character that made him a different man, and I began to harness his strengths. Guo also understood the Western mind and happily discussed his opinions on the Cultural Revolution and the history of China. But we could never draw him on the subject of the Army's suppression of the student uprising in Tiananmen Square in 1989.

'What will happen when Deng Xiaoping dies?'

'Nothing will change,' he replied.

'But don't you think the old guard will regain power and reverse the liberalization process and the move towards a market-orientated economy?'

'What old guard? There are few of them left now and, besides, the young people of today would not allow it to happen. They hold the power and the process of change is too far advanced. The Chinese people want to drive their own cars and make money from their own businesses. Look at me, for example. I have sold my car and mortgaged my house to raise capital to set up my own travel business. You see, when we get back, I will no longer be working for Xinjiang Nature Travel Service. That is a government company.'

'I thought you once said it was a military-owned company?'

'I did – it's the same thing.'

'Is that why the expedition was able to obtain all the necessary local permits for travelling through Xinjiang Province?'

'Precisely.'

'How long will you stay in Urumqi, Guo? After all, you went there with your parents from Manchuria, didn't you?'

'Yes, that's right, I think I have told you before. You know, Charles, I'm not sure. Maybe once I have made some money then I will leave. Many young Chinese people do not want to stay in Xinjiang Province now. It is too far away and the local people do not want us here.'

'Is that what all the bombings were about in June when Mark and I came over?' I asked, referring to the outbreak of bombings in Kashgar by Muslim extremists who aspire to ending the Han Chinese domination of their country.

'There have been many more since then, and also in Urumqi, Hotan and Shache. You know, these are very proud and independent people with a language, culture and religion that are different to ours. Now that the Chinese people are able to make money for themselves you will see many of the young ones leaving. Most of the Chinese families in Xinjiang, like my family, were forced to settle there forty years ago so as to keep the balance of Chinese to the minority peoples. Until now they could not leave but soon these things will change.'

We asked him about the Chinese law forbidding couples from having more than one child. It remains an emotive issue for it runs contrary to Chinese tradition. Besides, large families are an insurance policy against old age where, unlike in

Western society, the younger generation regard it as their duty to bring the aged parents into the home and care for them.

'It is the law,' he said with a shrug.

'Yes, but don't you want more children?'

'Of course, everyone wants more children but there is no room in China,' he replied, and for the first time I detected the Party line rather than Guo Jin Wei's usual frank opinion. I don't believe he was merely repeating the Party line but I do think he genuinely believed it was the only explanation. Perhaps there was no difference – autocratic societies are all about that.

With Lao Zhao the number of children he had was not an issue. At the age of 56 he belonged to a different era, the time before the Cultural Revolution, and as such had a more old-fashioned approach to life. Of his four sons, one ran an engineering factory, the second was a restaurant chef in Russia, the third was a car salesman and the fourth was still studying. There were two grandchildren.

'Aren't your children surprised at a grandfather crossing one of the world's worst deserts?' I asked one day.

'Not at all, I've been mucking around in the desert for thirty-six years now!'

Lao Zhao had become a popular figure with the British element. There was no side to him and of all the Chinese he worked the hardest. We never saw Calculus at the rear of the caravan, far from it – the difficulty was keeping him from taking pole position with the lead camel train as he had a tendency to select the most complicated and twisting route which totally ignored the trail laboriously made by the front scout. He had a marvellous way of saying our names which we soon mimicked and adopted – 'Rumper' (Rupert), 'E Marka' (Mark), 'Chasa' (Charles), 'Karleen' (Carolyn). And his forthright observations made us laugh. One evening we lingered around the camp fire after the usual meal of rice with packets of vegetables. Mark had been chatting to Calculus when he suddenly burst out laughing.

'Classic! Classic! You'll love this, Rupert.'

'What's that?'

'Old Lao Zhao here says that the reason why some of us have

black shit [referring to a recent medical condition that concerned us] is because the food causes us to shit like dogs. Dog shit, he says, is black!'

Lao Zhao's increasing popularity came from his growing affinity with us. He would initiate a conversation through Mark, and he was far less suspicious of us and our motives than were the other Chinese. Perhaps the fact that he was a generation older than the other three and had therefore been brought up before the years of the Cultural Revolution made a difference.

'He's a tough old bird,' remarked Rupert to me early in the morning as the camp was coming to life. The thermometer had registered a minimum temperature of minus 10° Fahrenheit during the night. It was bitterly cold and we blew on our hands and buried our backs deeper into our warm overcoats. By contrast, Lao Zhao, cigarette in mouth, was bent over the remains of the supper, sorting out the pans and cracking the ice in the water for the kettle. He had on his usual thin and baggy black trousers, collarless and filthy shirt and threadbare brown pullover.

'He's totally oblivious to it all,' I replied.

'I know, great chap.' Coming from Rupert that was a real compliment, because ever since we had entered the desert he had mistrusted the Chinese and resented their interference. In the first week he had experienced difficulties reaching the support team on the radio. At the time he was badly dehydrated and sick from dysentery, a combination which did nothing to improve his frame of mind. Unfortunately, Lao Zhao was unaware of his mood and suggested that Rupert's sloping wire for the radio set was pointing in the wrong direction, indicating with his outstretched arm the heading for Shache on the Silk Road. Rupert exploded.

'What does that interfering, silly old Chinese git know about it?'

'Not a lot, but he probably knows where Shache is,' I replied.

'They're bloody useless, the lot of them. I can't think why we have them with us. Tell me, what can they do? Do they navigate?'

'No.'

'Do they operate the radios?'

'No.'

'Do they operate the satellite link?'

'No.'

'The BBC recorder?'

'No.'

'Are any of them trained medics?'

'No.'

'Well what the fuck *do* they do, then?'

Fortunately those days were far behind us. Guo Jin Wei and Lao Zhao had both earned the respect of the British and their roles in the party were never questioned. The same could not be said of the other two. After thirty days in the desert, Zhang Bohua and Qiu Lei still caused friction and irritated the rest of my team. To be fair, the Spook, as we called Qiu Lei, had improved in the last two weeks. At least he understood the need for everyone to work together in the shared interests of survival, and would dig the water holes when the opportunity arose. It remained the most back-breaking chore of the day but he did make the effort. We had long since forgotten the notion that his heavy baggage contained secret radio equipment for reporting back to his controllers. He did take the odd photograph but many of them were amateurish attempts. Despite the punishment and hardship of the past month he surprised us by keeping up, although he was at pains never to over-exert himself. He held back just that little bit; that was enough to ensure he remained in better physical shape than the rest of us.

I had given up trying to get him removed from the crossing party at each of the resupply points, and had accepted that his presence was part of the deal for our continued clearance to undertake the journey. My overriding fear was that the Chinese authorities held it in their power to cancel our expedition at any time. If the Hong Kong talks misfired, or if something equally unrelated occurred, China's grudging acceptance of our presence might abruptly cease.

Two things, however, continued to annoy us about Qiu Lei. The first was his immaculate appearance in the one-piece white cotton oversuit that never seemed to get torn or dirty. 'Look at the big poof,' Mark would say, 'he looks just like a clean white sperm prancing across the dunes dressed in that thing!'

The second was Qiu Lei's hidden supply of personal luxuries. We could never find them and, to that extent, he was one step ahead of us in the game. But more often than not in packing up camp we would come across a crushed tin of mango juice or Pepsi in the sand where he had slept. The deceit of these acts of self-preservation angered us beyond description, especially since we were always at pains to reduce the weight of the camel sacks for the increasingly tired animals.

'Bring back Fagin, I say,' commented Carolyn. 'At least he would have been clip-boarding about the place and would have found the Spook's secret cache. I'm damned if any of us can.'

I repeatedly raised the subject with Guo and Qiu Lei but never with success. It remained an ulcer of discontent that festered and grew, particularly with Carolyn.

Finally, there was Zhang Bohua or Big Zhang, the fearless mountaineer who claimed to have climbed K2 without oxygen. The stories of that exploit, and of how his frost-bitten hands and feet were suffering now the nights were becoming colder, were repeated whenever there was a need to impress or restore credibility with the British. Such occasions were frequent. I liked Big Zhang but he was all bluff and coasted along with the minimum of effort. He was a disappointment. At first I had thought he would be a work-horse like Rupert, and they certainly matched each other in bulk and strength. In reality, he was lazy. And although he was the only Uyghur translator he never bothered to look after the camel handlers. Instead I conveyed all my instructions to Kirim through Mark. Zhang's place was normally at the rear of the caravan, striding along in his baggy blue jeans (all the Chinese wore baggy trousers except for Guo; by the end of the journey, however, he had lost so much weight that even his were baggy). In his right hand he carried a long walking stick, and on his head there perched a ridiculous-looking pair of ski goggles, presumably in case of the dreaded sandstorms that the Chinese feared could hit us at any moment.

The only time Zhang ever came to the front of the caravan was when we were within two hours or so of a resupply. Then, stripping off the tracksuit top he wore in all temperatures and with shirt sleeves rolled up, he would cruise ahead of the lead scout, hoping to show the unwatching world that he was a truly great desert explorer without whom none of the lesser British would have made it thus far.

At the outset of the expedition I had had visions of learning Chinese and coming away with a better understanding of the people and their culture. Somewhat naïvely, I had expected to leave the desert nearly fluent in Mandarin. By my own admission I failed on all counts. Niya marked the approximate half-way point in the crossing and I knew then the limits of my capacity to absorb anything more than the daily routine and my part in keeping it going. The squandering of the opportunity irked me. I tried not to judge the Chinese by my own standards or measure them against the attributes I saw in my own team, but it wasn't easy. Perhaps I was too orthodox in my assessment of other people's characters and contributions to the overall team effort. In some respects I was unjustifiably harsh on the Chinese. I did not intend to be, for they had become an integral part of the expedition and deserved their share of the credit for our accomplishment.

FIFTEEN

No More Star-gazing

The distraction of Niya soon disappeared, to be replaced by the wearisome drudgery of the march. What else was there to look forward to? The reality of crossing the desert for a further month to six weeks until Luobuzhuang at the eastern extremity of the Taklamakan was depressing in the extreme. We could not move any faster even had we wanted to. The dunes slowed our pace and the camels lacked the freshness and strength which had seen them through the deprivations of the first few weeks. On the leg from Tongguzbasti they lasted seven and a half days without proper watering; in that time they received only two buckets of water each, about ten litres, from our own dwindling supply. Even then we could not be sure they all received their share because of the chaos they caused in their desperation to get at each other's pails. The smell of the water drove them half berserk and inevitably much was wasted. Their plight would not have been so bad if there had been patches of scrub and camel thorn which are common in most deserts of the world. We came across some areas in the flatter dunes but they were never sufficient. The handlers had always maintained that the camels would die after four or five days without water. Fortunately their prophecy did not come true, but that naturally raised the question of how much they knew about camel husbandry, especially under such extreme conditions. Without regular watering the camels were unable to eat their full morning ration of corn spread out for them on a blue plastic tarpaulin. That was disturbing and I was conscious of how abruptly their eventual decline might come. Once a camel goes down and loses the will to live it is almost impossible to get it up again. It had happened to me once on the Lawrence of Arabia expedition. The Bedu remedy was to light a fire underneath the stranded animal and, on that occasion, it had worked.

The absence of water had shaken our confidence. but we had been lucky, very lucky. If Barney had not managed the emergency resupply I suspect we would have lost at least six camels, maybe more, from thirst and exhaustion. I could only be thankful that we had not crossed that stretch earlier in the journey when it would have been much hotter. Our chances of success had been jeopardized and each of us felt a renewed respect for the power of the desert. My gamble had paid off but it had been a close-run thing. Part of the problem was caused by the ancient river beds marked in blue dotted lines on the map along our route from Tongguzbasti to Yawatongguz. These suggested to me that we would be able to dig for water in the vicinity. When it came down to it, not a single one offered us that chance. They were ancient river beds all right, very ancient, and they had long ago completely dried up. Even after digging a hole six foot deep the sand was like dust. Little wonder that Carolyn called it the Valley of Death.

It was not until much later that we discovered why we had been so fortunate in finding water on the leg from Markit to Mazartagh. In discussions with Lao Zhao we reached the conclusion that the east-west line of the Mazartagh mountain feature acts as a dam for the meltwaters flowing north into the Tarim Basin from the Kun Lun mountains. In that way the water presumably finds its own table, having been deflected by the bedrock underneath the sand. That knowledge was gained from our own experience – no other source provided it.

Then, between Mazartagh and Tongguzbasti, we had been traversing the gap between the two largest rivers, the Hotan and the Keriya, that drained into the desert until they were eventually consumed by the sand. Even though they were dry at that time of year, the local people on the fringe of the desert confirmed that they flooded the low-lying areas near the Silk Road at least once a season. It was only east of Tongguzbasti that our luck ran out. It wasn't a question of being wise after the event because the route had never been attempted before. We were blazing a trail of discovery and any subsequent attempt would surely draw on our knowledge. That pioneering aspect of the venture kept us going. We never knew what we would find next. If anyone had told us that there would be nowhere to dig for water for seven days then our approach would have been totally different.

After the water scare a gradual change of emphasis occurred within the crossing party. At the beginning of the expedition we had focused upon our own personal weaknesses as being the likely cause of any failure or disaster. The camels were such large and stoical creatures, so fabled for their desert feats, each capable of carrying up to 150 kilos without complaining (or not that we noticed), that it never occurred to us that they might not make it. Naturally we were worried by the long periods when there was no water for them, but we supposed that their humps were keeping them supplied. The narrowness of our recent escape, however, combined with the deteriorating health of some of the animals, now forced us to question seriously our overall chances of success. Unless we kept the majority of the camels well and strong enough to carry the provisions at the rate that we needed to march, then we were unlikely to complete the route without serious mishap.

Out of our thirty camels eight were in poor physical shape. Six of them had nasty open wounds that Carolyn regularly treated. The female from Tongguzbasti still had maggots deeply embedded in her sphincter which we had been unable to eradicate. Finally, number eight camel (the replacement for the first number eight who had given us such trouble before) was worse than her predecessor – schizophrenic, thin to the point of starving and unable to carry heavy loads. She had been one of the two that had gone down the night before Niya. For some reason eight is a lucky number for the Chinese; perhaps that luck runs out when it comes to camels. Walking beside Guo one day I told him a story about the camel which I had learnt from the Arabs.

'Have you any idea why the camel looks at you as though you're inferior?' I asked him.

'No.'

'Well, according to the Bedu tribesmen of the Middle East, there are one hundred names for the Muslim god, Allah. The Arabs know ninety-nine of them, but it is only the camel who knows the hundredth.'

'*Aye ya!* Is that so?' Guo replied, and immediately he translated the story to the others who, in turn, passed it on to the Uyghurs. Surprisingly it did not really register with them and I put that down to the lack of deference they felt for the animals in their charge. In all his thousands of miles traversing deserts in Arabia with Bedu nomads, Wilfred Thesiger never once saw a camel harshly treated or beaten. On the contrary, the needs of the camels always came first, such was the high standing in which they were held by their handlers. It was not always the same with the Uyghurs in the Taklamakan.

Numbly resigned to the hardening climate and the lacklustre repetition of dunes and sand cones topped by tamarisks, we plodded the last few miles to a resupply point north of Yawatongguz on 24 October. There we halted for two days, submitting to the overwhelming need for rest. We were all aware of how physically and mentally tired we had become. The final two legs, 150 miles to Tatrang and then 190 miles to Luobuzhuang promised to be a real test of our remaining stamina. We still had an awfully long way to walk – nearly half as much again – and we longed to get it over and done with. The sheer daily drudgery of the walking, the never-ending sea of dunes and the meagre, unappetizing diet were beginning to pall. For the first time there was talk of finishing.

'The days-to-do syndrome,' Rupert said. 'Do you remember the "days to do" charts on operational tours in the Army?' he asked.

I did. They were invariably a double-edged weapon, maintaining morale on the one hand while on the other permitting an atmosphere of finality to creep in which could impair people's performance. Keith rejoined the party and his enthusiasm at being back in the desert allayed, to some extent, our staleness. He was a much-changed man since the Mazartagh leg. Somehow he had grown up and become more worldly, more travelled and less naïve.

'After more than a month with a bunch of crazy Brits, what do you expect?' he said.

As we started off on the next leg, on 26 October, I welcomed his company and the freshness of his conversation which countered what seemed to me to be increasingly snide and unhelpful comments that Mark and Rupert liked to make. I felt that both of them took pleasure in knocking anything and everything, and this chipped away at my equilibrium and peace of mind. Eventually I forbade them from walking together at the head of the caravan the whole time because they were becoming a clique. They weren't doing it deliberately but I was determined that we should remain a cohesive team and not break down into further sub-groupings.

'And another thing,' I told my team at the end of a day's march, 'you can stop walking together the entire time. I know the Chinese tend to be at the rear but I do not want an "us" and "them" situation. Otherwise we are forever leading the way like a pack of hounds, the Uyghurs are spread along the line leading the respective camel trains, and the Chinese are clip-boarding at the back.'

'With camel shit on their boots,' said Mark, characteristically seeking to raise a laugh.

'Be that as it may, we are not going to change them. Coping on an expedition is all about adaptability and compromise, and in this case it is the mountain which must move to Muhammad.'

'Oh! Purple prose!' added Mark. I ignored him.

The following morning, however, I did not take his next little dig so well. I had been making a recording on the BBC machine for a Radio 4 programme that we hoped to put together on our return when he approached me.

'I don't know why you bother with that thing,' he remarked in a thoughtless and offhand manner. 'There's no drama in this desert anymore so no one is going to want to listen to your ramblings.'

'For Christ's sake, will you stop being such a gloom merchant?' I snapped at him.

With that he backed off and gave me a wide berth for a while. I had not meant to lose my temper but I was irritated by his occasional jibes. We had developed a special affinity, especially after our week together in China and Hong Kong a few months before, and on that assumption I had welcomed his inclusion in the crossing party at Mazartagh. I did not want to ruin that. He sensed it too and apologized later. Perhaps he was unaware of the pressure I was under. I found I could talk to Mark on a very personal level; we often walked together for hours at a time. He told me about his childhood. And about his disabled father who lived in Norfolk near my mother; both lived alone and both shared a common interest in the lives of their young sons who were trekking across a formidable desert. I enjoyed listening to Mark, sharing the ghosts of his past and the anxieties of the future. In many respects he was a mirror of myself.

The weather had changed abruptly. The nights had become colder in the last week and it was common for the water in the containers to have turned to blocks of ice by the morning. Despite that, we still slept in the open under the stars. By dawn our bivvi bags, which formed the outer layer of our sleeping-bag arrangement, had a good covering of white frost hanging on the inside where the condensation had frozen. Concerned at the need to keep the batteries warm and charged up, we would retire each night with a varied collection of sleeping partners that ranged from the larger rectangular-shaped Racal HF batteries and the more compact Motorola ones to our GPS, torch, BBC recorder and camera batteries. There was barely sufficient room in the bags for our own bodies and there was little glamour in the arrangement but it did cause some laughter as we listened to each other's expletives as we tried to find a comfortable sleeping position.

There was no star-gazing now. It was a question of stripping off down to a T-shirt and pants, getting into the cold sleeping bag as quickly as possible to generate some heat and then battening down the hatches against the elements. The Uyghurs slept together in one line on top of as many camel sacks as they could lay their hands on. They would curl up in their sleeping bags with layers of rugs on top and all that showed were their six dirty white Muslim prayer caps at irregular intervals. Whoever got to be in the middle must have been as warm as toast.

The cold mornings made getting going much more difficult; our hands were frozen as we loaded the baggage and lashed it on to the camels, and I noticed how everyone moved at a much slower pace. Gone were the days of walking in a pair of shorts and a shirt. We were in trousers now and wore protective jackets for most of the morning against the wind-chill factor. By midday it would become quite hot and we would strip off but it was not uncommon, as early as the last days of October, for there still to be ice chinking about in my water bottle. The weather became yet another hardship and we quietly set our minds to coping with it.

On Saturday, 30 October, I wrote in my diary:

Day 37. The worst part of the morning is facing the cold when getting out of your warm sleeping bag. The full moon is still up at an angle of about 20° and the stars are out. It is dark. The struggle to dress and emerge into the chilly dawn is quite hard. Some are better at it than others. Mark is always the last to leave his warm snug. Putting my feet into my boots is left to the last possible moment; they are so painfully cold. Amazingly, Rupert and Carolyn are still not wearing socks for walking. We saw the silhouette of the Kun Lun mountain range for the first time. Very imposing until the rising sun obliterated all trace. To the west the pale moon, exhausted, was just descending below the horizon.

Dawn colours are pale and gentle, almost ephemeral. Breakfast of a mug of tea and some porridge with a chunk of Sven Hedin bread.* The thermometer recorded minus 12° Fahrenheit at 7.30 a.m.

---

*Our nickname for the local Uyghur bread which after two days became so hard that it could have been a hundred years old.

The following day was, for me, memorable for a very different reason. I felt depressed by the length of the journey, with 300 miles still to walk until the end. Our dream-like departure from Markit amidst the crowds and the pageantry of the bands seemed so, so far away. It had been over a month ago and in that time we had tramped across the empty desert for nearly 500 miles. My enthusiasm for the quest was now virtually spent. I could barely contemplate the ranges of dunes that lay ahead and the prospect of a further month among them. I knew that my body was tired and now my spirits began to flag as well. But there was no respite and no easy way out. As I solemnly trudged ahead of the caravan in the early afternoon I ascended the crest of a dune some 300 feet high. The sand came down over my legs in torrents, covering my boots completely, and I had to dig my stick in for support as I scrambled to the top. There, the scene in front was the same and I despaired at ever getting out. Our attempt looked utterly futile and I felt totally dejected.

Then, at that moment, my head was filled with a tune as though a band was playing beside me. It was Bert Kampert's 'Swinging Safari', one of my father's favourites. I had not heard it or even thought about it in connection with him for years. Suddenly images of him were kaleidoscoping all around as the tune played on: soft pictures of him smiling, one of him sitting in a wicker chair in my parents' house in Hong Kong tapping his foot to the beat and smoking his pipe, others of his face close up, each as though in a bubble floating all around me. I continued walking slowly and then, as I strode out further, I heard myself whistling the verses and the tears simply flowed down my dirty, sandy cheeks and into my beard as I cried without shame. I could feel the presence of my father right beside me and within me. He was there. It was an extraordinary sensation which left my heart racing with emotion. I did not wipe my tears but let them roll freely until I could taste their saltiness on my lips. The experience gave me strength. Later, once I had recovered from the shock of it, as I whistled and hummed the tune, I was immediately filled with a surge of happiness and comfort that only I will ever understand.

As the last days of October went by I dwelt increasingly upon my decision to leave the Army. As of 1 November I would officially be struck off the payroll. Certainly it was a novel way in which to finish fourteen years of service and I had joked with Barney about starting the expedition as a serving Major and ending it as a civilian. My time in the desert would act as a cushion between the one and the other, enabling me to get whatever wanderlust remained out of my system. Because I could not relate to being in civilian employment whilst I led the expedition I never seriously doubted my decision. I had had no reason to leave. Before the expedition I had been in a good career job as a staff officer in the Ministry of Defence, advising senior officers and civil servants on the restructuring of the Army. Promotion was just around the corner and one day I might command a Green Jacket battalion. More importantly, I enjoyed the Army. But something unquantifiable changed within me. Suddenly I had yearned to be different, to escape from an establishment and to see exactly what I was capable of in the so-called outside world. It was a maverick, almost masochistic decision when I had three young children to support. I knew there would be many aspects of Army life that I would miss – the camaraderie, the change in job every two or three years, the variety, the responsibility, the uniform and the sense of belonging. Yet in themselves they were not sufficient to justify staying. After all, I was going to leave at some stage, even if only on retirement, and arguably it was better to go earlier rather than later.

The one thing, above all else, that gave me comfort as I walked across the desert was that I had a job to go to in January. I was due to start work as the personal assistant to the Group Chief Executive of the merchant bank Robert Fleming. I had never aspired to be a banker. Frankly, the thought of working in the City after fourteen years of adventure all around the world filled me with horror. But it was a stepping-stone, and everyone has to begin somewhere. My only doubt was that I might merely be swapping one uniform for another.

The 1st of November came.

'Hello, Mr Blackmore,' said Barney on the evening radio schedule.

'Good evening, Major White-Spunner,' I replied.

'Now that you're a civilian you are totally dispensable so neither I nor Her Majesty will have to worry any further about your safety!'

'Thank you very much – most reassuring.'

'Perhaps, on reflection, you had better be known as Major Blackmore, retired; in which case I will look after your interests, for a bit anyway.'

Some of the most memorable moments in the crossing remained those when I was alone at the front of the caravan scouting ahead for the best route through the dunes. The temperature by early afternoon was a perfect 75° Fahrenheit and there was a crystalline clarity about the landscape set against the blue sky. The task of scouting was an absorbing one, looking to left and right, making quick mental appreciations and judgements as to the suitability of ascending one particular part of a dune rather than another. The sand was clean and pure, and I found pleasure in the sharp horse-shoe crescents, the deep cone-shaped depressions and the shadows of the rounded hillocks. And all the time, over the surface, there lay a fine patterning of wavy parallel lines some six to eight inches apart of larger, brown sand particles that had been blown along the top by the wind.

When the wind touched the crests of the dunes it gathered up the finest sand particles and blew them in a creeping mist about a foot high. The surface of the sand was in constant motion. The westernmost or leeward sides of the dunes were challenging to walk up, the sand being so soft and deep that it drowned my boots, filling them right up, and I would have to run to haul myself to the top. I used the long walking stick that I had picked up at Tongguzbasti as a permanent aid. It not only enabled me to balance on the steeper slopes, it also helped take some of the pressure off my knee. I still have that stick. The irony is that after walking with an injured knee across the desert, helped by the use of a stick, my knee turned out to be none the worse for such harsh treatment but I ended up with tennis elbow in my right arm.

Once at the top of the dune I would select the best route down the other side and plunge ahead in a cloud of sand and dust. On reaching the bottom the wind was gone and I would start to sweat again; then up the next dune until reaching the crest I could savour the gentle cooling breeze. I would then look back in the direction I had come towards the head of the caravan following in my tracks. Nothing impaired the perfection of the sand except the imprint from my footprints which, where they were exposed to the wind, magically disappeared as though someone was sweeping the trail behind me.

It was slow progress. The dunes were over 200 feet high in places and stretched in belts that ran from north to south, leaving us with no alternative but to roller-coaster over them. How simple it would be to cross the desert from south to north, or from north to south, I thought. Once I sat at the apex of a magnificent dune formation with the sand curling around the shape of my body like a comfortable armchair. It was warm to the touch and I played with the grains in my hand, letting them glide through my fingers and admiring their smallness and minute colouring. Most people would say that sand is yellow; but look at it carefully and you will see black particles, red, brown, white, orange and grey as well as yellow. I took my diary out of the breast pocket of my shirt to make an entry when a sudden breeze whipped the two photographs I kept of Tina and the boys away from between the book's pages. Off they went, somersaulting along the ridge of the dunes, going faster and faster until they were sucked into a depression. Momentarily I watched in anguish as the only possessions from my other life were taken from me. I could not bear the thought of losing that link. Frantically I dashed after them until I reached the lip of the void between the dunes and hurled myself down its steep sides in a cloud of sand, sending an avalanche of it cascading to the bottom. Clutching my precious photographs I lay there breathlessly, spat out a mouthful of sand and tried clearing it from my nose, ears and eyes. I looked at the faces of Tina and the boys. For a moment I imagined they were with me and that I was lying behind a sand dune on a beach holiday gazing up at the blue sky. Any moment now Oliver or Jack would come tumbling down the soft sand and lie beside me. I imagined I could hear the sea just over the lip of the dune and hear the cry of the gulls.

'God, what am I doing here?' I shouted aloud. Only the silence answered.

Reluctantly, wearily, I picked myself up and checked the equipment in my belt. The GPS and radio pouches were full of fine sand. I took a gulp of water and slowly climbed out of the depression and back to reality.

We made another exciting discovery on the leg to Tatrang. All morning we had been working our way through scenery not dissimilar to that around Niya except that there were fewer tamarisk cones and more evidence of some ancient flooding which had compacted a hard crust of pale clay. At intervals between the dunes it lay exposed with rock deposits that showed traces of marble. Mark was scouting the route ahead when he stopped and picked up a small fragment of black flint.

'What do you make of this?' he asked me.

'I'd say it's a worked flint, in which case we are talking of evidence for prehistoric occupation,' I replied.

Mark moved away and continued to search the ground. Carolyn had joined us and we decided it was as good a place as any for our lunch break.

'Carolyn, come and look at this,' Mark exclaimed. 'If Charles reckoned that was a flint then what do you call this?' He held up a solid piece of black flint about half the length and width of a wine bottle. I hastened across and there, on the ground beside him, lay a whole mass of worked flints which had been chipped off the one mother flint Mark was holding. Not only that, but beside them was a lump of rock twice the size of a clenched fist which looked like granite.

'That was more than likely the hammer,' I suggested.

'What do you mean?' asked Mark.

'Before man invented iron tools he used flints as knives, axe heads, arrow heads and all sorts. These flints have to be worked in order to get them to the correct shape and size. I should think the piece of flint you are holding was the source of the flints scattered around; in fact if you look closely you can see where they have been flaked off. And the tool which our Stone Age man would have used to chip away and break off the smaller flakes is that granite stone.'

The remainder of the caravan had caught up by now. The camels were couched in a circle and lunch was being collected from the saddle bags. Lao Zhao came across and started examining Mark's find. They talked together and I noticed that Calculus was quite excited by what he saw.

'Lao Zhao says the flints come from the Kun Lun mountains to our south. He reckons they are about 10,000 years old and prove that the Tarim Basin in prehistoric times was a fertile valley occupied by prehistoric man, hunter-gatherers he calls them, who would have roamed the forest in search of meat.'

'What about the granite?' I asked.

'He reckons that also came from the Kun Lun. He has found similar samples himself on climbing expeditions there.'

'Why does he think the flints are scattered around this precise area?' Carolyn asked. Mark translated.

'His theory is that we are looking at a place where prehistoric men stopped whilst they were out hunting and fashioned new flints from the mother stone. He says that it is the sort of size the hunters may have carried on them as a reserve for making new arrow heads and knives.'

It was difficult picturing the area when it was covered by watercourses and by riverine jungle, affording sufficient livelihood to a scattered semi-nomadic population of herdsmen, hunters and fishermen. It was like returning to a lost planet. For thousands of years the flints had lain undisturbed and now we had found them. In that time civilizations had come and gone, the surface of the world had changed, and the area that is now the Taklamakan had filled with sand. It made the span of a single human life suddenly seem very short and insignificant. We had no claim upon the desert; in ten thousand years there would be other deserts in the world where fertile plains and civilizations once existed: will someone be wanting to cross them then, simply because they are there?

SIXTEEN

Coping with Suleiman

'What's the matter, Guo?' I asked, having seen the Uyghurs gathered together near the camels and looking less happy than usual. It was the morning of 3 November, our eighth day on the way to Tatrang. We still had seventy miles to go and were not certain that we would be able to meet the support party at the point we had planned. Kirim had just finished talking to Guo with an intensity that attracted my attention. Immediately I walked over to them.

'He says last night there were thirty-one camels.' I tried to follow his meaning without success.

'I'm not with you, Guo.'

'Last night there were thirty-one camels but this morning we have only thirty.'

'That's all we're supposed to have.'

'I know that. In the night number eight camel gave birth.'

'Gave birth?' I exclaimed.

'Yes, but it was dead in the morning. The camel handlers are going to bury it. They say this is a bad omen for the expedition. They are superstitious, you know.'

I joined the Uyghurs. There on the ground lay the dead creature, about the size of a three-month-old Labrador puppy, curled up in the foetal position. There were tiny clumps of hair on its back and traces of blood which its mother had not licked off. It was a sad but inevitable fact of nature. Had we known number eight was heavily pregnant then we would not have taken her with us when we left Tongguzbasti. The camel handlers stood in a circle looking glum. Suleiman was the most affected.

'The only reason he's upset is because that represented sheer profit to him at the end of the expedition, the old rogue,' said Mark without malice.

'It certainly explains why number eight was in such a state,' observed Rupert, 'always the first to wimp out, unable to carry a decent-sized load and going along like a walking bag of bones. No wonder. Carolyn, don't you think as "Camel Doc" you'd better check the old girl out?'

Surprisingly, number eight seemed remarkably well. There had been a heavy discharge of blood down her thighs but this was now reduced to a thin trickle of watery crimson. She stood with her hind legs far apart in the resting position, the usual expression of 'What's your problem then?' written across her face. There was nothing that we could do about her condition except to ensure that for a few days she did not carry any loads. She was able to walk, albeit awkwardly, and managed to keep up with the others. It was just as well; I would have been forced to leave her behind if she had not been up to it.

The speed of the caravan was absolutely critical. Each day we had to cover as many miles as possible with the minimum of delays. The small margin for error between resupply points meant we must travel as fast as the dunes and the pace of the camels allowed. And the sudden drop in temperature which heralded the start of the Turkestan winter made it even more important to get a move on.

Every step we took across the wilderness of sand was one more that brought us closer to Luobuzhuang and the knowledge that we would have completed the first ever traverse of the Taklamakan Desert. Since overcoming the sand mountains before Mazartagh I had never seriously doubted that we would achieve our goal. Now, after everything we had experienced and survived, it seemed unlikely that some of us might not make it. The greatest danger lay in an accident with the camels. Whilst they had become more docile and obedient with the daily routine, nevertheless there were times when a camel would lash out, knocking one of us to the ground. Had any of

us sustained a serious injury we could only have headed at best
speed for the next rendezvous with the support team. There
was never a magic rescue formula.

Suleiman had developed an annoying habit of singing. Lucien's
performances had been stirring. By contrast, Suleiman
sounded like a funeral undertaker, and the miserable tune that
he sang over and over again in his dreary, flat voice was almost
more than we could bear.

'I've cracked it, Marko,' said Rupert, in the middle of an
afternoon when Suleiman had been singing particularly badly.

'What you do is hang back, and as soon as Suli starts singing
you hand him a boiled sweet!'

It certainly worked. Suleiman had hardly any teeth to speak
of and the appearance of a large boiled sweet from our survival
rations presented him with a dilemma – swallow it whole and
have that ghastly sensation of it sticking somewhere in the
upper larynx or try singing with it sliding precariously around
the palate. Fortunately, he worked out that the best thing was
to suck the sweet until it dissolved. That afforded us a ten-
minute break from the racket.

'And as soon as he starts up again,' Rupert added, 'you hand
him another. No flies on me, mate!' and off he went with a
laugh to the head of the caravan.

Suleiman was an endearing chap. He was 51 years old but
looked 70, and had slowly assumed the mantle of responsibility as head camel handler. This was just as well since our original four from Markit were novices in the business of camel
husbandry. As Suleiman's confidence grew he took to heading
the first camel train of five while mounted on the lead camel.
While we were loading the camels he would take his mount
aside and pad out the saddle and the space between its humps
with blankets and his old coat. He'd then ride off in the steps
of the scout, tucking his hands under his armpits and yelling
obscenities from the top of the camel as he lurched backwards
and forwards across the dunes. After a few days of this I spoke
to Guo.

'Suleiman can't keep riding the front camel. All he does is slow the rest of the caravan down and half the time he can't control the direction he goes in. In future the lead camel train must have a guide on foot. I don't care if Suleiman rides a spare camel but he can't do so at the front.'

Guo spoke to Big Zhang who, in turn, spoke to Suleiman and Kirim. I don't know what was said but the outcome was dramatic. From that moment onwards Suleiman led the front camel train on foot and at such a spanking pace that he was forever breathing right down the neck of the scout. It was impossible to shake him off. The poor camels were stretched to the limit and Suleiman himself seemed barely able to maintain the pace. At the end of the day he was all in.

'I reckon Guo threatened not to pay Suleiman at the end unless he kept up,' joked Carolyn.

'Either that or he offered him some of the camels for himself.'

It was wonderful to see with what sureness of foot the camels clambered up the steep inclines – inclines which we only climbed with the utmost exertion, slipping back at every step we took. As far as possible we kept to the same curving line of summits, so as to escape going up and down more than we could help. Nevertheless, we were often obliged to drop down when faced with too steep a slope. I loathed losing height, knowing full well that we would, sooner or later, have to regain it. When, after some hesitation, the camels began to slide down the loose sand, everyone had to be at the ready to prevent an accident and the sand would pour down after them in a torrent, covering them to the knees.

Aside from the odd bit of comedy, and incidents with the camels, the days blurred into each other with agonizing similarity though we never lost our feeling of vulnerability. I wondered why I did not pale with horror when my gaze swept eastwards over that unending ocean of fine yellow sand, its gigantic mounds rising up one behind the other for mile upon mile. Slowly we crept eastwards at a snail's pace. Sometimes the flatter ground afforded us the luxury of a brisk walk and the comfort of putting some mileage under our belts. But towards every point of the compass it was always the same monotonous, discouraging vista – one sand ridge looming behind another – a frozen ocean without a shore. Any occasion became an excuse to find mental respite from the tedium. And so we celebrated Mark's twenty-seventh birthday in style.

As a treat Carolyn took his turn of getting up first, rousing the rest of the camp and putting the breakfast on. She then brought Mark a mug of tea in bed. He lay there relishing the luxury, smoking a cigarette and stroking his ginger-blond beard which made him look like Tsar Nicholas of Russia. We all sported good growths by then but I had long since given up trying to compete with Keith and Mark. We each gave him a present. From Rupert there were two packets of our favourite custard and banana concentrate from the survival ration packs that he had saved especially for the occasion; Carolyn gave him a packet of digestive biscuits and one of her precious Mars Bars; Keith's present was a handwarmer which he suggested Mark use instead as a willy warmer; and I gave him my very last packet of Silk Cut cigarettes. For all of us these were highly prized commodities which assumed an unnatural importance in our existence. Mark went into raptures over the cigarettes; we had run out of our own brand some weeks ago and had since been smoking the rough Chinese ones. I had intended saving the Silk Cut for a celebration at the end of the journey but Mark's birthday seemed as good a moment as any.

In fact, Mark's birthday seemed to bring us luck. That day we covered the most distance, thirteen miles, that we had for some considerable time, and in the evening we chanced upon a patch of white salt crust that indicated the possibility of water below. We had not seen any sign of one for three days and, once again, the camels had become irrational in their behaviour for want of water. There was even less enthusiasm for digging a well than there had been a month previously. The only compensation now was that the hard work warmed us against the bitter chill of the night when the temperature would drop to minus 20° Fahrenheit. But it was clear from the frequency with which the diggers rested on their shovels that we were all on our last reserves of energy. The only thing to look forward to afterwards was a hot Chinese meal and a moment to relax before we sought the warmth and sanctuary of our sleeping bags. Gradually, shovel by shovel, the hole was widened and deepened until it was the depth of the men in the bottom. By then it was dark and the labour commensurably more arduous. Each shovel load had to be lifted to the high rim without it sliding off, and its weight became heavier as we reached moister sand. My body was racked with exhaustion, hunger pains continually gnawed in my stomach and I could feel my ribs sticking out because I had lost so much weight.

A kerosene lamp was brought over to aid our efforts. For two hours we dug until, at a depth of six feet, icy cold water reluctantly seeped into the hole. This presented a further problem because no one wanted to get their boots wet; the mornings were tough enough without having to put one's feet into frozen wet boots. On the other hand the water was too cold to go in barefoot; the simple pleasure we had taken in the early days of being below ground level in the coolness of the well now seemed an eternity away. Above, the camels crowded around impatiently, waiting for their first drink in three days. One of them collapsed the side of the well and nearly fell down; had Abdul Rasheed not reacted so quickly, Kirim and Rupert would have been crushed. Once as much sand as possible had been removed we left the well to fill up. After their meal the handlers would return and pull out the water in a bucket tied to a rope. Somehow, in the pitch black of night, they had devised a system whereby all the camels were watered but it was a lengthy procedure. Until the discovery of a place to dig that night I had been concerned that another water crisis was impending, for the terrain was no different to that around Niya and we had been no more fortune in finding any sites for wells.

After the Chinese had gone to bed, which they tended to do before the rest of the team, we sat around the fire talking and sharing the pleasure of each other's company. Many of the earlier tensions between us had been ironed out. There were bound to be moments of irritation, for no expedition is complete without them, but I was surprised at how few were of any real consequence. Kirim came across to our fire followed, at intervals, by the other Uyghurs. He handed Mark a wooden spit with some skewered meat on it.

'He says it is my birthday present from the Uyghurs.'

It was a touching gesture and we frantically racked our brains to work out what sort of meat it was, its age and where it had come from.

'You don't think it could be the aborted camel, do you, Kipper?' Rupert teased as Mark was chewing his first mouthful.

'Ugh!' exclaimed Mark. He would have spat it out had he not fully understood the rudeness of such behaviour in front of the handlers who were eyeing him with brotherly affection. In the end we all convinced ourselves that it had come from Barney's last resupply, but I could tell that Rupert's remark had left a lingering doubt in Mark's mind.

'Kirim says he thinks the British, the Chinese and the Uyghurs make an excellent team,' translated Mark. 'He also says that at the beginning they didn't give us a cat in hell's chance and thought the desert would have defeated us long ago.'

I looked at the faces of the Uyghurs and they smiled. I enjoyed watching them around the camp fire. Lucien habitually knelt in the sand with his backside resting on his heels, his back straight, his hands outstretched towards the flames and his head held fully back as he talked, that wonderful smile always on his face. Abdul Rasheed (Dopey or BP) tended to wrap up so well in his oversized Army great coat that he could barely be seen. Only his BP baseball cap and the elasticized goggles that he wore against the sand and wind were visible. He tucked his little legs under the coat, propped his head up on one hand, or against someone's shoulder, and sat there with a contented smile, the firelight reflecting off his two metal front teeth.

'They have never worked with Westerners before,' said Mark in response to a question from Carolyn to Kirim, 'but they have seen Pakistanis in Kashgar when they go there to the bazaar.'

'BP here owns a horse.'

'Bee Pee! Bee Pee! *Yakshee dos!*' (Good friend) exclaimed Rupert.

'*Yakshee*, huh?' and the little chap smiled proudly as Kirim translated.

'Emir here, on the other hand, used to be a cadre official of the Communist Party but apparently resigned because he had too many sheep to look after at home in Markit.'

Emir sat silently, his face long and grave, his heavy beard ingrained with dirt and sand, the dark fur collar of his coat turned up at the back. He never said very much but there again he didn't miss much either. We frequently saw him writing in a small book and called him the Poet. He was certainly a thinker and I was fond of him despite his sinister appearance. Of all the handlers he was the only one whom I never saw hitting a camel.

There was a squeak of delight from BP. He was busy feeling Carolyn's boots and the admiration on his face was palpable. His actions set the rest of them off and soon all aspects of our equipment were being discussed. Clearly we were in the final stages of the expedition now that the Uyghurs had started sizing up what they would like to take away with them.

'They say they're going to enjoy a big celebration when they take their first-ever flight on the aeroplane from Urumqi to Kashgar.'

I gained enormous satisfaction from those moments of communication at the end of the day when we could all relax. All too often it would have been easier to slip into one's own shell and say nothing, but such moments were an essential part of our teamwork.

Later, as Mark and I lay in our sleeping bags sharing one of his precious birthday cigarettes, he said, 'If the camel handlers thought that the desert would defeat us, I wonder what they imagined would happen to them? I can hardly believe that when they left their families at Markit they expected to be going to their deaths.'

'Would you have come on the crossing if you'd thought that?' I asked.

'I don't know. I'm not sure I ever thought about it; planning an expedition in England from incomplete sources a hundred years old hardly makes the actuality of doing it seem any more real. I mean, reading the name Desert of Death in print is not that off-putting.'

'It probably is if your village lies on the edge of it,' I remarked, 'and if your grandparents actually saw Sven Hedin off on his ill-fated journey. Being so close to the desert must have made the decision of the Uyghurs to accompany us very difficult.'

'If, in fact, they were allowed to make their own decision,' Mark added.

'What do you mean?'

'Well, I overheard one of the conversations between Kirim and someone else about the Chinese Communist Mayor of Markit having ordered them to go.'

'I'm not sure I believe that. After all, they are all intermarried in some way or another and, as I understand it, it was only because Esa Polta agreed that the others came.'

We lay in silence, our cigarettes glowing in the dark. There was no moon. I had enjoyed our fireside chat with the Uyghurs and knew that I would carry with me for a long time the memory of their faces, their good nature and their simple, uncluttered approach to life. I turned on my side and tried to make myself comfortable.

'But doesn't it make you feel rather humble?' Mark added after a while.

'In what way?'

'The fact that they trusted a bunch of foreigners, followed us and put their faith in our survival?'

'Yes, I suppose it does. Now I think about it, it makes me feel very small indeed.'

SEVENTEEN

A Costly Error

We reached our final resupply near Tatrang on 6 November, the forty-fifth day of the crossing. The 150 miles from Yawatongguz had taken twelve days. I estimated that the last leg of 190 miles to Luobuzhuang would take thirteen days but allowed sixteen for provisions. It was optimistic timing because the map led me to believe the going would be fairly flat as it had been on the final stage to Mazartagh. As it turned out, nothing could have been further from the truth. Keith left the camel party at Tatrang and we reverted to the core team of Rupert, Carolyn, Mark and myself.

Putting the map sheets of the route together for the final stage made me appreciate just how far we had walked. We were already counting the cost; there wasn't a single person without some ailment or another and we were all utterly worn down by the exertions of six weeks on the march, daily tramping through soft sand, up and down the gigantic sand-waves that piled up in pyramid masses. Our thin bodies and tired, lined faces were testimony to the hardship of the struggle. I looked at the pencil lines and camp sites marked on the map in the early days and it seemed as though they belonged to another time. We had been through so many experiences since then that it was impossible to share or recollect them all. When the expedition was over there would be few people, if any, who would ever understand what we had been through. It would not interest them for long because they would be unable to envisage it. The secrets would likely remain locked within us and only a person with a special key would ever open them up. But then any major experience in life is like that. People return from afar and someone will say, 'Oh, so you're back then?' and ask a couple of superficial questions and receive equally superficial replies. The next time they meet the conversation has moved on or stops at mundane, everyday topics. I didn't imagine that the returning Uyghurs would encounter the same apparent indifference: their stories would be told again and again, every detail absorbed and interpreted, ensuring that, in time, the fable of their undertaking would be preserved in communal folklore.

The support team were visibly ready for the end. Theirs had been an unglamorous role but they had carried it out with diligence and good humour – without them the crossing would never have happened. That is not to say that they didn't have their moments. One of their finest achievements was reaching the ancient site of Endere to the east of Yawatongguz at the northernmost limit of the Andir river. As with all the rivers it was dry and the vehicles found the going relatively easy for a change. With the benefit of a local guide they came across the site half a day's walk east of where they had left their vehicles in the dunes.

Stein excavated Endere in the winter of 1901 and again in November 1906. He discovered a fort close to a stupa and dated its most recent occupation to the eighth century AD after a lapse of two or three centuries. And it was in the fort in 1901 that he found some ancient chesspieces which are now housed in the British Museum. He recorded his regret at not recovering the chessboard as well but would have approved when a member of Barney's team chanced upon it in the sand along with numerous other artefacts from an occupation layer. Unfortunately the two have still to be reunited; the board was handed to the head of the Chinese support team at the end of the expedition and its whereabouts today remain uncertain. Barney also discovered two wooden coffins and the bones of their incumbents. Stein makes no reference to such a find – clearly the sandblasting and scouring action of the wind over the intervening ninety-odd years had gradually uncovered these gruesome relics.

In order to reach the vital resupply point at Tatrang we had been forced to abandon our original traverse line and head east-south-east. Now I was keen to regain that line and to do so we would have to march north for two days. The implementation of such a plan, however, was not without opposition.

'Madness. It is not possible,' said Guo, 'that is the worst part of the desert.'

'There will be nowhere to dig for water and the dunes are very high,' counselled Lao Zhao.

'Two years ago a well-equipped Japanese expedition costing many million yuan tried to cross the desert from Ruoqiang* to Yawatongguz. It failed after only one week.'

'Why?'

'Because the sand dunes were very big and very soft. The camels could not get through them so they went south to the Silk Road and walked near the edge of that instead. Afterwards they made a film and claimed they had undertaken a great crossing of the desert.'

'Let's face it, Charles,' argued Barney, in a separate conversation, 'the camels are pretty much all in, you lot are on your knees and you're all skin and bone yourself. Why don't you just head straight for Luobuzhuang. You'd still be crossing the desert. After all, the Silk Road is over eighty miles from where we are now, so your line across the map will still be authentic.'

As I listened and weighed up the advice I could not help feeling a slight temptation to take the easier option. I wavered, but only momentarily. As with many things that people achieve in life the brute challenge of what we were about to do had more substance to it than anything. In that regard Rupert remained my biggest ally.

'Let's just do it. No pussyfooting around,' he said bluntly.

Over the past week I had drawn increasingly upon Rupert's

---

*A town sixty miles south-east of Luobuzhuang on the Silk Road.

steadfastness and strength. He had become my unofficial deputy within the camel party and I had gradually reached the conclusion that if anything happened to me on the crossing it would be Rupert who would take charge and see things through to the end. Something of my belief in him and his ability generated the seed of an idea that we discussed while walking along together two days after leaving Tatrang.

'Have you ever thought of coming back and doing the crossing solo?' I asked.

'You really are mad' was his immediate response.

'No seriously, Rumper, how about the first ever lone crossing? With your experience now you would stand a good chance of succeeding. You know how to handle camels and where to find water, two of the most potentially awkward factors for anyone. You don't have any commitments back home in England and with all the contacts we have made in Xinjiang I'm sure we could get you the necessary permits.'

'Do you really believe it would be possible?'

'With the right plan and the right equipment, yes.'

We walked together in silence for a while as we selected the best route through an open landscape of flatter ground. In the distance lay rolling dunes set amid higher sand hills. The sand underfoot was firm and we walked with the measured stride and ease of two people whose fitness, despite our fatigue, had developed after forty-seven days of continual exercise. The weather was perfect for walking; it was warm, not hot, and the deep blue sky and crystalline clarity of the air heightened the yellow of the sand and enhanced the beauty of the rolling dunes. They looked friendly and unthreatening. For the first time since I had yearned to reach Luobuzhuang part of me almost didn't want the journey to end too soon. We had embarked upon a bold and seemingly impossible undertaking which had gradually come closer and closer to being accomplished. The fears and anxieties that we had all felt in those first few hundred miles were long gone. The planned resupplies had worked and we had proved that it was possible to survive a multitude of problems in a desert whose name now seemed its most frightening feature. We had adapted ourselves to its many hardships and in doing so we naturally grew more confident in our ability to conquer its legend once and for all.

That confidence, although measured, undoubtedly led to a complacency which lingered in the back of my mind like a warning beacon which I could acknowledge but couldn't actually do anything about. I was mentally half prepared for another dangerous situation even though I could not guess at what it might be. It seemed we had survived everything the desert threw at us – sand mountains, extremes of temperature, dysentery and sickness, days without finding water for the camels, navigating across a wilderness where each vantage point afforded the same view of sand and dunes stretching to the horizon, blind and maggot-infested camels, and a catalogue of minor accidents. Somehow we had coped and the desert had been kind. Yet I knew it would be naïve and foolish to assume that the desert had exhausted its repertoire of tricks. That knowledge caused me a degree of daily unease as we drew nearer to our goal.

'You'll crack the last leg to Luobuzhuang in about nine days judging by your previous track record,' Barney had said as I bade him farewell at Tatrang. 'Down hill all the way, Blackmore, you've pretty well done it now,' he added. It was easy to say it.

As we left the support team behind there was a tangible sense of us reaching the end. Everyone now wanted to get back home. The novelty of life in Chinese Turkestan and the romance of the adventure had waned. Traumas and obstacles had been overcome and we looked forward to the celebration at the end. Physically, despite being under-weight and under-nourished, we were in reasonable shape and our leg muscles were like iron springs as they pumped our bodies up and down the dunes. On the other hand our energy levels had been severely diminished. The drive and the surge of power that had given us the extra lift needed to get over the crest of a high dune had gone and we still had a huge stretch of virgin desert ahead of us.

'I'm like a racing snake on the flat,' Carolyn said, 'but it's become a struggle on the up – there's no oomph any more even though my body has never been fitter in its life.'

Our mental tiredness was more difficult to cope with. We were tired of the monotony of our existence, tired of the frugal living, the punishing mileage each and every day, and the exhausting business of loading and unloading camels, feeding them and digging a water hole. It was the same thing day in and day out. There was seldom anything to lighten the monotony: to relieve it we drew on simple pleasures like laughing at the victim of a direct hit from a mouthload of evil-smelling regurgitated camel food. Everything was reduced to basics to the extent that even our conversation degenerated and became monosyllabic.

My own mental fatigue was compounded by the need to plan ahead. Negotiations with the Chinese were still all too frequently fractious and at the end of the crossing I had yet to arrange how we would get all of our equipment out of China within a specified budget. Monetary concerns were high on my list of worries and I knew that the desert crossing was but one piece in the jigsaw. In that respect I relished the isolation the desert afforded me; I was out of reach and even if the expedition was thousands of pounds overdrawn there was little I could do about it. But I knew my escape was temporary. Until now Barney had borne the full brunt of administration and planning. As soon as I emerged from the desert they would become my responsibility. The realization that my temporary isolation was soon to come to an end only compounded my desire that the journey should not end too quickly.

'I would need to devise a different loading technique for being on my own,' Rupert said, returning to the conversation.

It is a curious feature of walking in pairs that a half-finished conversation can often be dropped for lengthy periods of silence and then picked up again as though the last sentence had only just been uttered.

'Those water containers are too much for a single man,' he continued, 'and I'd probably use a hawser and tackle arrangement instead. How many camels would I need, do you think?'

'Well, that would depend upon the number and location of your resupply points and it would be impossible to do it without them, as we've discovered. You would presumably use ours although my guess is that to really make it a solo first you'd want to strike farther north and miss out Yawatongguz and Tatrang. In which case the longest leg would be over 400 miles, from Luobuzhuang to Tongguzbasti if you chose to go that way first.'

'Why do you say that?'

'Because the biggest error I made in planning this venture was crossing from west to east, or left to right on the map. We have been heading against the grain, so to speak, for the entire route and now we are having to tackle the prevailing north-easterly wind head-on. The direction of the wind also means we have been going up the soft, leeward, side of the dunes and down the harder, windward slopes where the sand particles have been graded, rolled and packed by the wind. There's nothing like doing it the hard way! We would have found the going much easier had we started at Luobuzhuang and then headed west.'

'And hit those sand mountains at the end? I'm not sure about that. Anyway, I never have asked, why did you go from west to east and not the other way across?'

'I'm embarrassed to say there was little logic in it. I suppose I was initially influenced by Sven Hedin's account of his attempt at crossing from Markit to Mazartagh and assumed it was the natural way to do it even though it was never his intention to traverse the entire desert. And, I suppose that being right-handed I naturally drew the line on a map from left to right.'

'There doesn't seem to be a lot of science in that,' he chuckled. 'Just think, if General Slackbladder had been left-handed then we'd all be walking in the other direction. By such madness are the bare bones of history made!'

'Going back to the solo crossing idea, the biggest problems would be coping with the loneliness and the extraordinarily hard physical work. It's no mean feat digging a water hole on your own six feet deep and six feet square at the end of a hot day leading camels through the dunes. You could overcome that by resting for longer at the water holes but then every day you do that only puts off the inevitability of what you have left to face.'

We discussed other problems and logistical considerations. I could tell Rupert was attracted by the idea and, if nothing else, it gave him something constructive to think about.

'Mental exercise', Carolyn once said, 'is almost more difficult than physical exercise. It requires much more of you to focus the mind and harness its power to draw your conscious self away from the physical condition of your body and what you are doing.'

Mentally occupying ourselves during the long days of walking over similar ground was something of a challenge. For Rupert and myself it was slightly easier because we were navigating but, even so, I experienced periods of deep mental depression brought about by the boredom and drudgery of each day. In such moods the mind dwells on one's physical and mental weaknesses. Blisters on ankles and feet, and an aching knee, would prey on me until I became obsessed with their discomfort and with remedies to relieve them. My mind would single out a weakness in my character or my past and play on it until it blocked out all other thoughts and the only relief was a forced conversation with another member of the crossing team. If there was no one nearby when I was taking my turn as lead scout, then I would try to do some forward planning or invent a game of demanding mental agility. Such methods made me appreciate more fully the difficulties associated with long periods of solitary confinement. I had read of some people who actually overcame that by, for example, planning in their own minds the complete layout and construction of a home and a garden right down to the detail of each room and every piece of electrical fitting and plumbing. My own efforts were not successful and I found it easier to think back and relive the past. I envied those who could detach themselves from their surroundings and think ahead, or ponder something completely divorced from their present environment. James Bowden, a long-time friend and former fellow officer in my regiment, was one individual capable of that. At a particularly low point on our camel expedition retracing the journeys of Lawrence of Arabia, James had sat beside the camp fire in the bitter cold of dawn, drawing on a cigarette cupped between his hands, with a totally vacant look on his face. I had asked him what was the matter.

'Nothing really,' he had replied, 'I was actually thinking about Napoleon's piles.'

'Napoleon's piles?' I had exclaimed.

'Yes, did you know he had piles at the Battle of Waterloo and historians reckon the condition probably impaired his judgement? I was just thinking how different the history of Europe would have been had Napoleon not lost that battle.'

Unfortunately for me, in the Taklamakan, I was incapable of such abstract thought. Nonetheless, we discovered by chance another means of mental relief, and a way to pass the time. We began composing stories and then would tell them to the person we were with or to everyone at the end of the day. On the final leg to Luobuzhuang, when the temperature by day plummeted to minus 10° Fahrenheit and the prevailing wind gusted up to 30 m.p.h., blasting sand at us and whipping away our body heat as we leaned into it with our heads bowed forwards, we sought relief in creating our own little worlds of fiction. The competition to produce the best story became intense.

Mark quickly demonstrated a natural talent. He had an imaginative and original train of thought and was particularly good at making up poems and songs. He managed to keep me amused for many hours and by doing so took my mind off the great discomfort I was experiencing from my knee which liked neither the cold nor the cumulative effect of nearly seven hundred miles of walking. By then I had resorted to wearing an orthopaedic sleeve. It had steel joints on each side for support. The padding was tight and cut deeply into my skin, rubbing it raw. I welcomed any distraction from the dull arthritic pain and the uncomfortable brace. It took Mark two days to perfect a poem about Rupert's Uyghur haircut. To us, at the time, it seemed a masterpiece:

> Good morning, Mr Burton, the young man said,
> What a very fine hat on your hairless head.
> On that subject may I ask, if I'm not too late,
> Whatever did happen to your fuzzy brown pate?
> For 'tis rumoured, they say, that a Muslim did cut
> All trace of hirsuteness from your handsome nut.

Moreover, 'tis stated that this accident did happen
In the middle of a desert called the Taklamakan.
Now I can't help but notice the rest of your team
Are all wearing hairstyles of a sort rarely seen.
The leader, Lord Charles, more blond than black,
Grows hair at the front, both sides and the back.
Young Mark Kitto, whom I believe is one of your friends
Sports a fine moustache which curls at both ends.
In fact the only person with an all-smooth chin
Is Carolyn Ellis of Clinique-nurtured skin.
So the reason, Mr Burton, I really can't guess
To explain your state of scalpoid undress.
Does this courageous case of clean-shaven valour
Mean a sudden conversion to the ways of Allah?
Or does it mean that you've finally gone 'arty'
Or graduated in the school of camel karate?
For I must remark that you've taken some knocks
From the petulant camels whose ears you would box.
Perhaps in this manner you are far too lenient
And had better adopt the Uyghur expedient.
Step number one is to find a long stick.
For whipping the thinner, for whacking more thick.
This instrument when applied with unreasonable force
Accompanied for effect by language most coarse,
Will obtain a reaction you'll never have seen
Of yesterday's lunch in a high-speed stream.
(To protect yourself from this odorous affront
Ensure if you can, Guo stands to your front.)
But, Mr Burton, I fear that I do digress
From the subject which I did first address.
This was, if you remember, the length of your hair,
Or rather the absence of any up there.
One last question I ask. Will you be growing it long
To more keenly pleasure the girls of Hong Kong?
Of your success in that field I am more than certain
And so I bid you Good Day, Mr Burton.

The telling of stories was a particular feature of the last
hundred miles. We sat together, after supper, warmly wrapped
against the cold, having cherished all day the thought of listen-

ing to four stories, one from each of us, told in a different style and with a different and often subtle twist. Story-telling became our own form of entertainment and there would be a buzz of anticipation as we sat under the stars in a naked, cold desert waiting for the first author to unfold a tale. We relished our heightened affinity with each other and wistfully regretted the passing of story-telling in a world where television is so often the normal focus of family life in the evenings. But neither flights of fantasy in story-telling nor other attempts at taking our minds off the reality of the task in hand could disguise some of the very real difficulties we encountered within only three days of leaving Barney for the last time.

The brief euphoria of approaching the end soon faded as the sand hills became higher almost immediately when we struck out north-east of Tatrang and our daily mileage diminished accordingly. In some places the dunes rose to over 800 feet. Carolyn became properly ill for the first time and struggled valiantly to keep up with the camels. She was suffering simultaneously from vomiting and diarrhoea which rapidly dehydrated her.

'Jump on a camel,' I implored, 'you can't keep this up much longer otherwise you'll go down like a pack of cards and we'll have a real problem.'

'No thanks. I set out to walk every step across this desert and, whilst I'm able to walk, that's exactly what I intend doing,' she replied faintly.

'Well at least dump your back pack on a camel.'

'Not even that. Our main first-aid kit is in here and that way I know exactly where it is. If there is an accident and I can't find the medical kit because it's on the back of a camel somewhere, then it's not only unprofessional on my part but it could also make a huge difference to the outcome of the casualty.'

Nothing I did or said persuaded Carolyn otherwise and I was impressed by her courage and endurance. My own feet were suffering badly from unhealed blisters which had gone septic and were made worse by the friction of the sand. Putting on a bandage or plaster made little difference because the fine particles quickly penetrated everything. Added to that, I had swapped my Army desert boots for another pair of walking boots that Paul had brought to Tongguzbasti. Although they were half a size too small, they were far more comfortable and I had improvised by cutting out some of the inner lining. But by now the boots were causing me great discomfort and three toes on my left foot and two on my right had long since lost any semblance of feeling. Sand had got under the stitchwork, raising the soles of both boots into lumps and further compressing the sides. In short, unless my feet were half-frozen with cold and I could no longer feel them then the discomfort of the boots made walking almost unbearable. I sought relief by wearing only a pair of thick socks but it was short-lived: the socks wore through in less than two days and the sand was too cold to go barefoot for long. And, because walking in sand without footwear uses different calf and ankle muscles, I developed a stiffness and aching in my legs which I had not experienced before.

Carolyn's condition, however, forced me to put my own troubles to the back of my mind. At least I knew they were only a temporary inconvenience and that within a few weeks of leaving the desert my feet would probably look none the worse for their battering. But things seldom stay on an even keel. My diary entry for Tuesday, 9 November, the forty-seventh day of the crossing, and only two days out from Tatrang, recorded:

Woke feeling hot and sick in the pit of my stomach in the early hours. Bitterly cold. Did not get back to sleep. Felt very rough in the morning with a headache, upset stomach and aching joints. Mark felt much the same. Carolyn was worse off. She had been vomiting with attacks of diarrhoea at the same time. She didn't look too bad, but she had no energy at all. Rupert was in cracking form as normal. Tried some breakfast but couldn't face it. Decided that now was a good time to pack in smoking. I had fractional energy for leading the camels. I knew that I could not afford to dwell on it otherwise I would really go down. Instead I decided to carry the Hi-8 video camera as a means of keeping my mind off my body. Got some spectacular shots as the camels crested the high sand hills.

After two hours I began to feel worse. Difficult thinking myself out of the condition; my legs ached appallingly, my eyes were burning, I felt light-headed and I had hardly any energy at all. Tried keeping up at the front but had to walk three camel trains to the rear where the pace is slower. It is the worst I've felt so far on the crossing. It's interesting how alarmist one becomes, and the imagination runs riot. I even began thinking about death and how utterly ridiculous it would be to lose my life at this stage. I could not bear the thought of Tina having to bring up the boys on her own. My strength became less and less as the morning dragged on. By lunchtime I felt all in. At one point I thought I might black out. The caravan moved slowly over the difficult sand hills. The camels were weak and tired. I should think all of our immune systems have just about packed up by now.

One camel in Kirim's train dumped its complete load on the brow of a high dune. For some reason the girth was still fastened; the camel had somehow shaken off its load and then skipped out of the girth. Very nimble, but then it slipped and rolled down the side of the dune. Despite my failing strength I stopped to lend Kirim and BP a hand. I noticed the Chinese didn't but then I hadn't the energy to say anything. The problem about helping out at the rear is that it takes so long to catch up and everyone's instinct turns to self-preservation.

Stopped for lunch at 2.45 p.m. Did not feel like anything. All I wanted to do was lie down and sleep. The prospect of having to take my turn and lead over the dunes for three hours in the afternoon was quite daunting. Rupert and Mark offered to lead instead. I decided, however, that it would be a good bit of therapy for me. Otherwise one could easily slip into the mould of walking along at the back feeling ill and sorry for oneself.

A number of times I had to fight for breath at the brow of a sand hill. I needed to lean on my stick and rest. Wish I knew what was wrong with me. Feeling like this makes it real hell. After leading for an hour I realized something was seriously wrong. The dunes and sand hills extended north for mile after mile as far as I could see. My map plainly showed shading where the ripple dunes ended and then the route should have been fairly flat. The map is completely wrong. There is no flat! We are now in the middle of sand mountains which are becoming comparable in size to those of the first leg. Had a chat with Guo and Lao Zhao around the map at the top of a high dune. We had nearly lost a camel five minutes earlier when it slipped on the near-vertical sand wall which we were contouring. The sand was so soft that the animal plunged up to its belly and thrashed around in a cloud of sand; then it lost all its strength, went down and refused to budge. It was a two-hundred-foot drop to the bottom. Tense moment.

Guo insisted that he had told me my map did not compare with the Chinese one and that there was no flat area. I simply cannot remember. Had I known, I would certainly not have risked our lives by heading so far north into the sand mountains before then turning east to Luobuzhuang. Decided to head near east and set a bearing of 78° magnetic. It is 118 miles as the crow flies but probably more than 160 over the ground. In order to complete it within the twelve days for which we now have provisions left we must cover at least 11.3 miles a day. A very tall order. Will we make it?

EIGHTEEN

Camp of Death

Any feelings of complacency had vanished completely by 11 November. The landscape was a vast labyrinth of towering dunes far worse than we had crossed in the first week to Mazartagh. Then, at least, the ridges of sand rose to their summits over reasonably steady inclines of some distance. Now the dunes were vertical sand walls with no clearly defined passage through them. I felt an enormous responsibility for having led the expedition into such danger by heading north from Tatrang. The camels were far from strong and were carrying a heavy load of 1,000 litres of water and thirteen days' supply of camel grain plus our own provisions. Compounding our difficulties the satellite link had broken and other items of equipment were failing.

We were tired, very tired. The enormity of my mistake and my misplaced bravado weighed heavily on my mind. I wanted to dump all the stores and punch my way out of the interlocking dunes which menacingly surrounded us. The pressure to get on was enormous. Instead, the caravan moved more slowly now it was heading east again across the grain of the sand hills, and the sheer physical impossibility of what we were trying to achieve sparked rumblings of dissent among the Chinese.

I was resigned to losing some camels. It had always been talked about before but I only had to watch their exhausted movements now to know that it was entirely possible. They struggled to ascend the soft dunes, their legs floundering in the deep sand as they tried to leap forwards in bounds, urged on by the camel handlers who were almost invisible in the cloud of sand that was kicked up. The ropes between the camels snapped and people swore and cursed. Loads were dumped and camels panicked to escape from baggage dangling about their legs, their eyes wide with fright and their mouths open in a bellowing roar of protest. Each load scattered in the sand took up to fifteen minutes to reassemble and replace on the placated camel. The delays added up and soon the dunes were lit by the pale glow of evening light. There was no suitable place to camp. There was no water for the camels and no convenient tamarisk cones or ancient petrified tree stumps between the dunes from which we could gather timber for a fire. Instead, that night, we camped on bare flat ground on the leeward side of a high belt of sand hills that appeared insurmountable. I knew we should have climbed them before camping but the day was spent and with it the last of our and the camels' energy and enthusiasm for more dune-bashing.

There was little conversation during the evening meal. Guo was suffering from bad toothache and no amount of medicine from Carolyn relieved his plight. He told us he had never been to a dentist in his life. Carolyn's condition had marginally improved and she was able to treat some of the pressure sores on the camels. Bone-weary and shivering with cold, I retired to my sleeping bag with barely sufficient energy to write my diary.

That was the night a camel fell down a dune as it wandered away from the camp. It was pitiful watching the beast writhing in agony as we attempted to get it back on its feet. Our efforts were to no avail. Its neck was either broken or dislocated and after two hours in the freezing night air we tried to shut out the disasters of the day by wrapping ourselves in the warmth and security of our sleeping bags. I slept fitfully. A fever came over me and I thrashed about restlessly, haunted by images of waterless dunes waiting to consume our frail caravan and scared at the thought of facing the miles upon miles of sand still to be crossed.

The mood in the camp the following morning was sombre as we packed everything and loaded the camels. The execution of the camel just after dawn had had a profound impact on us all and, in particular, on the more superstitious Chinese. After Suleiman had cut its throat I had stayed to watch as he and Emir skinned the uppermost side of the camel and then hacked off one of its hind legs in its entirety. The meat was cut into manageable loads and wrapped in sacking. We would need the extra rations later.

The remaining camels had been visibly affected by the killing and, although we tried to load them out of sight of their dead companion, they were still very timid and nervous; sacks of baggage were thrown off and the animals bolted away from us in fright.

'They probably think they've got the same fate in store for them,' joked Mark.

'They're probably right if we keep going like this,' said Rupert.

It did not take long for the banter of the British contingent to be restored to its normal level. The Chinese, by contrast, remained particularly subdued and they were unable to meet my eyes. It was as though they blamed me for the fate of the camel, and for them it marked the beginning of the end.

'Charles, we must go back or head more to the south,' said Guo as we were completing the loading.

'I don't think that is necessary, Guo,' I replied.

'But if we carry on like this then more camels and maybe humans too will die.'

'Look, Guo,' I countered, becoming cross at his display of what I considered to be weakness, 'we always knew we would lose some camels. That was the risk. No one has done this before and we expected trouble. What happened last night was an accident which could have come at any time. The fact that it occurred at this moment in our crossing is plain bad luck.'

'But Charles, we must not lose any more camels. That will not be worth it. We have not found water now for two days and there will be none ahead.'

'Guo, we must be prepared to lose camels if we are to

succeed. We set out to make a complete traverse of this desert right the way across the middle. This is a great British–Chinese expedition and not a Japanese one. Don't worry, we will be fine.'

He looked utterly dejected and miserable. More worryingly, he was actually scared and, with the exception of Lao Zhao who took the whole thing in his stride, this had transmitted itself to the other Chinese. I suspect the pain Guo was suffering from his rotten teeth did not help but I was determined to stifle any talk of deviating from the plan and the goal we had set ourselves. What I had not told him about was the pact that I had made with Barney the night before entering the desert for the first time at Markit. He had asked how many casualties I was prepared to tolerate before cancelling the expedition. It was something to which I had given a great deal of thought, particularly after our visit to the British Embassy in Beijing when we discussed the arrangements for the repatriation of any bodies. My answer was that we would continue after the first death and reassess the situation after the second one. If the deaths were caused by an accident there would be no grounds for not continuing the complete crossing. If death was attributable to thirst and dehydration then the casualty limit would be two before I would either head south directly out of the desert or give up at the next resupply point.

The whole question of what to do with the bodies was more difficult. Theoretically there was a PLA helicopter on standby at Korla, some two hundred miles north of the desert's easternmost point, but its chances of reaching us, let alone locating us, in the desert were nil. We were the proverbial needle in a haystack. Therefore, on the assumption that external assistance was impractical, I had decided to carry the body on a camel for as long as it was hygienically possible and to bury the corpse in a marked grave when it became necessary to do so if we had not reached Barney by then. I had discussed the plan with my team at the outset but had deliberately avoided doing so with the Chinese and the Uyghurs.

As we ascended the sand hill that morning, 12 November, I looked down at the ill-fated camp of death. The corpse of the camel lay surrounded by a drying puddle of dark blood. If there had been bird life in the desert I suspect the vultures would already have been hovering, impatient for our departure. But there were none. The only things that lay near the dead camel were two empty and battered tin water containers. They had lasted well since Markit, but there was no point in retaining extra baggage once its usefulness had expired. On the tanks were their sponsors' logos – The Excelsior Hotel, Hong Kong, and United Biscuits (China). The names seemed out of place and communicated a hint of the outside world that had no relevance in the midst of such an unforgiving desert. I couldn't help wondering how many similar sights of abandoned stores and dead camels we might witness before the next 130 miles were through. There could be no doubting it; we had found the challenge now and I only hoped I would not live to regret it.

The spectre of Sven Hedin hovered about me that morning; he had been forced to leave living camels behind who could go no further. Killing our injured camel, by comparison, was an act of mercy. But I feared the agony of having to do as Hedin had done when he walked away from the first two camels.

In my imagination I saw the action vividly. It weighed upon my conscience like a nightmare, keeping me awake at night. I saw Babai lie down when Mohammed Shah left him. The other camel remained standing, although his legs trembled under him, and with expanding nostrils and shining eyes, followed the departing caravan with a wistful and reproachful look. But the caravan soon passed out of sight. Then I imagined him slowly turning his head towards his companion, and thereafter crouching down beside him. Their weariness increased; they rolled over on their sides with legs outstretched. Their blood coursed slower and slower, thicker and thicker, through their veins; the rigid torpor of death gradually stiffened their limbs. The pauses between their breathings became longer and longer, until at last the end came. In all probability Babai would die first, for he was the weaker. But how long did that death struggle last? We shall never know.

If the height of the dunes persisted and we did not find water in the next two days it would not be long before we would face similar scenes. It was ironic that, having come so far and survived so many ordeals, the expedition was now closer to failure and disaster than at any previous time.

It was a grim day, as my diary recorded:

A punishingly hard day and we only covered 7.5 miles. The dunes are immense, now up to 1,000 feet high, and face us in large sand walls perpendicular to our route. Everyone is more tired than ever before. Carolyn weak but walking well and still carrying her pack.

Three or four times the camels fell near the crest of dunes and were unable to rise. They are too weak and heavily laden. It is becoming a struggle to get them up these high dunes. Big Zhang particularly annoyed us by not helping at all. The man is completely useless and a bluffer. He stands at the rear of a train of five or six camels and merely watches while one of them refuses to go up a dune, the Uyghurs struggling in the sand and pulling on ropes, and the other camels prevented from moving further because of their fellow's refusal to budge.

The Chinese want to head south to the safety of the Qarqan river valley. They think we will all die if we continue on this route. No watering for the camels tonight – the third day without water. No scrub, no camel thorn – no old wood in sight either. This really is the most desolate part of the desert that we have been through, far worse than the Valley of Death near Niya and the earlier sand mountains. Feeling much stronger today but still not fully up to speed. It takes all my energy to get up these steep dunes, never mind having to help pull and encourage the camels up too. Camped at the top of a high sand mountain. Altitude of 2,000 feet. My sleeping bag is still damp from last night's frost which makes it cold and miserable.

I've been thinking about how long we can continue like this. In two days the camels will be just about at their end. There are no signs of the dunes getting better. I may have to concede and head further south-east to where we should be able to dig for water and the dunes are flatter. I'm concerned about our slow speed and the state of the camels. We are falling behind schedule now and the willpower is not there to pull it forward. Everyone in the British team is working hard but they are tired. These dunes are worse than those we faced between Markit and Mazartagh but then we also had the spirit of a new adventure plus our freshness to help. Now the reserves are gone. Every mile is beginning to feel like three and although we are making progress the end seems to get further and further away.

The scenery, however, still excites. It has been spectacular – the high dunes, their colours, shapes, shadows and the gentler light now it is cooler, all build up an enormous landscape of sand desert through which our tiny caravan wends its way. Walked behind a camel today with blood seeping out of a grain sack on its back. I then realized that this was all that was left to us of the dead camel.

That night marked the lowest point of the expedition. I instructed Rupert to work with Zhang Bohua and sort through all the camel sacks, discarding excess equipment and food. The events of the day had demonstrated beyond doubt that the camels were no longer able to carry such heavy loads through the belt of dunes we were having to cross. Somehow their loads had to be lightened. As the pile of excess provisions grew bigger I noticed the morale of the Chinese sink even lower. Our position on the sand mountain was very exposed and the bitterly cold wind made the simplest of tasks that much more difficult. Everything took a great deal of extra effort and energy. There was bickering between the Chinese and British about how much excess food and equipment belonging to each team had been dumped. Tempers flared and arguments broke out. The self-discipline which had previously knitted people together was beginning to break down and I could sense an air of impending disaster amongst everyone, the Chinese in particular. In the midst of all this the Uyghurs kept their distance, but later they added to the gathering chaos by looting the piles of discarded provisions and secreting their booty among their own things. It began to look like a rout.

In the meantime, after a lot of difficulty, Mark had managed to get through to Francis positioned 170 miles south-east, near Ruoqiang, on the HF radio. Francis was in charge of the support team in Barney's absence whilst he flew to Urumqi to organize our extraction from China with the authorities there. The Chinese were still prevaricating about letting the two vehicles travel across China and down to Hong Kong for shipment back to Southampton. We had been involved in lengthy negotiations over this aspect of the plan for over four months, and even a letter from Sir Edward Heath to the appropriate authority in Beijing had produced no result. Barney had decided on one last personal effort. Neither of the alternatives was attractive. Either the vehicles could be driven back over the Khunjerab Pass, which we were assured was closed in December because of snow and the danger of avalanches, or they and all the equipment could be left in Xinjiang until the following spring. If the latter were to happen I feared that the Chinese would hold the vehicles to ransom in order to elicit more money from us. It would be totally within their power and we were in a vulnerable position. After Francis had related Barney's movements I described the events of our own last twenty-four hours to him.

'So we are in a pretty tricky situation now,' I concluded, 'and I am pessimistic about what lies ahead.'

'Well, just make sure you reach Luobuzhuang by 23 November because all the celebrations in Ruoqiang and in Urumqi afterwards are being organized now around that date,' he replied. I shook my head in disbelief.

'Have the support team any idea of what it's like out here?' I asked Mark as an aside.

'Undoubtedly not.' We laughed. Francis sounded so calm and composed on the radio and that made our difficulties seem a little less grim.

'We'll do our best, Francis, but when you next talk to Barney I want you to emphasize the problems we have and try to come up with an emergency rescue plan with the Chinese in case it is needed, if that is at all possible.'

I got the last sentence in just before the radio batteries finally gave out. In the cold conditions their charge was not lasting long in spite of our efforts at keeping them warm at night. The portable battery charger that we plugged into the petrol generator only worked intermittently and it took a long time at the end of the day to get any life into the battery cells. If the generator itself packed up we would be in an even more dangerous situation without any means of communicating with the support team. Rupert had tried fixing the Ultralite satellite link without success. The sand had finally come out on top, degrading the performance of our equipment item by item.

Kirim had been missing from the campsite for more than two hours. No one knew where he had gone but one of the Chinese had last seen him heading in a southerly direction across the ridge. In the darkness, without a fire acting as a homing beacon, I doubted Kirim's chances of relocating us. After an evening meal of Chinese vegetables and rice there was still no sign of him.

'Fire some distress flares,' I suggested, and Rupert let off three red mini-flares. They arced high in the sky and then curved away, making the shadows and lines of the dunes dance briefly in the flicker of light. We shouted his name but there was no answer. Half an hour later a second volley of mini-flares was sent up and there, by the light of the final one, we caught sight of Kirim heading towards us. He appeared to be carrying a load on his back. When he reached us we found that he had a large bundle of tamarisk wood.

'What a player,' Carolyn said. 'Without so much as a prompting he took himself off in search of wood for a fire.'

'That's a good sign,' Mark added. 'Kirim says that there may also be a place to dig for water two hours south of where we are.'

Gratefully we built a small fire and the whole team huddled around it in a tight circle for warmth. The flames shot up in the frosty air. As we knelt together, Emir and Suleiman began hacking small chunks of meat off the hind leg of the camel and putting them on sticks before cooking them in turn over the fire.

'Camel kebab,' commented Mark.

'I'm not quite sure I can face that,' said Carolyn, and I watched the expressions of the others who seemed equally ill at ease.

'So this is the end of the brave camel who carried our water containers for nearly seven hundred miles over forty-eight days. Seems a shame to waste it – the first fresh meat of the expedition and who knows when our next meal will be,' remarked Rupert as he held up the cooked meat on its stick after Lucien had passed it to him. He pulled the top piece off with his teeth and handed the rest to me.

'Mmm, not at all bad.'

'Medium rare or well done?' I asked.

'Medium rare. No, actually a touch rare for my liking.'

Again, our sense of humour was there and I was proud of it. It always surfaced, no matter how serious things were. Once again, the situation emphasized the stark comparison between the British and the Chinese. They thought the camel kebabs in poor taste and none of their number would entertain the idea of eating the meat. Instead, they sat in silence and brooded, which only made Rupert and Mark play up even more.

At seven o'clock the following morning, 13 November, the stars were still glittering bright. The thermometer showed minus 20° Fahrenheit and there was thick frost over our sleeping bags. The water containers were frozen solid. The barrenness and remoteness of our sand mountain campsite exaggerated the cold face of dawn and the precariousness of our situation: no water for the camels; no more wood for a fire; a campsite littered with provisions that looked as though it had sustained an attack in the night; a Chinese team who were close to mutiny; sick, injured and exhausted camels; broken equipment; and still 120 miles to go through sand hills that rose in places 1,000 feet. Lao Zhao was there as always, pumping away at the dilapidated petrol cooker as he tried to keep the pressure up. The altitude and the cold made it difficult but he persevered and we were eventually rewarded with a kettle of hot water. I made myself a coffee and walked up to the highest peak of the sand mountain range in order to watch the dawn.

Mark was already there with his back to me, facing east and eating porridge out of an old metal tin. He was wrapped up in his down jacket. The wind coming off the Kun Lun mountains to the south was bitter and I couldn't take my hands out of my pockets for more than a moment. The coffee was cold by the time I reached Mark.

'I hope I'm not interrupting your moment of solitude?'

'Not at all. It would be a pleasure to share it with you.'

The view, as views go, was unforgettable. The long silhouette of the Kun Lun mountains occupied the entire horizon to the south, their peaks seemingly merging together in one line. I could almost imagine walking along their crest which had just welcomed the first touch of light, revealing a pencil-thin line of snow above the darker shade below. Between us and the mountains lay a rolling maze of sand hills still deep in shadow as the dawn appeared faintly in a pale, watery and wintry light to the east. As it gently grew, the horizon became a silver haze which slowly turned pale orange, then pale crimson and purple until all the colours of the spectrum stretched across the horizon and into the sky. Above, almost hanging on the temporary azure-blue divide between the white light of dawn and the darker night, was the bright star of Uranus with the thin slither of the moon nearby. To the north and to the east, I could see only the continual, threatening line of sand hills whose distorted shapes were exaggerated by the dark shadows that faced us. Behind and below me, to the west, the camp was slowly stirring into life and I picked out the dark shapes of the Uyghurs as they knelt in a line behind a low dune saying their prayers. I hoped they were saying one for all of us. In silence we contemplated the emerging dawn. As it unfolded in front of us, the shape and size of the dunes in the direction of the day's march became more easily recognizable for what they were – a terrifying barrier of obstacles which would slow our progress to a crawl and where there was little likelihood of finding somewhere to dig for water. I studied them more carefully as the light improved; it was as though some invisible hand was slowly turning up a dimmer switch until gradually the full reality of what lay ahead was completely revealed.

'Do you really intend sticking to the present bearing?' Mark asked, as though sensing the dilemma in my mind as the nature of the terrain became apparent.

'I said we would keep on the present heading for two days longer and reassess the situation then.'

'I know that, but seriously, Charles, just look at what we've got to go through. It will be more than a struggle and with the camels in the state they're in I really don't rate our chances at all.'

'It's not that that I'm worried about, although finding water within the next two days is a prime consideration or we will definitely lose more camels. My main fear is that we will be reduced to doing less than six miles a day and I don't think any of us, let alone the camels, can contend with a day longer than is necessary in these conditions.'

Mark was silent for a few minutes. I shifted my attention to the south-east. The slightly flatter terrain in the far distance was more apparent even though the depressions between the dunes were out of sight. I looked back again at the route to the north-east and the east. There was no doubt about it; the south-east would be easier.

'I'll leave you with one last thought,' said Mark as he stiffly stood up. 'When they first conquered Everest they didn't choose to do it by the most difficult route. We are still making a historic crossing, and the fact that we now head south-east for a few days in order to find water and make up a bit of distance will make less than no difference to the final outcome.'

Mark's reasoning became the catalyst for my eventual decision. I knew he was right, and the vantage point we were on had only confirmed the impossibility of maintaining our present heading. I took out my compass and read a bearing of 110° magnetic which would take the caravan to the south-east and hopefully more favourable terrain.

'We'll head that way,' I pointed, 'south-east, but don't say anything to anyone yet.'

Back at the camp, Rupert was waiting to tell me about the problems he was having in making the Chinese throw out their surplus kit. By comparison, the British element had jettisoned, probably rashly, a huge number of the heavy survival ration packs. I had instructed Rupert to work on the basis of carrying ten days' supplies. It was a big risk.

'I think you need to speak to Guo,' Rupert said, 'because they've done sod all about it and they won't listen to me.'

I did. It caused a fierce argument. Afterwards Guo stormed away and assembled his team around the pile of camel sacks.

'What's he saying, Mark?'

'I can't really make it out.'

Whatever was said, the result was a classic display of Chinese melodrama. First, an entire box of tinned congee was thrown on to the rubbish pile. Next, the fresh vegetable sacks were emptied and most of their contents followed the congee along with a huge quantity of packeted vegetables and rice.

'What about the tins of mango juice I know the Spook still has?' asked Carolyn.

'I told Guo to make sure they went too. He assured me there weren't any left.'

'Better bloody well not be.'

In a last dramatic gesture Guo emptied an entire jerrycan of petrol on top of all the discarded equipment and put a match to it. There was a thundering explosion which was soon followed by lesser poppings as the tins exploded. The reaction of the Uyghurs was difficult to gauge; on the one hand they probably enjoyed witnessing the Sino-British disagreements, and on the other they must have been perplexed by the way the expedition was going. Their opinion was not asked for, rightly or wrongly, and they were obliged to follow without question. Yet they had as much to lose as everyone else. Guo then examined the camel sacks of the British team and demanded to know why we carried so many boxes of digestive biscuits.

'Rupert, lend me a hand counting them out, will you?' I asked, quietly acknowledging the point Guo had made. We put aside sufficient for ten days. The surplus we carried over to where the camels were couched around the tarpaulin sheet eating corn. We unwrapped the biscuits and threw them into the centre. The camels went straight for them.

'Even honours, I reckon.'

'I should think so. Did you notice the tears in Guo's eyes when he was chucking out all their kit?' Rupert asked.

'I suppose he's becoming a bit tired and emotional. The bottom line is that he is scared. You can see it.'

'Have you decided what to do yet?'

'Yes, we're going to head south-east for a few days and get some mileage under our belts. I'll take point this morning and we'll be going on a bearing of 110° magnetic.'

It took nearly three hours to repack the remaining equipment, distribute it equally between the camel sacks and load the camels ready for departure. There was a visible listlessness and atmosphere of despair as people faced the prospect of yet another day's painful struggle through the endless dunes. Once the caravan was assembled I told them my decision.

There were no outbursts of joy: the south-easterly route was unpredictable and likely to be equally tortuous. Irrespective of the direction we went in we still faced another day of hard graft. I led off with mixed feelings. I was relieved the decision had been made and that the opportunity of studying the route ahead had confirmed the hopelessness of our situation. I did not feel I had given into the Chinese. In any case, I didn't care. But in heading south-east I felt I was turning away from the real challenge, from what should have been a perfect line across the map. In that respect I regretted taking the easier option and part of me wished I had stuck to my previously robust and uncompromising stance. Had it been earlier in the crossing when we and the camels were stronger then I would have done. But now, I reasoned, the camels were far too weak, our own reserves of energy had long ago expired, and we would only have been battering against a veritable brick wall by continuing due east. I hoped that we would still achieve our aim but I knew in my heart that the sand hills had defeated us. The desert had certainly held another trick up its sleeve. What none of us could be sure of on that depressing morning, as we descended the first steep gully of the sand hills, was whether the Taklamakan held any more secrets in the remaining hundred miles.

NINETEEN

A Sinister Twist

One of the main sensitivities concerning the route of our expedition for the Chinese authorities centred around their nuclear test site in the Lop Desert to the east of the Taklamakan. China's clandestine nuclear activities in that remote area were reasonably well known to the Russians and the Western powers. The Great Game of the last century, when the British and the Russians jockeyed for power and influence in Central Asia, has been superseded by a more sinister threat: the use of a nuclear capability to enforce bullying tactics and to defend the sovereignty of national boundaries. The threat of nuclear retaliation has altered the equation of national self-interest in and around Central Asia. Xinjiang borders the countries of Pakistan, India and the former Soviet republics of Central Asia, all of whom either have a proven nuclear capability or are close to developing one.

Naturally we knew that the Chinese nuclear test site lay to our east. I had been briefed about it, in general terms, by the Ministry of Defence prior to my departure, and our proximity to Lop Nor accounted in part for the unexpected addition of Qiu Lei (the Spook) to the crossing party. The Chinese intelligence service would have done its homework well: the presence of three serving and two former members of the British armed forces accompanying an expedition in a province which was, until recently, closed to foreigners and to which access is still strictly controlled, would unquestionably have raised more than a few Beijing eyebrows.

It was, therefore, a major concern when, during the first week of our crossing to Mazartagh in September, we heard that China had detonated a surface nuclear device in the Lop Desert. News of that development was relayed to us by Barney on the radio one evening.

'I thought it would amuse you to hear that the Chinese have disclaimed the test', Barney added, 'by announcing to the international press that there has been an earthquake in the Uyghur Autonomous Region,* but because no one lives in the area there are no reports of any casualties.'

'That's all very well,' I replied, 'but it doesn't take account of the fact that our caravan is approximately a thousand miles downwind of Lop, and the prevailing wind is from the north-east.'

We were continually reminded of the international community's interest in the region by the number of satellites plainly visible in the night sky. Rupert and I often lay in our sleeping bags looking up and counting the constant activity as satellites criss-crossed back and forth with such regularity that spy coverage of the region must have been virtually complete. But, in the course of events, we had forgotten about the incident until the last week of the crossing as we neared Luobuzhuang, the point where we hoped to leave the desert once and for all.

Barney's team had moved to the town of Ruoqiang eighty miles to the south-east in preparation for our anticipated triumphant exit and to co-ordinate the local celebrations there. Ruoqiang is the last major oasis at the eastern end of the southern Silk Road as it skirts the fringes of the Taklamakan. From there the road, no more than a track of loose gravel chippings, heads due north to Luobuzhuang *en route* to Korla, conveniently dividing the line of the Taklamakan and Lop Deserts.

But Luobuzhuang turned out to be a surprise. Marked as a settlement on the map, there was in fact nothing there when Barney arrived for a reconnaissance with his vehicles. Nothing, that is, except for a few deserted buildings bearing signs of temporary military occupation. The plain reinforced-concrete

---

*Another name for Xinjiang.

walls bore evidence of destruction. What alarmed Francis, however, was the equipment and paper scattered on the ground with recent seismic measurements scrawled all over them. Both he and the others in the support team reached the conclusion that Luobuzhuang had probably been used as one of the sites for measuring the effects of the nuclear testing further to the east in the middle of the Lop Desert. The surrounding desert was flat and cheerless with no glorious sand dunes of striking colours and shapes; it was an unlikely spot for the ending of an expedition such as ours.

'I'm not hanging around here,' he told Barney, 'otherwise I might start glowing in the night.' Keith felt the same and Barney told me on the radio of his unease over Luobuzhuang.

'It probably explains why the Chinese authorities in Ruoqiang were so jumpy when I headed up here alone without the usual Chinese entourage.' His vehicles were not allowed to leave Ruoqiang unescorted again when the authorities finally caught up with him.

Jokes about having been downwind of a nuclear explosion were plentiful from then onwards. Francis had told us that we should have been carrying a geiger counter to measure nuclear radiation. He certainly would have been happier walking around Luobuzhuang if he had had one. But there was a more serious concern. For some reason the backs of both Mark's hands were covered in large blisters filled with light yellow fluid that caused him some discomfort. It was a recent condition that could not be attributed to the sun which, by that stage, had lost its earlier intensity.

'He's a leper,' Rupert teased, 'we ought to put a camel bell round his neck so he can go around saying "Unclean, unclean!"'

Carolyn treated the blisters as best she could, but the faint chance that Mark had somehow picked up something from a contaminated area did dawn on us. In circumstances like ours, removed from the outside world and dependent upon a code of survival, it was easy and natural for one's imagination to run riot. What made the idea more convincing was the fact the blisters looked very similar to the many photographs we had all seen during our Army training for nuclear, biological and chemical warfare. At the expedition's end, and during the press conferences in Hong Kong and back in England, we deliberately made no mention of the subject of nuclear testing. Neither did we talk about Barney's encounter with the *laogai* when his vehicle got bogged down on the way to Dandanuilik. Had we done so, I am sure that media coverage of the expedition would have been far more sensational and extensive. We decided instead on a simple story of exploration.

After the near-mutiny of the Chinese team on the sand mountain, the night after the mercy killing of the camel, our relations with them became even more strained. With 100 miles still to go and 680 miles already covered conflict was never far from the surface and it was tempting to let things fall apart, each national team racing under its own steam and on its own route to the finish.

The day after my decision to head south-east there was further disagreement over the route which brought matters to a head. As the dunes became less formidable and difficult to cross, I had gradually swung back on to a bearing of due east. We then hit a massive sand wall perpendicular to our chosen axis that towered overhead. The sand was so soft and deep that it required a considerable effort for the camels to make any headway. They bellowed in outrage and stood immobilized with their legs trembling. With the right leading and coaxing, and enormous patience on our behalf, it was not impossible to get them up, and the first train of six with Lucien dragging them from the front reached the crest with Mark and Carolyn. Rupert and I had gone ahead, blazing the trail as we called it. 'Bite the dune' was my favourite expression for heading in a straight line rather than 'winky-wanking' around. In this case we certainly did bite the dune but were rewarded for doing so. Had we gone for an alternative route it would have taken us a further hour. Unfortunately, that is what the Chinese did. Walking at the rear of the caravan they watched the beginning of our assault on the near-vertical sand wall and told the remaining Uyghurs to head due south. Mark and Carolyn had

seen them alter direction but because they were already struggling knee-deep in sand half-way up the slope, they were
unable to influence the course of events. We rested the camels
for ten minutes then continued through an area of lower, undulating dunes no more than sixty feet high where I halted the six
camels and waited for the remainder to catch up. It was an hour
before I saw them, the trains gradually emerging from all directions; some had obviously traversed the sand wall to the south
and Suleiman had taken things into his own hands by going
north with Emir. I was furious. Not only was it dangerous to
split the caravan but the whole episode had wasted time at a
point in the crossing where every hour over ground covered
was vital to our chances of success.

'Charles, you've got to sort this out,' Rupert said, 'those
bloody irregulars are always calling the tune at the rear of the
caravan.'

'I know. It's time Guo and I had a showdown.'

But it wasn't me who took the first step. Once all twenty-
nine camels were assembled and couched, Guo gathered the
Uyghurs together and shouted at them, blaming them for following without thinking, for tiring the camels by going up
impossibly steep slopes and for failing to look for the easier
route. I kept my patience just long enough for him to have his
say. Then I lost it completely.

'Guo, it is not the fault of the Uyghurs. You have no right
to accuse them. Their job is to lead the camels and follow the
tracks of the people at the front who are navigating.'

'You are going to kill all the camels if you go on like this, and
probably some humans also,' he countered.

'We've been through all that more than once. I am leading
this expedition, not you. I select the route and I do not expect
people at the back to change things. It is dangerous and it
wastes time.'

'You are dangerous. These camels can go no further. We can
go no further.'

I studied his face and I saw how close he was to tears. The
strain of the expedition had been building up within us all over
the fifty days that we had been in the desert. Guo stood at one

end of the Uyghurs and Chinese who either sat, squatted or knelt in a loose huddle. I stood at the other end, Rupert beside me. Across the group we blazed furiously at each other. All our pent-up anxieties and emotions spilled out as insults were flung from one to the other.

'None of you Chinese have ever walked at the front. Only Lao Zhao has a compass and the rest of you just walk at the back with your thumbs up your bums and your minds in neutral.'

At this point Rupert waded into the mêlée and added, 'Guo, if you didn't like Charles's leadership then you should have pulled out on day one. It is the British who are doing everything; navigation, radios, medical care. We're even paying for the expedition. What have you paid?'

This led the argument on to very delicate ground but at that point I no longer cared.

'Precisely, Guo, the British are paying for everything here. These are my camels, my food, I pay for the Uyghurs and I even pay for you!'

The viciousness of my outburst silenced him and I detected a flicker of hurt in his eyes. I had overstepped the mark but the strain of seven weeks in the desert continually having to mend the fences of relations within the team had suddenly become too much. There was a cold fury inside me which despised the petty bickering of the Chinese and their lack of spirit. I felt the British had given everything of themselves in drawing a line of exploration across the Taklamakan that no one had dared attempt before. The Chinese had merely piggy-backed upon our initiative and drive; if that had not been the case then the desert would have been conquered by an all-Chinese expedition long ago since it lay in their country. Instead, it had been a team from a small island thousands of miles away who had engineered the scheme, financed it, and ultimately showed the courage to pursue the challenge with the tenacity and stubbornness that was a prerequisite for success and survival. And now the weaker ones were scared and sought an easy escape route just when the ultimate test lay before us.

'The camels are carrying too much. They cannot keep going

like this any further,' Qui Lei said after a few moments of silence in which Guo and I stared at each other with barely concealed hostility.

'What the hell do you know about it?' I shouted. 'You're only a journalist, so-called, and you've done nothing for this expedition. You wouldn't even know the difference between a loaded camel and an unladen one. So you can shut up, for starters.'

Even without a translation he clearly got the drift of my reply.

'Steady on a bit, Charles,' cautioned Mark in a whisper, 'you don't want these guys to lose too much face, especially in front of the Uyghurs, or you'll end up with a slit throat when you're asleep one night. They harbour grudges for a long time.'

Realizing that co-operation between the Chinese, the Uyghurs and the British hung in the balance I stepped through the group and touched Guo on the shoulder. He knocked my hand away with an expression of disgust. I tried again.

'Come on, Guo, let's go over there away from everyone and share a cigarette. We are the leaders of this crossing and we cannot afford to fall out like this in front of our teams. Someone has to hold them together.'

He looked at me sadly like a small and frightened boy. I noticed the lines of tiredness and strain that were deeply etched on his face and realized how much he had aged since the beginning of the crossing. Having put him down I now had to build him up again. We walked off to one side and I lit a cigarette which I handed to him. There were tears in his eyes and I regretted the things I had said so cruelly. In my heart I knew Guo was right and I had grown fond of him as a friend; I also felt uncompromisingly determined to see the venture through to the bitter end, even at the risk of losing more camels or possibly a member of the team. Ours was a daring and dangerous plan; we were trying to push back one of the last frontiers of exploration in a way which was no longer a common or fashionable feature of modern-day travel. Only we knew how far we had gone to achieve it and how much we had gambled on fortune and providence.

*   *   *

The cold became our worst enemy during those last hundred miles. The icy wind from the north-east cut relentlessly across the bare and exposed dunes, flinging sand particles at us which stung the skin. My body was racked by the weariness of long marches through wind-whipped dunes. On some days the sky and the desert merged into such a blanket of wintry greyness that the division between the two was barely visible. The air was full of dust and sand which clothed us permanently but by that stage we were beyond noticing: survival became the prime objective and the deteriorating weather was only one more thing to cope with.

To a man we now yearned for the end. Our bodies had been punished severely and we knew that we could not continue much further. We were utterly tired of struggling against the rigours of desert life and sought only to emerge intact and claim the prize of conquest which we had truly earned. As I watched the increasingly tired and pitiful attempts of the weaker camels to ascend the deep, soft sands of the higher dunes during those final days I realized how close we had come to the limit and how negligent we had been in caring for their needs. Now everything depended on keeping them going and on us finding adequate water. Whilst I openly scoffed at Guo's fears about the camels lasting much longer, I knew that he was right: everything hinged on us keeping going for just ten more days. Ten days. That was all. We had come too far against over-whelming odds to deserve failure just before the end. But I knew, too, that in heading north from Tatrang we had over-stepped the mark. We had gambled once too often, had dared to play with the desert's power and had arrogantly ignored the warnings of those who said I was courting disaster by heading so far north into its more dangerous heartland.

Thoughts of finishing dominated my day as I trudged along, silently cursing the overpowering sterility and bleakness of one of nature's most desolate landscapes. I dreamt of the acclaim and public recognition as I held on to visions of a triumphant return to civilization. Yet the more I thought of finishing, the longer each hour took and the harder the march became. More and more often I checked to see how far we had walked that day, subtracting the figure from the mileage that remained, and I grew impatient when the sum total never appeared to have been reduced sufficiently. The journey seemed to last forever. I could scarcely remember any other life outside our simple and rugged existence. Even my own family seemed a distant and barely real memory, and I became deeply ashamed at the lack of emotion that any thoughts of them aroused in me. The other world had receded into artificiality and I only knew of my routine within the crossing party.

There were other days, less destructive ones, when the deep blue of the sky and the yellow of the undulating dunes were accentuated by the crystalline clarity of the cold. Those days brought out the braver and more contented side of my explorer's temperament as I relished the physical challenge and savoured the uniqueness of our surroundings. Then the palpable sadness of our proximity to the end of our quest enabled me to delight in the freedom of our existence and the bonding of the British, the Chinese and the Uyghurs. During such times nothing was taken for granted and our slow pace allowed me the luxury of observing the smallest of details, from the colours of the sand and the ungainly walk of the camels to the characteristics of each and every member of the team as they went about their tasks. I surveyed the scene like an old man near the end of his days who hopes to take the memories with him when finally the time comes to go.

I stopped at the base of a dune and admired the artistry of the ripples of sand, noticed the tiny avalanches silently sliding down from the thin line of the crest, and marvelled at the shapes and formations of the surrounding dunes. I removed from my jacket three plastic sample bags and knelt down. I filled each small sachet with sand and spoke aloud as I did so, as though performing a ritual, 'This is for you, Oliver . . . this is for you, Jack . . . and this is for you, little Toby.' I then kissed each in turn before writing the names of my sons on the white labels. They would be my present from the desert, I decided, as I tucked the little offerings away in a safe place. Then I took a longitude and latitude reading and marked it as an entry in my diary under Saturday, 13 November.

The following day Mark walked straight into a desert fox as he was leading ahead of the caravan. It was our first and last sighting. He was full of excitement and described the animal in detail as each of us relished the change in conversation.

'I don't know who was more surprised, me or the fox,' he recounted. 'It was larger than a normal dog fox you'd see at home, with a huge brush, small mask and very small ears. Its coat was a white and pale sandy colour. I stood motionless six feet from it. We looked at each other for nearly a minute before it realized that something was amiss and calmly walked away, keeping its head and eyes permanently fixed on me before disappearing between two dunes.'

Minor ailments were rife. Abdul Rene and Guo both suffered appalling pain from rotten teeth which caused huge swellings to the sides of their faces. Nothing Carolyn gave them from her medicine chest seemed to counter the discomfort and we contemplated rudimentary dentistry if their condition worsened. Suleiman had a bad dose of diarrhoea as well as an eye infection that left it red and highly inflamed. Carolyn's Achilles tendon, snapped whilst sprinting in an athletics championship ten years earlier, had steadily deteriorated – she limped continually and had difficulty keeping up on occasions. We were a sorry-looking crowd. My knee was aggravated by the cold and I had to hobble along, totally reliant on a walking stick to ascend and descend the dunes. Even the Brufen anti-inflammatory pain-killers I took each day no longer made any difference – my system had probably got used to them. Everyone's inner thighs were raw from the rubbing of their trousers which hung low and were baggy as a result of so much weight loss. In the cold the skin cracked and the discomfort was such that people often walked awhile with one hand under their crutch in an attempt to minimize the friction.

The option of riding an unladen camel was no longer taken up because of the cold. Some of us tried it but soon dismounted half frozen and barely able to move our stiff joints. The only exception was Lao Zhao who remained apparently unmoved by the extremes of temperature. I admired his extraordinary toughness and strength of character. He still wore the orange kagool, less bright after fifty-three days' wear and tear, and the same thin cotton trousers. His only visible concession to the cold was the purple outer cover of a sleeping bag which he wore on his head beneath his battered VW baseball cap. He looked like an old granny on a winter's day and his wonderful eccentricity amused us greatly.

The state of the camels remained unchanged. Some of their worst infections had healed but countering maggot-ridden sores was still a daily chore. Suleiman surprised us one evening by tackling the tongue of a camel with a pair of nail clippers that he had borrowed from Carolyn. We couldn't work out what he was up to as he attacked the long tongue of the poor animal who had been firmly trussed up with ropes beforehand. Blood sprayed everywhere whilst Suleiman snipped around the edges of the tongue as it slipped this way and that in his hands like a freshly landed fish. Eventually we discovered that he was cutting out maggots from areas of dead skin.

Maintaining my diary entries became more difficult and I repeatedly had to stop and warm my frozen fingers after a few words, gently unbending the claw-like joints from the pencil. Stupidly, I only wore a pair of old Army fingerless mittens, having inadvertently left my prized arctic gloves with the support team a long while back. During those bitter days I cursed my oversight a thousand times.

My diary entry for Tuesday, 16 November, recorded:

Desert Camp 44 (39° 13.04′N, 87° 21.42′E). Day 54
The bleakest and most arduous day, weather-wise, that we have encountered to date. Freezing cold NE wind gusting up to 40 or 50 m.p.h. at times. A minus 10° Fahrenheit wind chill factor all day. The water containers were frozen and I noticed icicles around the eyelashes and mouths of the camels. Set off at 10.30 a.m. with Mark leading on a bearing of 25° magnetic. The wind was horizontal and we walked bent double against its penetrating cold. Visibility was down to a few hundred yards as we entered a belt of sand hills. It was dramatic and exciting: a howling wind, sand being blasted against us, a silvery sky with the silver-bright halo of the sun trying to break through the dust storm; sand being whipped up by the camels' hooves as they struggled up the steep

dunes; the sight of people going up and down the long line of the
caravan urging the camels on, waving their sticks in encourage-
ment and then rubbing their hands and pumping their arms across
the body to generate some heat. I felt the surge of adventure: the
camel caravan in the middle of the unknown battling against the
elements, gamely fighting to reach the final destination and
thereby achieve the hitherto unthought-of crossing of the Desert
of Death. It was us against the desert. We battled on, heads bowed
defiantly against the battering of the wind and sand combined,
feeling elated by the achievement of crossing the dune obstacles in
our path.

I talked with Guo this evening about what he had gained from
the expedition. He said that he had learnt a lot about himself; initially he didn't think he would be physically able to complete the
crossing. Now he is more confident. I appreciated how much I
owed Guo. Without him in China many things could not have
happened. He has done more than one realizes for the planning
of the venture.

Carolyn can become really British and almost introverted
sometimes. Today she annoyed me with a remark after I had
offered Abdul Rene and Lucien some crushed and stale biscuits
during the break. She sounded surprised and said, 'They've got
plenty of their own, you know,' in a superior manner.

'I'm aware of that,' I replied brusquely, 'but it is only polite to
offer. Anyway, it's not an us and them situation.'

I cannot stand this attitude of this is ours, that is theirs, etc. It is
so pernickety and unnecessary. In the desert the code is one of
sharing and you offer your last one of anything to someone else if
they are nearby. But to give her credit, she is quite outstanding the
way she gets around everyone, patching them up, making sure
they take their pills and tending to the camel injuries.

Despite the cold and the effort involved Rupert continued
to take sand samples and measurements as he had done
throughout the crossing. These were being recorded for
Oxford University and it was important that the expedition
should be able to produce a complete set of samples from west
to east across the middle of the desert. At least something tangible would come of it and the opportunity had not been
wasted. In some respects I regretted that we did not have more

to show for our efforts. True, there had been the discovery of the ancient site, the flints, the primeval forest and the secret of the water supply for Dandan-uilik, but I always felt we could have done more and possibly contributed further to science and geography. There again, the task of crossing the desert had in itself been all-consuming. We never had the luxury of time or plentiful water and supplies to enable us to conduct more serious studies. It had been a question of grabbing what we could. Just surviving was a full-time chore.

Rounding the summit of a dune one morning we came across a dead goose lying frozen rigid in the sand. There was no telling how long it had been there although it was perfectly preserved. Its feathers were white and there was a splash of orange on the crown of its head. From its final position it appeared to have died while sitting on the surface of the sand, its black bill tucked under a wing for warmth and protection. I could picture the scene of migrating birds battling high above the desert on their way south to warmer climes. Perhaps this one had been sick or too weary to fly any further and had circled out of the sky and come to rest there in front of us. Once down it could not get up again and so resigned itself to a slow, lingering death brought on by starvation and the extremes of temperature. It was a melancholy sight. Surprisingly it was the only such discovery. We had had thoughts of finding the sites of crashed aircraft, lost and unknown in the desert, but there had been nothing, only the untouched and unexplored labyrinth of dunes.

TWENTY

A Desert Conquered

The end, when it came, was an anti-climax. The desert changed and the dunes gave way to a flat, pebbled terrain scattered with tamarisks. Before we knew it we had left the billowing ocean of sand behind and we mourned its passing. The dreary landscape set against a grey, overcast day was not the way we wanted to remember our last moments. So deliberately, with only twenty miles to go, we stopped short and camped. We drew back from the very edge of our prison and our home, almost afraid to let it disappear forever. Now that we had done it, and survived, we looked back with nostalgia and emptiness; we were not ready to be abruptly catapulted back into the world. The lure of the desert and the unknown, and the simple camaraderie of our existence had sustained us well for two months. Suddenly we did not wish the spell to be broken.

But just before the halt, Abdul Rene, who was mounted, saw in the distance a camel coming towards our caravan. As it got closer we noticed the size of its splendid humps and the thickness of its fur. It was a large bull camel and it was wild. Attracted by the smell and sight of so many of its kind it timidly circled at a distance, not quite sure what to make of us.

'Big Zhang,' I said, 'tell the handlers to try and capture it.'

He translated but there was no interest among the Uyghurs in the chase. The biting cold of the wind had numbed their minds and bodies into inertia. It was only then that I realized they did not regard our remaining miles in the desert in the same way. As far as they were concerned, the quicker they reached Luobuzhuang the better. Our mentalities were quite different, which was why we had been driven to explore the desert in the first place. With a sudden spurt of energy I took off across the gravel plain at a run, urging Mark to follow. Together we moved at a speed which surprised me and soon outflanked the wild camel. It turned uncertainly and looked from Mark on one side to myself on the other. We closed in. The camel started towards the main caravan, first at a slow walk and then at a trot. In something of a panic it crashed directly into the line of the second camel train and became entangled in the ropes between them. As we delivered the catch to them, the handlers excitedly sprang into action. Suleiman made a lasso from a rope and slipped it around the neck of the animal who, by then, was foaming at the mouth with fear. It was a huge beast, far bigger than Chumbar, our largest, and a beautiful specimen, much more healthy-looking than many of the ones paraded before us so long ago in Markit.

'Well, you started with thirty camels and it looks like you're ending with thirty,' said Carolyn.

'I should think it will fetch a high price in a camel market on the Silk Road,' Rupert added.

The adrenalin from the chase soon passed and I suddenly felt extremely cold and tired. We pushed on for another few miles, Rupert and myself leading and the long line of the caravan slowly plodding behind. The only sounds were the gusting of the wind and the toll of the camel bells. We were soon far ahead and after three hours found a sheltered place to camp in the lee of a low dune. When the others caught up I was surprised and disappointed that the wild camel, our prize catch, was no longer with them.

'Apparently it broke its rope and bolted,' said Mark, although he had not witnessed it.

Suleiman was not unduly concerned and, from his manner, I detected that he had probably not made much effort to prevent the camel's escape back into the wild. I could understand why, and in many respects I was glad it had gone and would not be subjected to the camel bazaars of Turkestan.

There was a restrained atmosphere around the camp fire that last night. We had experienced too much to realize that it was nearly over. We were also completely exhausted and drained by our journey. Lao Zhao was the only one with any spark and he made a point of coming over to where we were sitting. From his pocket he produced a piece of dirty cloth which he carefully unfolded in front of us. Holding it in the palm of his hand he revealed a collection of glittering stones that, at first glance, looked like diamonds.

'He says they are a precious stone which he found in the Mazartagh mountain line,' Mark told us. With that Lao Zhao took the largest stone and gave it to Carolyn.

'He says it is a gift for a woman who is like the great British Prime Minister, Mrs Thatcher. Carolyn, Lao Zhao wants you to know that you too are an "Iron Lady" – in fact, you will be known as the "Iron Lady of China".'

He then picked out three small stones and put them in my hand. Once again Mark translated.

'A present from the Mad Professor to the Mad General, and lots of other complimentary stuff, Charles, which I won't translate because it will make you too big-headed! But, in summary, he wants you to know that the expedition would not have succeeded without your leadership and he pays tribute to that.' I was touched and humbled by the gesture.

On the morning of Sunday, 21 November, the fifty-ninth day of the crossing, we loaded the camels for the last time. It did not take long because we had discarded so much on that desperate night when the Chinese came so near to mutiny. We had also given the last of our water to the camels. Afterwards I gathered the team together. The sun was up and the sky was clear. We stood self-consciously in a circle, almost afraid to hear the words I was about to utter. They did not come easily. I was half choked, knowing that one of the greatest of all desert journeys was over. It was the end of the dream I had nurtured, planned and fought for for so long. In ten miles our two-month quest would be over, our life in the desert at an end. It had been kind to us after all.

'I think we should all say a prayer for our safe deliverance from the desert. Its name – "you go in but you won't come out" – is no longer true. Two months ago we went in and today we come out.' Mark translated into Chinese and then Big Zhang did so into Uyghur. 'You must be proud of that achievement. We did it by teamwork – the British, the Chinese and the Uyghurs. And the camels. None of us could have done it without the other. Tell your families when you return home safely that you were the first ever to make the complete crossing of the Taklamakan. And the friendships that we have made will stay with us forever. In my mind I will always think of you; in my speech I will always talk of you; and in my heart I will always feel for you.'

With that I went around the team and shook their hands silently in turn. Everyone did the same. There were embraces and there were tears. It was not a moment for bravado or celebration. It was our own silent and special ceremony in front of the camels who had served us so faithfully. We turned our backs on the desert and walked to the east. For the first time I had no need of a map and simply stuck to a bearing of due east knowing that, after a few hours, I could expect to see the vehicles of the support party.

'What are you feeling, Rumper?' I asked Rupert as we walked side by side over those last remaining miles.

'I'm not sure. What about you?'

'I don't feel anything. I'm trying to but there is nothing there. No elation and no sadness. I simply feel numbed by it all.'

'It's the same with me. I want to believe it is all over but, there again, I don't. What does a man do after this?'

'What indeed? It is a difficult act to follow.'

My father's Union Jack was the first thing I saw. It flew proudly on a pole from the highest point that Francis had been able to find. At first it was barely perceptible until I made out the colours. The flag transfixed me as the distance narrowed; it burned ahead like an eternal flame, marking for me the many facets of my past and my character that I had had to come to terms with in the desert. I drew strength from the knowledge that my father's star had watched over and guided me. At that moment nothing else mattered. I spoke aloud the words of the seventeenth-century Gaelic blessing and thanked Him for our deliverance:

> May the road rise with you
> The wind be always at your back
> And may the Lord hold you in the
> Hollow of his hand.

The desert had been conquered.

Epilogue

I had mixed emotions as we drove north towards Urumqi on the third day after coming out of the desert. From Urumqi we would fly to Beijing and then on to Hong Kong before returning to England. I sat beside Barney in the cab of the Pinzgauer and realized the expedition had come full circle. The last time we had been together had been on the journey from Markit to the edge of Taklamakan. Then we had exuded the bravado and freshness wholly appropriate to the beginning of a great adventure. Now we were seasoned explorers, tried and tested. I studied the deep cracks in my hands and the wrinkled, weathered skin caused by the extreme cold; they did not seem to belong to me but rather were those of a very old man. Outside, the pale, wintry sun was setting over Chinese Turkestan amid a dust haze as Barney negotiated the pot-holes and drifting sand. Over to our left lay the Taklamakan, to us at least no longer quite the same fearsome desert shrouded in mystery, death and legend. But it had been kind to us; future travellers may not be so fortunate. To our right was the Lop Desert, the area of the Chinese nuclear test ground, and beyond that the vast open tracts of the Gobi.

I glanced around the cab, noting bits of equipment, now redundant and each with a different story to tell of their part in the grander scheme of things. Thick layers of fine sand coated everything like talcum powder. It felt as though we were taking the desert with us. I put a tape of Fauré's *Requiem* into the cassette recorder, sat back with my feet on the dashboard, and listened to the Sanctus. Images of the sand dunes and the camel caravan drifted past me in the twilight as the music encapsulated the human transcendence of suffering. It was uplifting and triumphant, an ending to a challenge that none of us had dared believe achievable.

After we had unloaded our faithful camels at Luobuzhuang for the last time, we had been driven at breakneck speed by Chinese drivers to Ruoqiang, an experience nearly as frightening as crossing the desert. The camels walked there and arrived two days later. The celebrations in Ruoqiang were not on the scale of our send-off from Markit but the colour and excitement were as vivid. I proudly carried the Union Jack through the streets and Guo Jin Wei walked beside me with the Red Flag as firecrackers were let off in front of us. Behind came all the expedition members carrying bouquets of plastic flowers presented by schoolchildren and wearing red sashes of greeting. The welcome and rejoicing were touching. At night we feasted and danced to local music around an open fire in the main square.

There were further receptions during the two-day drive to Urumqi. The biggest was at Korla where we were received with a traditional Mongolian welcome. Each of us in turn had to drink *bai jiu* from bowls of gold, silver and jade, held by singing boys in Mongolian costumes who urged us to down the contents in one. Then we were seated for a colourful re-enactment of the life of Genghis Khan set to the music of the rolling plains of Mongolia. The play ended with a candlelit procession of exquisite girls accompanying the body of the great warlord to his final resting place.

By the time we reached Urumqi our minds and bodies were beginning to rebel against the unaccustomed noise and pace of 'normal' life, the alcohol and the rich food. We looked back with envy to the simple routine of the desert. Waiting in Urumqi was a faxed copy of a letter from Buckingham Palace which read, 'Her Majesty was quite delighted to hear of the successful outcome of the Joint British-Chinese Taklamakan Desert Crossing . . . and sends you and all those who took part the heartfelt congratulations of herself and His Royal Highness.' We could not have sought more recognition than that.

With each day the desert grew further and further away and with it went everything that had sustained us throughout the journey. The breaking up of the nucleus of our endeavour happened just as quickly. We had left the camels in Ruoqiang. They were now somewhere on their 400-mile journey home to Hotan on the Silk Road, led by Suleiman's brother and another handler. We said a poignant farewell to our Uyghurs in Urumqi, the capital city that none of them had ever seen before. Now they were to fly, for the first time in their lives, back to Kashgar and their families at the Seven Stars Commune at Markit. John and Anne Thomas, with their son Kevin and two friends who had flown out, remained behind in Urumqi. They faced the difficult task of getting the two vehicles and our equipment back to England. The Chinese had refused permission for an overland journey to Hong Kong and John would have to use the dangerous route through the Khunjerab Pass to Pakistan in mid-winter. Before they left, the authorities confiscated every sample of sand that Rupert had painstakingly collected twice a day across the entire desert for the Oxford University project. It was strange behaviour and we could not understand what harm there was in taking sand out of the country. Only later did we link it to the nuclear incident and realize that they were worried lest Western intelligence take radioactive readings from the sand and thus gain proof of the Lop Nor nuclear test. After a two-week journey John's team eventually arrived at Karachi and the vehicles were shipped safely back to Southampton, arriving there in January, seven months after first setting out.

Deep snow covered the ground the morning that the crossing party and the remainder of the support team flew from Urumqi to Beijing. Guo Jin Wei and Lao Zhao came with us to the airport. Despite two days of frenzied negotiations with Guo over the final fee for the Chinese, and my fear that in leaving John behind with the vehicles we were offering a hostage to fortune, I knew it was going to be a great wrench

saying goodbye. We still keep in touch: Guo is now running his
own travel company, while old 'Calculus' continues to potter
around the edge of the desert gathering scientific data.

At Beijing Airport Tina was waiting. She stood on the far
side of the Customs exit, having arrived an hour earlier from
Hong Kong. For a while I watched her surrounded by crowds
of Chinese. Although it was only two and a half months since
she had driven me to Heathrow Airport, I knew the scale of
the experience I had been through made it seem far longer for
both of us. I hesitated. It was one of those moments I had
planned so often in my imagination as I walked across the
desert. Now that it was suddenly upon me I was no longer sure
how to react. Then I approached her. Either she didn't notice
or she didn't register my presence until I was by her side and
she gasped at my appearance. I stood there awkwardly, a thin,
bearded figure two stone underweight and still wearing my
dirty desert clothes and clutching my stick. I felt like Moses
emerging from the wilderness. And then we embraced. My
body trembled with relief and emotion as she held me and I
knew, for the first time, that I had really made it.

It took me a while to appreciate what Tina herself had been
through while I was in the desert – long days and nights of worry
and loneliness, and anxiety over the boys as they occasionally
lashed out with frustration and anger because they could not
understand why their father had gone. From the outset she had
thought I might not survive. The desert's formidable reputation
did nothing to alleviate those fears. Worse still, after my departure, she had found, under her pillow, an envelope I had left her
containing a letter and my signet ring, dress watch and military
identity card. She remembered my own story of entering the
dining-room of my parents' home in Nepal when I arrived for
my father's funeral. The first things I saw were his signet ring,
watch and identity card all neatly laid out on the table. To Tina
it seemed that history was repeating itself.

Our Beijing reunion was not an easy one. There were too
many gaps which only time would bridge. Although we had
moments alone as we toured the Forbidden City and the
Summer Palace, and picnicked on the Great Wall of China,

Tina found it difficult to accept that my spirit was still in the Taklamakan and that my preoccupation with the expedition eclipsed everything. Surprisingly, considering the extensive Chinese media coverage of our exploits, the three days in Beijing were not marked by official banquets, press conferences or other ceremonies. To some extent this suited us as we tried to readjust to life outside the desert, and the future.

Since our return from China the members of the team have gone their own ways. Barney is still in the Army and has been promoted; Carolyn runs her family's garden centre in Devon; Rupert is in Africa working for an organization that clears mines left by former conflicts there; Keith is in California with his photographic work; Mark has left the Army and works in London, travelling to China on business from time to time; Richard heads up the Shanghai office of a merchant bank; John and Anne Thomas continue their business ventures in Wales; Francis has returned to the City and his former job as a fund manager; Paul is painting; and Krishna is a journalist. The bond between us all remains strong and we are supremely aware that, together, we shared a unique historic experience that will remain with us for the rest of our lives. There are moments, particularly if I feel vulnerable or unsure of myself, when I think back to the desert and draw strength from the knowledge that I made a dream come true.

Dawn was just breaking over the valley in Hampshire when I came home in early December. A friend from the village met Tina and me at the airport. I could not face going straight into the house and seeing the children. I needed a few moments alone. And so I walked in the half-light of dawn along the lane beside the river that leads to the house. The morning was, in its own way, as silent and beautiful as the desert. I looked at the moon and the few remaining stars, and thought back to when I had sat with Mark on the high sand mountain contemplating the jagged lines of dunes and the delicate silhouette of the Kun Lun mountains far to the south. Just as I uttered out loud a prayer of thanks for my safe return and for my father, I heard children's voices in the darkness shouting, 'Daddy, Daddy!' I was home.

Members of the Joint British-Chinese
Taklamakan Desert Crossing,
September–November 1993

Crossing party

Charles Blackmore	Expedition leader, navigator
Rupert Burton	Check navigator, communications
Carolyn Ellis	Medic
Richard Graham	Chinese interpreter (from Markit to Mazartagh only)
Mark Kitto	Chinese interpreter and communications (from Mazartagh to the end at Luobuzhuang)
Keith Sutter (USA)	Photographer (from Markit to Mazartagh, and from Yawatongguz to Tatrang: otherwise on the Silk Road)
Guo Jin Wei	Chinese team leader
Lao Zhao	Government scientist
Zhang Bohua	Uyghur translator
Qui Lei	Photographer and central government representative
Esa Polta	Head camel handler (evacuated injured at Mazartagh)
Kirim Yunus	Camel handler
Abdul Rasheed Mohammed	Camel handler
Rosa Khorta	Camel handler (evacuated with Esa Polta at Mazartagh)
Lucien Hussein	Camel handler
Emir Ishmail	Camel handler
Abdul Rene	Camel handler (from Tongguzbasti to Luobuzhuang)

Suleiman Rosa	Camel handler (from Tongguzbasti to Luobuzhuang)

Support Party

Barney White-Spunner	Leader and expedition deputy leader
Lord Francis Seymour	Administration and driver of 'Bella' vehicle
John Thomas	Driver of 'Thomas' vehicle
Anne Thomas	Administration
Krishna Guha	Research on ancient sites (joined in China)
Paul Treasure	Official expedition artist (in the crossing party from Tongguzbasti to emergency resupply near Niya)

Chinese support team with four to six assistants in three vehicles